Race, Class, and
the Death Penalty

Race, Class, and the Death Penalty

Capital Punishment in American History

Howard W. Allen
and
Jerome M. Clubb

with assistance from
Vincent A. Lacey

STATE UNIVERSITY OF NEW YORK PRESS

Published by
State University of New York Press, Albany

For information, contact State University of New York Press, Albany, NY
www.sunypress.edu

Production by Diane Ganeles
Marketing by Michael Campochiaro

Library of Congress Cataloging-in-Publication Data

Allen, Howard W., 1931–
    Race, class, and the death penalty: capital punishment in American
history / Howard W. Allen, Jerome M. Clubb.
        p. cm.
    Includes bibliographical references and index.
    ISBN 978-0-7914-7437-2 (hardcover : alk. paper)
    1. Capital punishment—United States—History. 2. Discrimination in
capital punishment—United States—History. 3. Discrimination in
criminal justice administration—United States—History. I. Clubb,
Jerome M., 1928– II. Title.

HV8699.U5A725 2008
364.660973—dc22   2007033225

10 9 8 7 6 5 4 3 2 1

For our wives, Lorie and Vera

Contents

List of Illustrations   ix

Acknowledgments   xiii

Introduction   1

Chapter 1   The Death Penalty in National Perspective   9

Chapter 2   The Colonial and Revolutionary Eras   27

Chapter 3   The Early Republic, 1786–1865   47

Chapter 4   The South and the Border, 1866–1945   67

Chapter 5   The Northeast, 1866–1945   93

Chapter 6   The Western Regions, 1836–1945   119

Chapter 7   Social Perspectives   147

Chapter 8   The Death Penalty after 1945   167

Chapter 9   The Death Penalty in American History   183

Appendix   191

Notes   205

Index   229

Illustrations

FIGURES

1.1 Average annual number of executions per year by ten-year period, 1606–1945   11

1.2 Average annual rates of execution of African American and white per 100,000 population combined by ten-year period, 1636–1945   17

1.3 Average annual rates of execution of African American and white per 100,000 population by ten-year period, 1636–1945   20

1.4 Ratio of African American to white rates of execution, 1606–1945   22

1.5 African American and white executions for known nonlethal crimes as a percentage of total executions, 1606–1945   24

4.1 Average annual rates of execution of African American and white population: The South, 1866–1945   71

4.2 African American and white executions for nonlethal and unknown offenses as a percentage of total executions: The South, 1866–1945   73

4.3 Average annual rates of execution of African American and white population: The Border, 1866–1945   78

4.4 African American and white executions for nonlethal and unknown offenses as a percentage of total executions: The Border, 1866–1945   80

4.5 Average annual rates of lynchings and of lynchings and executions of African Americans and whites: The South, 1886–1925   86

4.6   Average annual rates of lynchings and of lynchings and
        executions per 100,000 population for African
        Americans and whites: The Border, 1886–1925   87

5.1   Average annual rates of execution of African Americans
        and whites and proportional increase in African
        American population: New England, 1866–1945   99

5.2   Average annual rates of execution of African Americans
        and whites and proportional increase in African
        American population: Middle Atlantic, 1866–1945   103

5.3   Average annual rates of execution of African Americans
        and whites and proportional increase in African
        American population: East North Central, 1866–1945   107

5.4   Rates of lynchings and of lynchings and executions of
        African American and white population: East North
        Central, 1886–1925   109

TABLES

1.1   Annual number of executions by ten-year period and
        ethnic group, 1606–1945   13

2.1   Number of executions by region and ethnic group,
        1606–1695   30

2.2   Average annual rates of execution per 100,000
        African American and white population by region,
        1606–1695   32

2.3   Number of executions by region and ethnic group,
        1696–1785   34

2.4   Average annual rates of execution of African American
        and white population by region, 1696–1785   37

2.5   Ratio of African American to white rates of execution by
        region, 1636–1785   44

3.1   Number of executions by region and ethnic group:
        The Northeast, 1786–1865   50

3.2   Number of executions by region and racial and ethnic
        groups: The South and Border, 1786–1865   53

3.3   Rates of execution per 100,000 of African American
        and white population by region, 1786–1865   56

3.4   Ratios of African American to white rates of execution
        per 100,000 population by region, 1786–1865   57

3.5   Percentage of African Americans and whites executed
      for nonlethal and unknown crimes: New England,
      Mid-Atlantic, South, and Border, 1786–1855   61

4.1   Number of executions by racial and ethnic groups:
      The South, 1866–1945   70

4.2   Number of executions by racial and ethnic groups:
      The Border, 1866–1945   76

4.3   Number of lynchings and legal executions by racial
      and ethnic groups: The South and Border, 1886–1925   84

4.4   Number and rate of lynchings of African Americans and
      whites per 100,000 population: Kentucky, 1866–1925   89

5.1   Number of executions by racial and ethnic groups:
      New England, 1866–1945   97

5.2   Number of executions by racial and ethnic groups:
      The Middle Atlantic, 1866–1945   101

5.3   Number of executions by racial and ethnic groups:
      The East North Central, 1866–1945   105

5.4   Rates of execution of Italian Americans compared to
      African Americans and native-born whites of native-born
      parents in seven Northeastern states, 1906–1935   113

5.5   Ratio of rates of execution in the Northeast to rates of
      execution in the South and Border, 1866–1945   115

5.6   Ratio of rates of executions and lynchings per 100,000
      population in Middle Atlantic and East North Central
      to rates of executions and lynchings in the South and
      Border, 1886–1925   117

6.1   Number of executions by regions and racial and ethnic
      groups: The West, 1836–1945   121

6.2   Rates of executions by racial and ethnic groups:
      The West, 1836–1945   124

6.3   Rates of executions of Asians, Mexicans, Native
      Americans, and whites by state and ethnic groups:
      The West, 1856–1945   127

6.4   Number of lynchings by racial and ethnic groups:
      The West, 1886–1925   133

6.5   Rates of lynching and rates of lynching and executions
      of African Americans, Asians, and whites: The West,
      1886–1925   134

6.6   Ratio of African American and Asian American to
      white rates of execution per 100,000 population
      by region, 1866–1945   139

6.7   Ratio of rates of executed and lynched African Americans
      and whites in the Western, Southern, and Border regions,
      1886–1925   141

6.8   Ratio of rates of African Americans and whites
      executed in the West to rates executed in the South
      and Middle Atlantic, 1866–1945   143

7.1   Percentage of African Americans and whites ages 15–34
      executed, percentage of African Americans and whites
      ages 15–34 of total population, and percentage
      of African Americans and whites of unknown age,
      1896–1945   154

7.2   Comparison of execution rates in 1880, 1920, and 1940
      in the ten largest cities in 1900 with rates excluding the
      cities in the states where they were located   159

8.1   Number executed by region, race, and ethnicity,
      January 17, 1977–December 31, 2005   172

8.2   Number on death row, July 1, 2005, by region, race,
      and ethnicity   174

8.3   Ratio of the percentage of racial and ethnic groups among
      those executed between 1996 and 2005 and the death row
      population that each group represented in the regional
      populations in 2000   175

8.4   Rates of executions of African Americans and whites by
      region and by selected ten-year periods   177

A.1   The summary file as a percentage of total known
      executions by region, 1606–1945   193

Acknowledgments

No scholarly effort is ever conducted without heavy indebtedness to others. This is particularly true of efforts that rest as heavily as this one does upon data collection efforts carried out by others. Our largest debt is, of course, to M. Watt Espy. Without his continuing effort, this study would have been impossible. We are profoundly grateful to him and hope that our efforts prove to be a credit to his work. We are indebted as well to the National Science Foundation for providing the support required to make the initial version of the collection available for general use. We also are grateful to John Ortiz Smykla for his work in preparing the collection for use. We are pleased to once again express our indebtedness to the Inter-university Consortium for Political and Social Research for maintaining and providing access to the computer-readable version of the collection and to the collection of historical census data. Victoria Schneider contributed to the preparation of the data collection for use and first brought it to the attention of one of us. Although she decided not to participate in the effort reported here, her early assistance was of considerable value. We are grateful as well to Erik W. Austin of the Inter-university Consortium for Political and Social Research who advised us of characteristics of the various data collections we have used. Special thanks also to Walter Stubbs, government documents librarian, and to other members of the staff of Morris Library at Southern Illinois University at Carbondale.

James Q. Graham read an early version of our manuscript and made many helpful comments and suggestions. We appreciate his efforts. We also are grateful to several anonymous readers. Although we were unable or unwilling to follow all of the suggestions, their comments made this a better book. The two authors are, of course, equally responsible for its shortcomings.

Introduction

This book is concerned with the long-term trends in the use of capital punishment in the United States, and in areas that would become part of the United States, from the colonial period onward. The book focuses on four basic questions: How frequently has the death penalty been used, and how has the frequency of use changed? Where was the death penalty used most frequently? What were the offenses charged? What were the characteristics of the executed? As will become clear, the first two questions can be addressed more successfully than the third and fourth. All four, however, are fraught with serious ambiguities.

We also attempt in what follows to take lynching into account. Lynching was, of course, a criminal act whether carried out by vigilantes, Klansmen, or unorganized mobs, and as such it might be seen as being outside the purview of a book concerned with the legal use of the death penalty. The line between lynching and the legal use of the death penalty, however, was often far from clear. To distinguish between lynching, on the one hand, and a legal execution, on the other, of an African American following a hasty trial before a white jury, carried out under the watchful eye of a nascent lynch mob and explained as necessary to prevent a lynching, might seem a distinction without much in the way of meaningful difference.[1]

How many such "legal lynchings" actually occurred will never be known. It is clear, however, that during the nineteenth and the earlier twentieth centuries lynching had the approval of many leading political figures and, at least in some areas of the nation, a sizable segment of the public. Lynching was treated as, and many probably believed it to be, a legitimate alternative to legal processes. These matters to the side, lynching claimed large numbers of victims and was, as a consequence, an important element in the context of the legal use of the death penalty. In some regions and time periods victims of lynching exceeded the number legally executed and effectively negated trends in the legal use of the death penalty.

1

The issues addressed in what follows are, we believe, of considerable intrinsic importance, although aside from the work of specialists they often are left unconsidered in studies of American social and political history. They also reflect, however, a number of broader and interrelated issues bearing upon the changing nature of national culture and institutions. Three of these issues were of particular importance in shaping the temporal and geographic change and variation in the incidence and nature of capital punishment.

One involves the characteristics and development of the institutions, laws, and practices governing criminal justice in the United States, which were themselves also reflections of the larger society. In his concluding chapter of the history of crime and punishment in the United States, Lawrence M. Friedman writes that

> . . . the criminal justice "system" is not a system at all. This particular mirror of society is a jigsaw puzzle with a thousand tiny pieces. No one is really in charge. Legislatures make rules; police and detectives carry them out (more or less). Prosecutors prosecute; defense attorneys defend; judges and juries go their own way. So do prison officials. Everybody seems to have veto power over everybody else. Juries can frustrate judges and the police; the police can make nonsense out of the legislature; prison officials can undo the work of judges; prosecutors can ignore the police and the judges.[2]

The history of capital punishment well illustrates the point and, if anything, adds additional dimensions. If the notion of system implies a measure of uniformity—the same crimes, same legal procedures, same sentences, and same implementation of sentences—then the use of capital punishment has historically lacked systemic properties. The use of capital punishment has not only changed over time, its use also has varied from one area and jurisdiction to another and from one ethnic, racial, and social group to another. Variation is compounded when lynching is added to the context of the legal use of the death penalty. In these terms change and variation in the use of capital punishment provide an indication of the characteristics and patterns of development of the criminal justice system and, in some sense, of society more generally.

A second broad issue concerns the social biases characteristic of the United States and its various regions and jurisdictions. It will come as no surprise to learn that African Americans have been executed in disproportionate numbers during the history of the United States. Members of other ethnic and racial groups also were executed in disproportionate numbers. Apart from matters of race and ethnicity, it also will come as no surprise that the large majority of those put to death, whatever their race or ethnicity, appear to have been of low economic status.

These disparities cannot be taken as no more than indications of a discriminatory law and criminal justice system. We know on other grounds that the historical law and criminal justice system was massively discriminatory and placed the poor at a disadvantage. The available evidence indicates, however, that violent and criminal behavior was not evenly distributed across the various groups that made up American society, and it is reasonable to believe that most of those put to death actually committed the offenses charged or were guilty of similar offenses. We also know that other and deeper social conflicts and tensions within American society both shaped the law and criminal justice system and played a major role in shaping individual behavior. Disparities in the use of capital punishment can be seen, then, as providing a crude indication of these deeper conflicts and tensions.

The history of capital punishment also reflects a third aspect of American history, the incidence and role of violence. This is not to assume that the historical incidence of capital punishment is a reliable and consistent indicator of the incidence of violence in America. The large majority of those executed were charged with violent offenses, usually some form of homicide often accompanied by other offenses. Thus it is reasonable to at least suspect that the frequent use of the death penalty tended to occur in areas marked by high levels of violence. Similarly, the weaker assumption that the incidence of capital punishment provides in any straightforward fashion a satisfactory indicator of the incidence of homicide or other capital crimes also is untenable. While a relation undoubtedly did exist, such an assumption is undermined by historical change in the definition of capital crime and by a wide variation in the incidence of capital punishment from one time period, jurisdiction, and ethnic, economic, and social group to another. These variations allow ample room for the intervention of other factors in addition to crime rates in determining the incidence of capital punishment.

The incidence of capital punishment is, however, a measure of one type of violence. Capital punishment is, after all, a form of violence, and the most extreme form that organized society can legally impose on its members. As such, one measure of the role and incidence of violence in the history of the nation is the frequency and the conditions under which capital punishment has been used to maintain social order, however social order has been defined and whatever has been presumed to be the relationship between punishment and the maintenance of order.

Although concerned with the long sweep of American history, this study is limited in a number of respects. The bulk of the investigation focuses on the years prior to 1945. During the years immediately following, the use of capital punishment declined sharply—it was briefly discontinued in 1972 but resumed in 1977. The years after 1977 seem to constitute something of a different era in the use of the death penalty. The numbers put to death have not reached the levels of the pre-World War II years, and a degree of centralization of control over capital punishment has occurred largely through the intervention of the federal courts. Examination of the incidence of capital punishment and sentencing after 1977 indicates both persistence and change in trends and patterns characteristic of the years before 1945. These differences and elements of continuity have provoked considerable scholarly controversy centering in part on questions concerning whether, or in what degree, they reflect persistent systemic racial, ethnic, and class discrimination. We note these disagreements and touch upon some of their dimensions. We do not attempt to reconcile them.

Our examination of the history of capital punishment is primarily descriptive in nature. We trace and examine long-term trends and regional variations in the use of the death penalty, and we attempt to place these trends and variations in the broader context of American history. At various points, but particularly in concluding chapters, we note explanations sometimes offered for violence in American history as they seem to apply to capital punishment, and we suggest rather obvious factors that are clearly related to change in the use of the death penalty. Racial and ethnic discrimination and the relations between racial and ethnic groups more generally are clearly among these factors, as are differences in economic condition. Although difficult to demonstrate, change in the age structure of the national and regional populations was probably also a factor shaping the history of capital punishment.

We have found as well that trends and patterns characteristic of the history of capital punishment seem to parallel formulations developed by Norbert Elias. Elias describes a "civilizing process" characteristic of the development of societies that shaped manners, personal behavior, and the relations between social groups and also worked to control and regulate violence.[3] These formulations, particularly as applied to punishment by David Garland, provide suggestive explanations for aspects of the history of capital punishment across the sweep of American history.[4] We do not attempt, however, to demonstrate or weigh the precise relevance of these factors and possible explanations through rigorous causal or other analysis. Our primary goal is to trace and demonstrate trends and patterns in the use of capital punishment across the course of American history.

Similarly, we have not attempted to dramatize our examination of the use of the death penalty, although it would be easy to do so. Ample descriptions are found of gruesomely botched executions as well as those that were carried out with at least a measure of humanity and dignity, although to combine deliberate infliction of death with notions of humanity and dignity may appear as something of an oxymoron. Many stories exist about trials that were no more than kangaroo courts, but also about trials that seem eminently fair. Similarly, abundant examples are found of crimes so horrid that execution hardly seems an adequate retribution. On the other hand, many examples of the use of the death penalty seem far out of proportion to the offenses committed if, indeed, an offense was actually committed. We have attempted, however, to minimize the use of anecdotes. The simple fact is that given the paucity of evidence, it is impossible to know which of the many available anecdotes could be seen as in any sense typical of the general practices of particular times and places. In our view, the selection of anecdotes inevitably provides a biased perspective. In our view as well whether capital punishment is supported or opposed, its history is in itself a sufficiently sad and tragic story and requires no embellishment or dramatization.

DATA SOURCES

As in the case of other forms of violence in the United States, an examination of long-term historical trends in the use of capital punishment has presented major obstacles. Historical information bearing upon the use of the death penalty has existed only in scattered and often fugitive form. Historical record keeping was imperfect, the decentralized nature of the nation meant that records also were decentralized, and records of the use of the death penalty, as other historical records, have been subject to the usual ravages of time. Even limited work in the relevant historical sources, moreover, sometimes gives the impression that during much of their history Americans were often indifferent to the use of capital punishment with the consequence that careful records of its occurrence were not always kept. Newspaper and other accounts of historical executions often treated them as being of only passing significance and, aside from an occasional spectacle, of limited and transitory interest. Characteristics of the executed that are important from a historical perspective were seemingly often of little interest to people at the time. These matters to the side, the nature of historical source material has been a major obstacle to the systematic investigation of the use of the death penalty.

To examine the history of capital punishment we have drawn upon several bodies of data. The most important of these was collected by M. Watt Espy. Indeed, it is due to Espy's work that it is possible at least to begin to address basic questions concerning the historical use of the death penalty. In 1970, working out of his home in Headland, Alabama, and on the basis of his personal financial resources, Espy began the work of systematically identifying and collecting information on all legal executions in the United States, or in areas settled or occupied by Europeans that would become part of the United States. The magnitude of this task will be apparent. On the order of two thirds of all executions in American history were carried out at the local level. To identify and collect even limited information on these executions involved widely scattered and diverse sources, including a variety of local repositories, court and other governmental records, local and regional newspapers, and local histories, as well as other sources.

Espy subsequently moved the project to the University of Alabama, and by the mid-1980s he had compiled information on over 14,000 executions, beginning with the first European executed in Jamestown in 1608. Working at the University of Alabama with the assistance of Professor John Ortiz Smykla, and with support provided by the National Science Foundation and the University of Alabama Law Center, this segment of the collection was organized and converted to usable computer-readable form. This version was then supplied to the Inter-university Consortium for Political and Social Research (ICPSR) to be distributed for scholarly use. Corrections subsequently provided by Espy were then made, and a second version of the collection was released in 1992. Although information for particular cases and variables understandably is sometimes missing, the collection includes the ethnicity, sex, and age of the executed, the place of conviction and execution, the method of execution, and the offense charged, as well as limited additional information.[5] The Espy project continued, and by March 1996, Espy had identified and collected information bearing upon well over 4,000 additional executions. Espy's project is ongoing, again being carried out in his home in Headland and on the basis of his own resources. There can be no doubt that his work will produce evidence and information about still additional executions.

In what follows we draw upon the 1992 revised computer-readable Espy file supplied by the ICPSR. Espy also has been kind enough to supply us with summary information bearing upon over 4,000 executions identified between 1985 and early 1996. We have combined this additional information with the 1992 revised ICPSR version of the collection. This combined data collection provides the primary basis for our examination of capital punishment.[6] Data from executions after 1945 are from the Death Penalty Information Center.[7]

Characteristics of the combined Espy collection are discussed in greater detail in the Appendix of this book, which explores as well some of the strengths and weaknesses of the collection, and the characteristics of the collection are noted in the text and footnotes that follow as they relate to particular generalizations or categories of generalizations. The Appendix also describes work directed to assessing the reliability of the collection. These include comparison with other and more limited compilations, with a variety of relevant secondary works, and a limited examination of original sources.

On the basis of this work we have developed considerable confidence in the collection as a source of a reasonably accurate view of the use of the death penalty in American history. As the Appendix indicates, it is likely, as would probably be expected, that the collection is relatively less complete for the earlier years and for the Southern and Border states. It is likely as well that in the future additional executions will be identified either by Espy or others, and it is virtually certain that the collection includes an unknown number of spurious cases. Even so, we believe that the collection provides a sound basis for an approximation of the ethnic, geographical, and temporal distribution of executions in American history. Our confidence is increased by the degree to which the patterns and relations identified through the examination of the collection conform to prior expectations. Information bearing upon the characteristics of the executed, the offenses charged, and the methods of execution is less complete, as we indicate. In these areas as well, however, the observed patterns are highly predictable, and our confidence in our findings is thereby increased.

To avoid possible confusion, we should note that we do not treat the Espy collection as a sample in either the dictionary or technical sense of that word. In the first place, the collection was not intended as a sample but is an effort to collect information on the total universe of legal executions carried out in American history. Because of the nature of historical sources and record keeping, that effort could not be entirely successful. However, the direction of biases characteristic of the collection is known or can be reasonably assumed, and the consequences estimated in at least general ways. One consequence of this approach is that we often treat small numbers as real values—as approximations of historical reality—not as only the possibly erroneous products of inadequate sampling.

Sources for examination of lynching and their characteristics also are discussed in greater detail in the Appendix. These sources present many of the same difficulties as sources for the study of capital punishment in even more serious ways. Sources of information are widely scattered, often in the form of local and regional newspaper accounts. The problem is compounded by the fact that lynching was a criminal act that usually did not result in official records, except on the rare occasions that perpetrators were the subjects of criminal action. As a consequence, nothing exists that approaches a complete list of lynchings or of the names and characteristics of victims. Here again, however, we have benefited from the work of others. Stewart E. Tolnay and E. M. Beck supplied data on lynching for ten Southern and, in our definition,

Border states for the years 1882–1930 that they used in their study *A Festival of Violence: An Analysis of Southern Lynchings, 1882–1930.*[8] For three additional Border and Southern states we have used compilations published by George C. Wright and W. Fitzhugh Brundage.[9] For the rest of the nation, several older compilations, including the National Association for the Advancement of Colored People publication *Thirty Years of Lynching*, have been used.[10] The characteristics and limitations of these sources also are discussed in an appendix. Richard Maxwell Brown, in *Strain of Violence: Historical Studies of American Violence and Vigilantism*, provides estimates of the numbers lynched by organized vigilante groups from 1767 through 1904.[11]

In relating the incidence of executions and lynchings to population, we have used the extensive files of historical computer-readable data also drawn from U.S. Census reports related sources, maintained by the ICPSR.[12] In using these data, however, we also have drawn upon the corrections and additions at the state level to the original census reports provided by the *Historical Statistics of the United States*. We have also relied upon the *Historical Statistics* for estimates of the colonial population.[13]

All of the data sources that we have employed are imperfect, and all are marked by an error of one sort or another. We attempt to call attention to these imperfections as they may affect our interpretations and inferences. Suffice it to say here that the data sources provide an approximate view of the historical incidence of capital punishment. The degree of approximation varies from one time period and region of the nation to another, as does the possible type and magnitude of error. We believe, however, that what follows is a valid approximation of historical reality.

This book is, in short, based upon "secondary analysis," that is, mostly upon data collected by others in some cases for purposes other than historical investigation. We have spent some time working in the relevant primary sources mainly for purposes of verification. We have come to recognize that the limitations of the data that we have used are in considerable measure a reflection of the primary sources and to appreciate the work of original data collectors.

Chapter 1

The Death Penalty in National Perspective

From the very beginning capital punishment has been an integral part of American history. The first execution of a European in what would become part of the United States was in Jamestown in 1608, only a few months after the colony was founded.[1] During the next twenty years only occasional executions took place. By mid-century, some fifty people had been executed. By the end of the seventeenth century, on the order of 300 European, African, and Native Americans had been put to death. One hundred years later, the number had grown to almost 3,000. While the number of executions steadily grew, the population grew at a more rapid rate. As a consequence, viewed in relation to population, the use of capital punishment actually declined. Even so, by the end of 1945, more than 17,000 people had been legally put to death.

This chapter examines the trends in the incidence, racial, ethnic, and gender distribution of executions in the continental United States, or what would become part of the continental United States, from 1608 through 1945. The incidence of capital punishment is examined both in terms of the actual number of executions and in relation to population. Both perspectives are, of course, valid and useful but for different purposes, and each provides support for different generalizations.

In recent years, as is well known, a disproportionate number of those put to death have been African Americans. This disproportion appeared early in American history. Beginning in the early eighteenth century, a majority of those executed in most years were of African descent, and the pattern persisted. African Americans, of course, never constituted a majority of the colonial or national population. When other racial and ethnic groups are combined with African Americans, whites appear as a distinct minority of those executed. The gender distribution

9

of capital punishment is considered only briefly later. In American history, the death penalty has been, very largely, a male monopoly.

FREQUENCY OF EXECUTION

During most of American history capital punishment has been characterized by a long-term rising trend. The shape of that trend from the early seventeenth century through 1945 is summarized in Figure 1.1. Viewed in detail, the incidence of capital punishment, particularly during the earlier years, fluctuated widely from one year to the next. To somewhat smooth out these fluctuations and to facilitate relating the number of executions to population at a later point, the figure gives the average number of executions per year for each ten-year period through 1945. For these purposes, each period is centered on the decennial census year and is defined as beginning with the year ending in six, as 1886, and closing with the next year ending in five, as 1895.[2]

Even when smoothed out in this fashion, the series is marked by rather wide fluctuations. Despite these fluctuations, the rising trend in the number of executions is clear. During the ten-year period from 1606 through 1615, the data collection records only two executions, both in Virginia. The number rose to an average of about six per year for the ten-year period from 1686 through 1695, and to approximately forty each year during the ten years centering on 1790. One hundred years later (1886 through 1895), an average of about 120 people were executed each year, roughly two per week. High points in the number of executions were reached during the twenty-year period from 1926 through 1945. Over 1,500 individuals, an average of almost three each week, were put to death during the years 1926 through 1935 and 1,491 during the next ten-year period. Thereafter, the incidence of executions declined.

Since we know that data collection is continuing, and that additional executions will be identified, it is reasonable to ponder the degree to which the trend in Figure 1.1 is a reflection of historical reality. It is certainly possible that some of the extreme fluctuations, particularly during the earlier years, may be indicative of executions that actually occurred but have not yet been identified. At later points we discuss other factors that also help account for some of these fluctuations. These include the Revolutionary War and the Civil War, both of which were accompanied by comparatively heavy use of the death penalty, and help account for two of the peaks in the time series in Figure 1.1.

A more serious question concerns the degree to which the trend in Figure 1.1 is the product of error in the form of executions that have not yet been identified rather than actual historical change. As discussed briefly in the Introduction and at greater length in the Appendix, it is

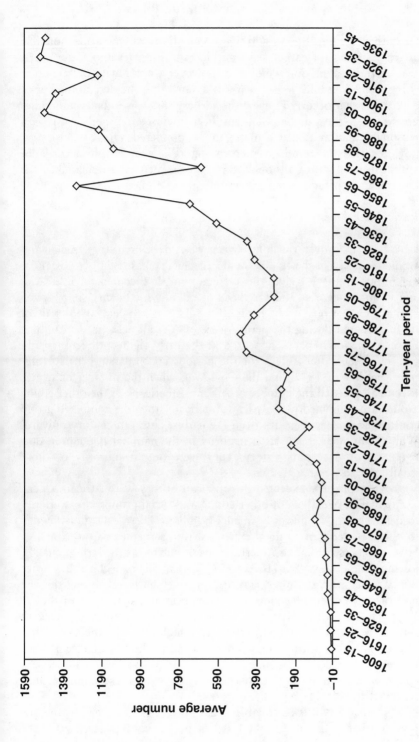

Figure 1.1 Average annual number of executions per year by ten-year period, 1606–1945

likely that identification of additional executions will disproportionately affect the series for earlier years and have less impact upon later years. Even if this assumption were valid, however, to eliminate the apparent rising trend it would be necessary to assume that the actual number of executions that occurred during the earlier years was in fact many times greater than the number that has been identified. Whether this is a reasonable assumption is a matter to be pondered. Our conclusion is, however, that the trend given in the figure is generally in accordance with historical reality, although it might be somewhat attenuated by the identification of additional executions in the future.[3]

Race and Ethnicity

It is clear that over the long sweep of American history, racial and ethnic disparity in the use of the death penalty has been of substantial magnitude. Table 1.1 gives the average number executed for five racial and ethnic categories and for those of unknown ethnicity summarized by ten-year periods, as in Figure 1.1.[4] As can be seen, about half of those executed during the period were of African descent. As can also be seen, this discrepancy appeared in the early eighteenth century and continued thereafter except for the periods encompassing the Revolution, the War of 1812, and the Civil War, when the number of whites executed exceeded the number of African Americans. If the other ethnic groups are combined with African Americans, then the combined group constituted a clear majority from the early eighteenth century onward. Whites, of course, made up a majority of the national population during most of American history. They were only a minority of those legally put to death.

Most of those executed in American history were African American or white. Members of other ethnic and racial groups also were put to death, but in significantly smaller numbers. These executions tended to reflect patterns of national expansion and settlement. Comparatively large numbers of Native Americans were put to death during and following King Philip's War (1675–1676). The numbers declined thereafter but rose again in the nineteenth century to high levels during the last half of that period reflecting the penetration and settlement of the far West. The number of Hispanics put to death also rose in the nineteenth century and continued at comparatively high levels in the twentieth.[5] Execution of Asians, usually Chinese, began in the late nineteenth century and continued in the following years. As will be seen in subsequent chapters, executions of members of all three of these ethnic groups followed predictable regional patterns.

Here again, it is reasonable to ask whether, or to what degree, the patterns that appear in Table 1.1 are the product of imperfections of the

Table 1.1. Annual number of executions by ten-year period and ethnic group, 1606–1945

	African American	White	Native American	Hispanic	Asian	Other	Unknown	Total
1606–15	0	2	0	0	0	0	0	2
1616–25	0	3	0	0	0	0	0	3
1626–35	0	4	0	0	0	0	0	4
1636–45	1	17	2	0	0	0	0	20
1646–55	0	23	0	0	0	0	0	23
1656–65	2	14	5	0	0	0	9	30
1666–75	2	17	10	0	0	0	6	35
1676–85	5	42	44	0	0	0	0	91
1686–95	9	38	5	0	0	0	10	62
1696–05	11	27	14	0	0	0	1	53
1706–15	56	13	14	0	0	0	2	85
1716–25	43	133	5	0	0	0	36	217
1726–35	55	47	10	0	0	0	8	120
1736–45	166	99	7	0	0	0	5	277
1746–55	145	104	1	0	0	0	15	265
1756–65	123	92	5	0	0	0	12	232
1766–75	236	174	6	0	0	0	31	447
1776–85	156	274	5	1	0	0	45	481
1786–95	193	150	4	1	0	0	61	409
1796–05	225	63	4	1	1	0	9	303
1806–15	122	161	11	1	0	0	10	305
1816–25	212	159	20	2	0	0	13	406
1826–35	250	147	15	20	0	0	13	445
1836–45	342	206	25	6	1	0	22	602

continued on next page

Table 1.1. (Continued)

	African American	White	Native American	Hispanic	Asian	Other	Unknown	Total
1846–55	434	235	27	17	0	0	25	738
1856–65	528	682	52	12	3	0	47	1,324
1866–75	299	249	28	19	3	0	84	682
1876–85	543	408	53	21	13	1	94	1,133
1886–95	637	394	50	21	11	0	91	1,204
1896–05	834	474	27	36	12	0	108	1,491
1906–15	811	510	8	23	12	0	68	1,432
1916–25	584	530	4	46	14	1	34	1,213
1926–35	727	701	6	31	19	1	26	1,511
1936–45	766	641	7	27	10	0	34	1,485
Total	8,517	6,833	474	285	99	3	919	17,130
Percent	49.72	39.89	2.77	1.66	0.58	0.02	5.36	100.00

available data rather than reflections of historical reality. As can be seen, the number whose ethnicity is unknown is sometimes troublesomely large. It is impossible to know the ethnicity of these individuals, but it is possible to ponder on the basis of assumption how the distribution of capital punishment between these ethnic groups would appear if the ethnicity of these individuals were known.

If it were assumed, for example, that all of those given in the table as being of unknown ethnicity were actually white, probably an extreme assumption, then whites would still appear as a minority of those put to death. Those classified nonwhite would still constitute a majority of those executed both in terms of the total number during the entire period and during most ten-year periods after the late seventeenth century. African Americans would still constitute the largest ethnic group among the executed, again both in total numbers across the period and during most ten-year periods. The margin of difference between whites and other groups taken individually or in combination would be narrower, but whites would remain in the minority. Various other assumptions of different degrees of plausibility also could be made. These would not undermine, however, the basic pattern characteristic of the table. Groups classified nonwhite have been more frequently executed in American history. Whites have been in a minority, despite their majority status in the national population.

Gender

We have information on gender for approximately three fourths of the known executions prior to 1945. The large majority of these individuals were male, and less than 3% were women. Although the number of women executed tended to increase until the late nineteenth century, women constituted a declining percentage of those put to death. Of those executed during the seventeenth century for whom information on gender is available, thirty-nine were women. In the eighteenth century the number rose to ninety-eight and to 178 in the nineteenth. In the twentieth century prior to 1945 only twenty-eight women were executed. For each century women constituted, respectively, approximately 25%, 7%, 3% and less than 1% of the total number put to death.

The available evidence suggests that the ethnic distribution of the women put to death was characterized by, if anything, a more pronounced racial disparity than the total group of those executed. Of all women executed, some 57% were African Americans as compared to about 35% white. About 6% were of unknown ethnicity, and 2% were members of other ethnic groups. If more complete information was available, then it is unlikely that these ethnic disparities would be much changed. It seems unlikely as well that more complete information would show that women constituted a significantly larger proportion of the total number of people put to death.

RATES OF EXECUTION

The number of individuals executed is of considerable historical interest. The data series summarized in Figure 1.1 indicated that prior to the mid-twentieth century the death penalty was used with increasing frequency and became an increasingly prominent fact of national life. From one perspective, that increase is as would be expected. All other things the same, as the population increased it might be expected that the number executed would also increase, unless there was some change in the factors governing the imposition of the death penalty, the change in the rates of capital crimes, or some combination of the two. It also is the case that if increased reliance was placed upon the death penalty as a means to cope with crime and violence, then it could be expected that the rate of executions in relation to population, not simply the number of executions, would increase.

This is not the pattern that appears. Figure 1.2 gives the average number of executions per 100,000 population for each decade from the early seventeenth century through 1945.[6] In estimating the number of executions for this calculation, the same procedure was used as in preparing Figure 1.1. That is, the average number of executions per year was calculated for each ten-year period, and the averages were then divided by the national population as estimated or enumerated at the end of each decade to extract the rate of execution per 100,000 population. Calculations for the years before 1790 are based upon estimates of the colonial population at each decade. Those for 1790 and after are based upon the decennial censuses of the United States.[7] The population figures used in the figure are for the white and African American populations.[8] Other population groups were not consistently enumerated until the late nineteenth century and in some cases even later.

As figure 1.2 indicates, the rate of executions in relation to population is marked by historical decline rather than increase.[9] As Figure 1.1 indicated, only a small number of executions are recorded as occurring in the seventeenth century. While the number of executions grew prior to independence, it remained small in comparison to later years. In this sense it is accurate to say that the colonists made relatively little use of the death penalty.[10] Because of the very small population during these years, however, this small number of executions translates into very high execution rates. The two executions during the years 1606–1615 translate into a rate of approximately 5.7 persons per 1,000 population, or approximately 57.1 per 100,000. The rate of executions quickly declined to an average of approximately 13.0 per 100,000 in

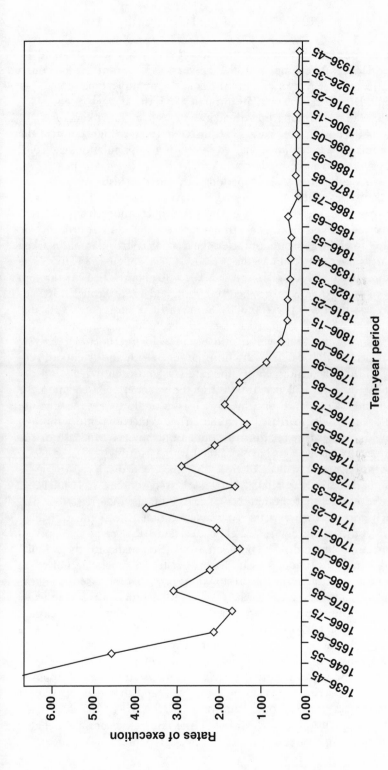

Figure 1.2 Average annual rates of execution of African American and white per 100,000 population combined by ten-year period, 1636–1945

the following ten-year period, and succeeding years were marked by further decline. As examples, in the ten-year period, from 1686 through 1695, the average rate of executions remained at approximately 2.2 per 100,000. During the years 1756 through 1765, the average rate was 1.4 per 100,000. This compares with an average rate of approximately 0.12 per 100,000 during the years 1926 through 1935, a high point in the total number of executions. Viewed in relation to population, the colonies appeared to have made considerable use of the death penalty, at least when compared to later periods in American history.

The series given in Figure 1.2 is marked, particularly in the seventeenth and eighteenth centuries, by sharp fluctuations from one ten-year period to the next. The trend, however, is downward. In the seventeenth and eighteenth centuries, the trend was irregular and marked by sharp surges, especially in the periods 1676 through 1685 (to a little over three per 100,000), 1716 through 1725 (to about 3.7), 1736 through 1745 (to approximately three per 100,000), and 1766 through 1785 (to slightly less than two per 100,000). Some of these surges are explicable in terms of unusual events discussed in the following chapter. In the later years of the century the rate began a long-term and relatively regular decline that carried over into the nineteenth and twentieth centuries. In the nineteenth century the rate was consistently below .4 per 100,000 and below .2 per 100,000 in the twentieth. Based upon the sheer numbers of executions, in short it is accurate to say that the use of the death penalty increased from the early seventeenth century through the 1930s. Viewed in relation to population, however, the use of the death penalty appears to have declined rather steadily.

Once again, it will be obvious that the trend displayed in Figure 1.2 is marked by bias related to at least two sources. It is likely, as discussed earlier, that the number of executions is underreported, particularly for the earlier years. At the same time, the population data used in constructing Figure 1.2 almost certainly underreport the actual African American and white populations. The estimates for the colonial period, it is likely, underestimate both the African American and white populations, although the underestimate is probably more serious in the case of African Americans in the seventeenth century.[11] It is very likely that the census enumerations also involve undercounts of magnitudes on the order of 10% or more for the early years. The censuses became progressively more accurate for later years, although even the most recent censuses are thought to involve undercounts.[12]

It will be recognized that these two sources of bias have opposite effects on the series displayed in Figure 1.2, and that they also affect calculation of rates for other purposes. Obviously, to the degree the number of executions is undercounted, the rate of execution is deflated below the actual values. To the degree that population is underestimated, the rate of executions is inflated above actual values. There are no grounds, however, for assuming that the two sources of bias cancel each other out, although they do work in opposite directions. At the same time, there also are no grounds for believing that the downward trend in the average yearly rate of executions can be accounted for solely as a consequence of the biases or other inaccuracies characteristic of the available data. To eliminate the trend shown in the figure, it would be necessary to assume very large, and probably unlikely, undercounts of the population or executions, or a combination of both.

It appears, then, that the rate of executions in relation to population has diminished rather consistently, and by a considerable magnitude over time. To illustrate the point, if the rate of executions per 100,000 population for the years 1786 through 1795 (.81) had persisted, then an average of almost 1,000 people would have been executed each year during the period 1926–1935 rather than the actual average of approximately 152 per year. It is unlikely that a decline of this magnitude in the annual average number of executions can be explained by incomplete data or other configurations of data error.

These elements of bias also affect in unknown ways execution rates calculated for racial and ethnic groups. Execution rates for African Americans and whites taken separately are given in Figure 1.3.[13] As indicated earlier, rates for other groups cannot be calculated because of lack of population data. As can be seen, after the seventeenth century the execution rates for both groups tended to decline. The decline in white rates, however, began earlier and is more precipitous than the decline in the rates for African Americans. The African American rates also tend to be more volatile and marked by more and wider fluctuations. Particularly for the earlier years, this characteristic is in part a product of the smaller African American population. The very high figure for the period 1636–1645, for example, reflects the execution of a single African slave in 1641. The colonial population of African descent is estimated as being less than 600 in 1640.

What is striking about the figure is the marked disparity between the African American and white rates. Beginning early in the seventeenth century, African American rates of execution have been, with a single exception, consistently higher than the rates for whites. The drop in white rates compared to the rates for African Americans also is apparent. By the mid-seventeenth century white rates had dropped below four per 100,000 and to below one per 100,000 by the middle of the following century. Before the end of the nineteenth century they had fallen below .1 per 100,000 and remained essentially stable at these levels. In contrast, African American rates did not fall consistently below one until late in the nineteenth century, and they never fell below .56 per 100,000.

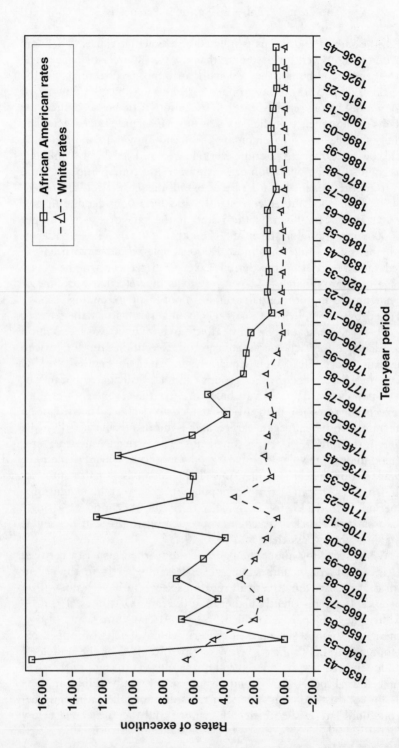

Figure 1.3 Average annual rates of execution of African American and white per 100,000 population by ten-year period, 1636–1945

The differences between the two groups shown in Figure 1.3 are of very considerable magnitude. The point can be made more clearly by looking at the ratio of African American to white average rates of execution in Figure 1.4.[14] As will be recognized, a ratio above 1.0 indicates that African American rates were higher than white rates, and a value below 1.0 indicates that African American rates were lower. The ratio of African American to white execution rates tended to rise across the entire period, although the series is quite irregular. In the eighteenth century the ratio rarely exceeded 6.0. That is, the African Americans were rarely executed at rates more than six times that of whites. In the nineteenth century and the first half of the twentieth, the ratio was usually above 8.0. During the last decade (1935–1945) of the period, the ratio of African American to white rates of execution was over 10.0.[15] Put differently, from the early nineteenth century through the mid-twentieth African American rates of execution were, on average, nearly nine times that of whites.

Viewed in relation to population, use of capital punishment declined during the course of American history for both African Americans and whites. It is probable that the rate at which other ethnic groups were put to death also declined, but that can be only a matter of speculation, since information about population is unavailable for these groups. The comparative pattern of change in rates of execution for African Americans and whites, however, was more than a matter of simple decline. From the mid-sixteenth century onward, the rate in relation to population at which African Americans were put to death almost consistently exceeded that of whites. While rates of execution declined for both groups, the discrepancy between the groups increased. In the twentieth century the difference between the groups was greater than it had been in the eighteenth.

CAPITAL OFFENSES

The number of offenses defined as capital was smaller in the North American colonies than in England at the time. Even so, a lengthy list of offenses in the various colonies could result in execution, and the list was certainly longer than it would become in later years. Beginning as early as the latter seventeenth century, capital punishment was increasingly restricted to offenses that involved the death of a victim. The death penalty was never restricted exclusively to lethal offenses. Various other crimes remained subject to execution, but by the 1940s the number was relatively small, and in practice executions for these offenses were rare.

This process of redefinition, both in de jure and de facto terms, can be observed behaviorally by examining the offenses that led to

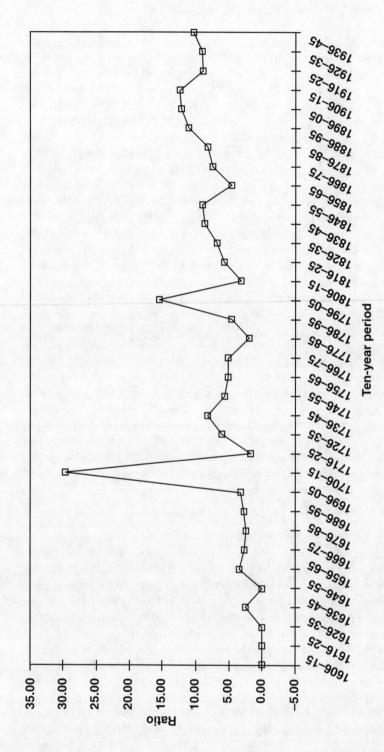

Figure 1.4 Ratio of African American to white rates of execution, 1606–1945

execution. That examination will be imperfect. Information is available on the offenses charged for approximately 75% of known executions from the beginning of the colonial period through 1945. The precise number of executions for offenses that did not involve a death cannot be established. It is possible, however, to establish the approximate minimum number that were put to death for such offenses.

In the colonial and revolutionary period, only about half of all known executions were for offenses that involved the death of a victim. The rest were for a variety of other offenses with various forms of theft and robbery, including forgery and counterfeiting, which constituted the largest category—about three out of ten executions. In the years that followed, lethal offenses accounted for an increasing proportion of all executions. During the period 1786 through the end of the Civil War approximately seven out of ten executions were for offenses that involved a death. The proportion rose to nine out of every ten executions during the period 1866–1945. (The other offenses that led to execution are discussed in somewhat greater detail in following chapters.)

Change in the crimes that led to execution can be seen more clearly in Figure 1.5, which provides for known executions of African Americans and whites the percentages that did not involve the death of the victim. For the seventeenth and eighteenth centuries the series is quite irregular, and no clear trends are apparent. During the following years, in contrast, the percentage of executions for nonlethal offenses declined steadily and relatively consistently for both groups. After the Civil War, however, the percentage of African Americans executed for nonlethal offenses gradually increased, and in the ten-year period, 1936–1945, it reached levels not seen since the early nineteenth century. The white percentage of nonlethal offenses also increased, but the increase was substantially less than that for African Americans and limited to the period 1926–1945.

Beginning in the late eighteenth century the series takes on a clear bias for African Americans. The percentage of African Americans executed for nonlethal crimes was consistently higher than the percentage of whites. For both groups the percentage executed for lethal crimes increased across the nineteenth and twentieth centuries, but the percentage was consistently higher for whites than for African Americans. Although the differences persisted, they were smaller after the Civil War than in earlier years. While capital crime was redefined, the consequences were, in practice, usually more beneficial to whites than African Americans.

While execution for most nonlethal offenses either declined or was discontinued prior to 1945, rape, attempted rape, and rape with other offenses such as burglary or robbery were exceptions.[16] Here again, executions for these offenses were marked by a clear ethnic bias. After

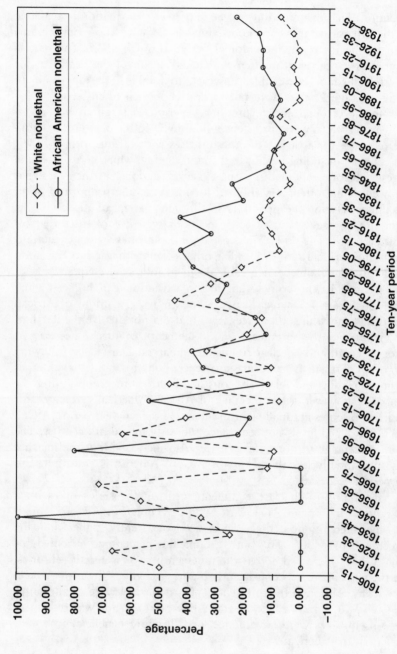

Figure 1.5 African American to white executions for known nonlethal crimes as a percentage of total executions, 1606–1945

the seventeenth century the percentage of African Americans put to death for rape was consistently greater, often many times greater, than that of whites.[17] Moreover, in the decades of the late nineteenth century, the percentage of African Americans executed for rape increased.[18] Most of the increase in the number of African Americans executed for non-lethal offenses was due to the increase in the number put to death for rape. The number of whites executed for rape also increased in the early twentieth century, but the numbers were far smaller than for African Americans. The offenses for which other ethnic groups were executed underwent little change. The large majority of these groups, around 90%, were executed for crimes that involved the death of a victim. Native Americans and Hispanics were sometimes executed for rape, but the number was small.

From the seventeenth century through the 1930s the United States made increasing use of the death penalty, however, this did not increase as rapidly as the national population, and the rate of execution in relation to population declined. Neither trend was entirely consistent, but their presence is unmistakable. Capital crime was redefined particularly from the latter eighteenth century onward. The number of offenses that carried the death penalty was progressively reduced, and execution was increasingly restricted, although never exclusively, to offenses that involved the death of a victim. This progressive redefinition of capital crime helps explain, at least in a direct sense, the decline in the rate of execution in relation to population. From the early eighteenth century onward, the use of capital punishment was characterized by clear racial disparity. Although a majority of the national population, whites constituted a minority of those put to death. The rate of capital punishment for whites declined earlier and to lower levels than the rate for African Americans, and the disparity between African American and whites tended to increase. While capital crime was redefined for both groups, the redefinition tended to be more meaningful for whites than for African Americans.

A complete explanation for the gap between the number and rate of African American executions as compared to white executions is not available. A racially discriminatory legal system and pervasive racial prejudice within white society were certainly part of the explanation, as we discuss more fully at various points later. The legal system also placed the poor at a disadvantage, which impacted more heavily upon African Americans, who were disproportionately poor. Research concerned with the years since 1945 indicates that rates of violent crime are higher among African Americans than among whites. If the same pattern prevailed in earlier years, it would also help explain the interracial gap in numbers and rates of execution. The hypothesis that historical crime rates were higher among African Americans than whites is in some degree self-confirming. In a number of areas of the nation, particularly the South and the Border regions, many more crimes carried the death penalty if committed by African Americans than if committed by whites. African Americans also resisted slavery and white domination by slave rebellions and during and after slavery by individual and other forms of group action. To the degree that resistance was violent, execution could be the result, which also worked to inflate the number and rate of African American executions.

These issues to the side, it is certainly possible that in the past other forms of violent offenses were committed more frequently by African Americans than by whites. Unfortunately, these possibilities cannot be tested. Systematic and reliable data on historical crime rates do not exist. It is possible—even likely—that all of these as well as other factors, and their interaction, contributed to the historical gap between African American and white execution rates. We have no way to distinguish between and assign relative importance to these various possibilities. We do know, however, that racial discrimination and prejudice were part of the story.

Chapter 2

The Colonial and Revolutionary Eras

The use of capital punishment underwent radical change over the course of American history. It also differed from one part of the nation to another, and for that matter, from one jurisdiction to another. The United States has never been homogeneous in cultural, demographic, economic, or even institutional terms. As would be expected, the use of the death penalty and the history of that use have reflected these differences. When the history of capital punishment is viewed in national perspective, in the preceding chapter, many of these differences are masked. This chapter begins the process of examining in greater detail some of these temporal and regional differences.

The colonial and revolutionary years, in the use of capital punishment, stand out as sharply different from later periods in American history, just as they do in many other respects. Criminal justice in these years often has been seen as rigid and harsh in the extreme. More recent scholarship suggests that this picture is overdrawn. In the first place, there was no single colonial criminal justice system. English law and criminal justice practices were modified both deliberately and inadvertently in the transit to the new world. What was imported to the colonies often varied considerably, depending upon when given colonies were founded, the characteristics of particular groups of colonists, and prevailing needs and conditions. These differences were enduring, and to further complicate matters, well before the end of the colonial period what amounted to separate criminal justice systems for African Americans and whites had emerged.[1]

It appears as well that in practice colonial approaches to criminal justice could be highly flexible and were not as rigid and unbending as they have sometimes been made out to be. Laws and the letter of the law

27

were sometimes ignored and not enforced; more serious charges could be replaced with those less serious; alternatives to criminal proceedings could be found and apparently often were preferred; and in the case of capital punishment, milder penalties often were substituted for execution.[2]

On the other hand, if the use of capital punishment is an indication, then it also appears that criminal justice in this period was harsher than it would become in later years and certainly harsher than in the latter twentieth century. Viewed in relation to population, the colonists made heavy use of the death penalty—comparable, it appears, to use in England during the same period. The offenses defined as capital differed somewhat among the colonies, but in most colonies a dozen or more offenses were punishable by death. Practices that now seem to involve little more than personal and morality preference could result in execution. In the interest of deterrence and retribution, methods of execution were sometimes used that seem cruel and barbaric in the extreme by modern standards, although the use of such methods may have been more the exception than the rule. Lesser penalties included whipping, branding, and mutilation.

To accommodate differences in the use of capital punishment and for purposes of summarization, this chapter and those that follow adopt a regional approach. Of course, no regional scheme can fully accommodate the heterogeneity characteristic of the colonies or the later United States. To better reflect historical reality, it also is sometimes necessary to shift the perspective to individual colonies and states.

THE SEVENTEENTH CENTURY

Depending on how it is defined, the colonial and revolutionary period encompasses over 175 years of American history, almost half the period considered in this study. During these years the colonies underwent extensive change and development, and these changes were reflected in use of the death penalty. In view of these changes it is useful to examine the seventeenth and eighteenth centuries separately, although the distinction is somewhat arbitrary. The seventeenth-century colonies were frontier settlements with characteristics that resembled but were probably harsher than those of the nineteenth-century West. Across the period the population grew, and the area of settlement expanded, but growth and development also were marked by setbacks and reversals. A measure of instability, periodic conflict, and hardship were facts of seventeenth-century colonial life, and these characteristics undoubtedly colored the use of capital punishment.

Only a relatively small number of executions took place in the seventeenth-century colonies, as the preceding chapter indicates. Approximately 270 whites, Native and African Americans, and individuals of unknown ethnicity were executed during the years from the first execution at Jamestown through 1695. Table 2.1 gives the number and ethnicity of those executed for each ten-year period from the founding through 1695.[3] For comparison with later periods, the executions are grouped in four regions.[4] As can be seen, most of the seventeenth-century executions (approximately 64%) took place in New England. The best estimates indicate that only once during the seventeenth century did New England account for as much as 50% of the population of the mainland colonies. As the population increased, the number put to death also increased, as did the ethnic diversity of the executed. The large majority of those executed in all regions were of European extraction. The next largest group was composed of Native Americans. In New England, during one conflict-ridden period that included King Philip's War, more than four times the number of Native Americans than whites were put to death.

It is not entirely meaningful to look at the seventeenth-century colonies only in regional terms after the fashion of Table 2.1. The number of colonies was small, and the use of the death penalty tended to be concentrated in a few areas. Over half of all executions took place in what would become Massachusetts. Connecticut accounted for about one in ten and Rhode Island for about one in twenty. All of the executions in the South took place in Virginia. In the Border region, some thirty-five were executed in Maryland and two in Delaware. Of the executions in the Middle Atlantic colonies, thirteen are known to have occurred in New York, eight in New Jersey, and one in Pennsylvania.

The number of executions in New England, particularly in Massachusetts, increased sharply during the closing decades of the century. The increase was in part a reflection of population growth, but it also reflects several well-known and well-documented events. Forty-two Native Americans were executed in New England, thirty-seven in Massachusetts, many of them probably in connection with King Philip's war and its aftermath. The number of Native Americans executed was probably larger than indicated in Table 2.1. It appears that during the war and its aftermath an unknown number were put to death immediately upon apprehension under circumstances that did not or may not have involved legal proceedings.[5] Twenty more individuals, fourteen of them female, were executed for witchcraft in Salem, Massachusetts, in 1692.[6] The frequency of executions in Virginia also increased during the latter part of the century. Almost two thirds of the executions recorded in the seventeenth century occurred during the ten-year period 1676–1685. At least twenty-three of these took place in connection with what has come to be known as Bacon's Rebellion.[7]

While the number of executions was small in comparison to later years, the seventeenth-century population also was small, and viewed in

Table 2.1. Number of executions by region and ethnic group, 1606–1695

	1606–15	1616–25	1626–35	1636–45	1646–55	1656–65	1666–75	1676–85	1686–95	TOTAL
New England										
African American	—	—	—	—	—	—	1	4	1	6
White	—	—	1	13	16	9	12	10	26	87
Native American	—	—	—	2	—	1	6	42	5	56
Unknown	—	—	—	—	—	6	6	—	10	22
Total	—	—	1	15	16	16	25	56	42	171
Mid-Atlantic										
African American	—	—	—	1	—	—	—	1	6	8
White	—	—	—	2	3	1	3	—	5	11
Native American	—	—	—	—	—	—	3	—	—	3
Unknown	—	—	—	—	—	—	—	—	—	—
Total	—	—	—	3	3	1	3	1	11	22
South										
African American	2	—	—	—	—	—	—	—	2	2
White	—	3	3	—	—	1	—	27	—	36
Native American	—	—	—	—	—	—	—	—	—	—
Unknown	—	—	—	—	—	—	—	—	—	—
Total	2	3	3	—	—	1	—	27	2	38
Border										
African American	—	—	—	—	—	2	1	—	—	3
White	—	—	—	2	4	3	5	5	7	26
Native American	—	—	—	—	—	4	1	—	—	5
Unknown	—	—	—	—	—	3	0	—	—	3
Total	—	—	—	2	4	12	7	5	7	37
Grand total	2	3	4	20	23	30	35	89	62	268

relation to population, rates of execution were high (see Table 2.2). The colonial population grew across the period. The New England population in 1650, for example, is estimated (probably underestimated) as approximately 23,000 whites and 380 of African descent. The number of Native Americans is, of course, unknown. By 1690, the estimated population of the region had reached 86,000 whites and 950 of African descent, probably underestimates in both cases.[8] Population growth was not accompanied by commensurate growth in execution rates. Rather, execution rates tended to decline irregularly. Even so, at the end of the period execution rates remained high compared to later years. During the period 1686–1695, twenty-six whites and a single African American were put to death in the New England colonies, an average rate of about three per 100,000 population for whites and eleven per 100,000 for the African American population.

As would be expected, seventeenth-century execution rates appear even more erratic when viewed at the level of individual colonies. In Connecticut the execution of one African American, out of an African American population estimated at thirty-five in 1670, meant an average yearly execution rate of 286 per 100,000. During the next ten-year period, the execution of three African Americans in Massachusetts, with an estimated African American population of 170, netted an average execution rate of approximately 176 per 100,000.[9] These very high execution rates were not typical, as the table also indicates. During most ten-year periods, the average yearly rates were significantly lower, and in many periods no executions are known to have occurred. Even so, the rates of execution were high compared to more recent years.

The erratic nature of the execution rates in Table 2.2 and imperfections of the available data complicate generalization. It appears, however, that many more executions took place in New England, primarily in Massachusetts, than in the other mainland colonies, where settlement and population growth were slower. New England execution rates, however, were not consistently higher than execution rates elsewhere in the colonies. Execution rates, whether viewed at the regional level or at the level of individual colonies, tended to decline irregularly across the period. Few African Americans were put to death prior to 1695, however, the African American population also was very small. The small number put to death resulted in very high rates of execution, usually much higher than the rates for whites. In contrast to whites, African American execution rates showed no clear and consistent indication of decline.

THE EIGHTEENTH CENTURY

In the eighteenth century the population of the British mainland colonies increased by a factor of a little over ten, from approximately 275,000

Table 2.2. Average annual rates of execution per 100,000 African American and white population by region, 1606–1695

	1606–15	1616–25	1626–35	1636–45	1646–55	1656–65	1666–75	1676–85	1686–95
New England									
African American	—	—	—	—	—	—	26.67	85.11	10.53
White	—	—	5.57	9.64	7.13	2.76	2.33	1.47	3.02
Mid-Atlantic									
African American	—	—	—	43.10	—	—	—	7.02	25.10
White	—	—	—	10.36	7.29	2.03	—	—	1.50
Border									
African American	—	—	—	—	—	25.38	8.13	—	—
White	—	—	—	34.31	8.53	3.35	3.59	2.64	2.74
South									
African American	—	13.76	—	—	—	—	—	—	1.79
White	57.14	—	12.00	—	—	0.36	—	5.38	—

African Americans and whites in 1700 to a little less than 3,000,000 in 1780. The older areas took on a measure of stability and maturity, but the area of settlement continued to expand, and in the new areas what amounted to frontier conditions usually prevailed. The ethnic composition of the colonial population also changed. Slavery was legal in all of the colonies and became the dominant labor system in the Southern and Border colonies and, for a time, in parts of the Middle Atlantic region as well. With the adoption of the slave labor system, the population of African descent also increased, in some areas more rapidly than the white population.

As population increased, the use of the death penalty also increased. During the period 1696–1785, there were 2,166 known executions in the mainland colonies, roughly an eightfold increase compared to the period 1608–1695, somewhat less than the growth of population. In the eighteenth century, the colonies also diverged in their use of the death penalty, as Table 2.3 indicates.[10] While the number put to death increased in all four regions, the largest growth was in the Southern colonies. During the period the number of executions carried out in the Southern colonies grew with relative consistency. About 45% of all executions during the period 1696–1785 took place in the South. The New England population also grew in the eighteenth century, but that growth was accompanied by little if any growth in the number executed. In the seventeenth century, most executions were carried out in New England; in the eighteenth century, most took place in the Southern colonies. Frequency of executions increased to a greater degree in the Middle Atlantic and Border regions than in New England. Growth in these regions, however, was neither as pronounced nor as consistent as in the South, particularly if the large number of executions, most of them of whites, in the Middle Atlantic region during the revolutionary period is excluded.

The ethnicity of the executed also changed. At the beginning of the century more whites than African Americans were put to death in the mainland colonies. By mid-century, the pattern was reversed. The change was largely due to the Southern and, to a lesser degree, the Border colonies. In the South, beginning in the period 1726–1735, African Americans consistently outnumbered whites among those put to death often by a margin of two or more to one. In the period 1696–1785, approximately 65% of those executed in the South and 46% in the Border colonies were African Americans. After mid-century, the number of African Americans executed in New England and the Middle Atlantic regions tended to decline, although the numbers were consistently greater in the latter colonies than in the former. Native Americans continued to be executed, usually charged with murder. As Table 2.3 indicates, approximately half of the Native Americans known to have been executed

Table 2.3. Number of executions by region and ethnic group, 1696–1785

	1696–1705	1706–15	1716–25	1726–35	1736–45	1746–55	1756–65	1766–75	1776–85	Total
New England										
African American	1	3	4	2	5	6	3	2	—	26
White	11	3	38	7	13	5	3	9	31	120
Native American	6	8	4	6	5	1	6	6	—	37
Unknown	1	1	—	4	1	2	1	3	5	18
Total	19	15	46	19	24	14	8	20	36	201
Mid-Atlantic										
African American	5	30	12	10	44	10	7	15	8	141
White	5	0	17	14	20	25	61	56	178	376
Native American	—	3	—	1	1	—	2	—	1	8
Unknown	—	—	3	2	3	11	6	14	40	79
Total	10	33	32	27	68	46	76	85	227	604
South										
African American	4	21	22	32	72	87	80	191	129	638
White	8	—	36	4	42	30	12	89	40	261
Native American	7	3	1	3	0	0	1	—	—	15
Unknown	—	1	32	2	1	1	3	8	—	48
Total	19	25	91	41	115	118	96	288	169	962
Border										
African American	1	2	5	11	44	42	33	28	16	182
White	3	9	42	22	25	44	16	19	24	204
Native American	1	—	—	—	1	—	—	—	—	2
Hispanic	—	—	—	—	—	—	—	—	1	1
Unknown	0	0	1	0	0	1	2	6	—	10
Total	5	11	48	33	70	87	51	53	41	399
Grand Total	53	84	217	120	277	265	231	446	473	2,166

were put to death in New England, most of them in Massachusetts. The total number was small in comparison to African Americans and whites.

The series displayed in Table 2.3 is often marked by irregularities. As in the seventeenth century, some of the valleys in the series may reflect as yet unidentified executions; some of the peaks are explained by particular events. The unusually large number of executions in the Middle Atlantic region and New England during the period 1776–1785 can probably be accounted for by revolution and war. Some of these executions were for war-related offenses, such as treason, spying, and desertion; others were for more ordinary offenses, such as murder and robbery, reflecting the troubles and dislocations of the period.[11]

Earlier fluctuations in the series also reflect particular events and circumstances, some of which are worth summarizing for the indications they provide of the nature of colonial use of the death penalty. British efforts to stamp out piracy, in which the colonies participated, perhaps sometimes reluctantly, help account for the large numbers of executions during the early years of the century. Of the fourteen executions in New England during 1696–1705, recorded in the Espy collection, six were for piracy and were carried out in Massachusetts on June 30, 1704. A few years later more concerted efforts to eliminate piracy resulted in larger numbers of executions. Six more were executed for piracy in Massachusetts on November 15, 1717. On July 19, 1723, twenty-six were executed in Rhode Island. Executions for piracy also took place in Virginia and South Carolina. In Virginia, four were executed in 1718 for that offense, and twenty-one more were executed in South Carolina on August 11, 1718. All of the executions for piracy were by hanging. The bodies of at least two of those executed in British North America were left hanging in chains at harborside, where they could be observed both from shore and from passing ships and could serve as a warning.[12]

Mass executions carried out for an alleged slave revolt also account for fluctuations seen in Table 2.3. Two of these, both in New York, are particularly well documented. In 1712, twenty African American slaves were executed for slave revolt, in this case an alleged conspiracy to burn the town. One was hung in chains, possibly while still alive, four were burned, and the rest were hanged.[13] Again in 1741, thirty African American slaves and four whites, two of them women, were executed for what was believed to be a conspiracy to poison the water supply. In this case thirteen were burned, and the others, including all of the whites, were hanged.[14] What has come to be known as the Stono Rebellion in South Carolina in 1739 also resulted in the death of a substantial number of whites and African American slaves. The exact number is unclear but probably included between twenty-five and forty slaves. How many, if any, of the "executions" of slaves involved any form of judicial proceeding also is unclear. Some were certainly put to death without trial or other legal process.[15] None are included in the Espy collection.

Obviously the particular events and circumstances summarized earlier complicate the identification of trends and differences in regional rates of execution in relation to population. Even so, on examination of the average annual rates of execution for each ten-year period given in Table 2.4 reveals racial and regional differences and similarities. The most obvious of these is the difference between African American and white rates of execution. With few exceptions, African American rates are higher than white rates in all time periods and all four regions. The exceptions are New England in the period 1776–1785, when no African Americans are known to have been executed, and the three Middle Atlantic colonies during the same period. In the latter colonies, it was not simply a matter of decline in the number of African Americans put to death. While in all three colonies the number of African Americans executed declined, the number of whites executed increased sharply. The Border colonies, Maryland and Delaware, during the twenty years from 1706 to 1725, constitute the other exception. For the rest, African Americans were consistently executed at higher rates than whites. The pattern persists when the perspective is shifted to the rates for individual colonies. Viewed at this level, the execution rates behave more erratically, and more exceptions appear. Even so, in most of the colonies during most time periods, African Americans were executed at rates higher than whites.

Executions in Louisiana merit special comment. Colonial Louisiana was, of course, not British, but was it ruled first by France, then by Spain, and briefly again by France. Its ethnic makeup, legal system, and traditions were different from those of the British colonies. In its use of the death penalty, however, Louisiana tended to resemble the British colonies, particularly the Southern and Border colonies. The number of known executions in eighteenth-century Louisiana is small (forty-one), and the list may not be complete, but most of those executed (twenty-four) were African Americans. Eleven of the African Americans executed, eight of them on the same day in 1730, were charged with slave rebellion. A single Native American slave also was put to death. These executions are included in Table 2.3, but because of lack of population data, they are not included in the calculation of rates of execution in Table 2.4. An estimate of the Louisiana population in 1785 is available and suggests that execution rates were at least roughly comparable to those of the British colonies.[16] The average annual execution rate for African American slaves during the twenty years from 1776 to 1795 was more than eight per 100,000 and less than one per 100,000 for whites. It appears that in Louisiana, as was usually the case in the

Table 2.4. Average annual rates of execution of African American and white population by region, 1696–1785

	1696–1705	1706–15	1716–25	1726–35	1736–45	1746–55	1756–65	1766–75	1776–85
New England									
African American	6.0	11.6	10.1	3.3	5.9	5.5	2.4	1.3	0.0
White	1.2	0.3	2.3	0.3	0.5	0.1	0.1	0.2	0.4
Mid-Atlantic									
African American	14.2	52.5	11.9	8.9	28.5	5.2	2.6	4.5	2.0
White	1.0	0.0	1.7	1.0	1.0	0.9	1.6	1.1	2.6
South									
African American	2.1	7.5	4.8	4.3	7.0	5.3	3.4	5.5	2.8
White	1.1	0.0	2.7	0.2	1.5	0.8	0.2	1.0	0.4
Border									
African American	3.0	2.4	3.8	6.2	17.6	9.3	6.5	4.1	1.8
White	0.9	1.9	5.9	2.2	1.8	2.6	0.8	0.8	0.7

British colonies, African Americans were executed at substantially higher rates than whites.

More surprising in some respects is the comparison of rates of execution between the regions. Particularly during the earlier years of the eighteenth century, African Americans were executed in New England and the Middle Atlantic colonies at rates that often equaled or exceeded those of the South and the Border region. Here again, the same pattern tends to appear when individual colonies are compared.

Trends in rates of execution are more difficult to diagnose. Seen in relation to population, the use of capital punishment declined in New England, particularly if the high rate for whites during the revolutionary years from 1776 to 1785 is excluded. Although the trends are not entirely consistent, both African Americans and whites were executed at lower rates at the end of the period than earlier in the century. The pattern also tends to hold for all of the New England colonies viewed individually. The pattern is less clear in the Middle Atlantic region. African American rates of execution apparently did decline, even if the high rates produced by the executions for slave revolt in 1712 and 1741 are disregarded. White rates, however, show little trend viewed either at the regional level or from the perspective of individual colonies. In the Southern and Border colonies, white rates of execution declined irregularly. No clear trend in African American rates is apparent.

THE DEATH PENALTY IN COLONIAL AMERICA

The evidence suggests that capital punishment was in many respects a different institution in the colonial period than it would come to be in later years. Many more offenses were subject to the death penalty, and viewed in relation to population, the colonists applied heavy use of the death penalty at least by modern standards. As an example, during the period 1746–1755, the execution rate for the combined African American and white population, the only population data available for the colonial period, was 2.13 per 100,000 (see Figure 1.2). In contrast, during the ten-year period 1926–1935, which encompassed the years with the highest number of executions in American history, the average execution rate was .13 per 100,000 for the total population of states with the death penalty. For the period 1996–2003, the average rate was .02, again for the total population of states with the death penalty. African American rates were much higher, 6.1, .61, and .3 per 100,000, respectively, for the three time periods.[17]

Any effort to explain this frequent use of the death penalty involves elements of speculation. It is clear, however, that the use of the death penalty by the colonists was in accordance with their experience with English practices. Only a few estimates of English use of capital punishment are available. One estimate has it that between 1530 and

1630 as many as 75,000 were put to death, and this in a nation that ranged in population from an estimated 2.77 million in 1541 to 4.7 million in 1621. English execution rates, estimated at twenty per 100,000 in the latter part of the sixteenth century, fell to an estimated ten per 100,000 in the 1630s and to one or two per 100,000 in the 1750s.[18] These rates are roughly comparable to or a little higher than colonial rates for whites with variations from region to region and one colony to another. African American rates were, of course, much higher (see Tables 2.2 and 2.4). If the colonial rates for whites and African Americans are combined—1.5 for the period 1696–1705 and 1.9 for the period 1746–1755—then they appear roughly comparable to English rates.

It also is reasonable to believe that colonial attitudes toward death were different from those of more contemporary times, and different in ways that might be seen as conducive to frequent use of the death penalty. Experience with death was closer, more direct, and more frequent during the colonial years. The death rate was substantially higher, and people usually died at home with their families, not in a hospital or hospice. Religion also may have contributed to a different view of death. For the devout, and many colonists were, death could be seen as little more than a transition from one life to an eternal life of reward or punishment. It also was the case that before the invention of prisons few facilities or resources were available to the colonists to support the long-term incarceration of those who committed serious offenses. From these perspectives infliction of death might be seen as both necessary and of lesser significance than it would be seen in more recent years.

Executions also played a different role in colonial life. They often had, exactly how often is unclear, some of the characteristics and served some of the purposes of a morality play. They were carried out in public, drew large crowds, and were intended to do so. What amounted to a ritualized pattern was followed, which served the purpose of deterrence by warning onlookers and others of the consequences of evil acts, worked to demonstrate that retribution inevitably followed such acts, and sought the repentance of the condemned and, vicariously, that of the watching crowd. Sermons preached at executions, and the last words of offenders, or words attributed to them, often were published and disseminated to, it appears, an eager public.[19] What proportion of colonial executions actually followed this pattern is uncertain, but many of them probably did in at least some respects.

Colonial use of the death penalty also differed from that of more recent years in other ways, including the offenses for which people were executed, the methods of execution employed, and even the treatment of the bodies of those put to death. In colonial America people were executed for their religious beliefs, for various sexual offenses, for witchcraft and, among other offenses, for theft, counterfeiting, and forgery, as well as for homicide. Extreme methods of execution were used, burning and breaking on the wheel among them. Some offenders were hung in chains or dismembered after execution as a warning and deterrent to others, and as a form of retribution that was intended to continue after death.

That executions for offenses of this sort did take place, and that extreme methods of execution were used, is well documented in the secondary literature. On the other hand, how many were executed for such offenses, and how often extreme methods of execution were used, is less clear. The available data are of at least limited value for addressing such questions.[20] On the basis of these data, it appears that at least 16% of known executions during the colonial and revolutionary period were for offenses that involved homicide, sometimes in connection to other offenses such as rape or robbery. At least 30% of those known to have been executed were charged with offenses that apparently did not involve a death. Put differently, we do not know how many were executed during these years for offenses that involved the death of a victim as compared to offenses that did not involve a death. We do know, however, that a substantial proportion of known executions was for offenses not involving a death.

Information on the offenses that led to execution varies in availability from one region and colony to another. The percentage of available information is largest for New England (about 64%), smaller for the Middle Atlantic colonies (56%), and still smaller for the South (about 46%). For the Border colonies the offenses charged are available for only about 16% of known executions, too few to be useful. In the former three regions, nonlethal offenses accounted for a substantial portion of all known executions—approximately 42% of known executions in New England, 38% in the Middle Atlantic colonies, and 31% in the South. Offenses that involved a death accounted for roughly 22% of known executions in New England, 18% in the Middle Atlantic region, and 16% in the South. Information concerning the offenses charged is unavailable for a large number of known executions. It would be possible to assume that all of these executions were for offenses that involved homicide. Even with such an assumption, however, it would remain the case that a large proportion of known executions was for offenses not involving a death.

The capital offenses for which colonial America is most notorious, particularly in the popular literature, may have rarely led to the death penalty. The available data indicate that only a little over 1% of the known colonial executions were for witchcraft, and the episode in Salem accounts for most of those. Approximately 9% of the executions in colonial New England were on charges of witchcraft, and the available evidence indicates that executions for this offense were almost exclusively confined to that region. Another 1% of known executions involved sexual offenses such as adultery and bestiality, and most of those also occurred in seventeenth-century New England.

Lethal offenses, often accompanied by some other offense, constituted the largest single category of offenses that led to execution. The other offenses that led to execution also are of interest. The second largest category of offenses that resulted in execution was some form of theft or robbery, including a few cases of counterfeiting and forgery. Around 12% of those executed were charged with offenses of this sort. The percentages varied, however, from one region to the other. Only about 4% of those executed in New England were charged with some form of theft. In contrast, 19% of those executed in the Middle Atlantic colonies were charged with such offenses, more than were charged with lethal offenses. About 12% of executions in the South were for offenses involving theft. Approximately 18% of those executed in New England were charged with piracy. Less than 1% of those executed in the Middle Atlantic region and 3% in the South were charged with that offense. It is possible, of course, that more complete data would show that executions for offenses of this sort constituted a larger proportion of colonial executions. However, the data available suggest otherwise.

The apparent harshness of colonial approaches to criminal justice also was mitigated in various ways, some of them formal and others less so. We know from anecdotal evidence that juries sometimes refused to convict when the death penalty was seen as excessive for the offense charged, or when mitigating circumstances seemed to justify or explain the offense. Juries or court officials sometimes falsified the value of stolen goods in order to bring the value below the threshold that required execution. Charges were sometimes reduced, although the letter of the law would have required otherwise to avoid the death sentence. And doubtless, other subterfuges were found to escape a capital conviction.[21]

More formal change also occurred. In some of the Northeastern colonies, what amounted to symbolic execution was sometimes substituted for actual execution for offenses such as adultery, blasphemy, and incest. The convicted offender was sentenced to stand on the scaffold with the noose around his or her neck for some period of time—a half hour or an hour, for example—followed by whipping, branding, or the severance of an ear or other appendage, or perhaps all three, but death was not inflicted. Such sentences were apparently sometimes imposed for other crimes at the discretion of magistrates or other officials. Last-minute reprieves also were used. A reprieve was granted by an appropriate official with the understanding that it would be announced to no one—particularly not the condemned—until the last minute before execution.[22] Execution was avoided, although the fear and anticipation of death were still experienced by the offender and by onlookers. Here again, however, it is uncertain how often actions such as these were taken to avoid the death penalty.

Harsh methods of execution, including burning and breaking on the wheel, were used, but here again, it is uncertain how often such methods were actually employed. We know the methods used in about half of known colonial executions. Information for New England is most complete; methods are known for approximately two thirds of known executions in that region, about six in ten for the Middle Atlantic colonies, roughly half of those in the South, but for only about 15% of the executions in the Border region, too few to be useful. If these data were taken at face value, then it would be necessary to conclude that hanging was by far the preferred method of execution in colonial America. About 45% of known executions were by this method—over 60% in New England, a little over half in the Middle Atlantic colonies, and a little less than half in the South. Shooting was employed in about 1% of known executions, most of them in New England, and it appears that Native Americans were more frequently executed by this method than members of other ethnic groups. Pressing was used at least once, although, strictly speaking, this was not a method of execution but was employed to secure confession. Burning was used more frequently and was seemingly used more frequently for African Americans than for whites. Over 5% of African Americans executed during these years, but less than 1% of whites, were burned. Taken in total, extreme methods of execution account for only about 3% of known executions. Most executions using methods of this sort occurred in New York and the Southern colonies; only a few took place in New England.

Punishment of the condemned did not always end in death. After execution, bodies were hung in chains and left to decay or to be consumed by birds or other scavengers. The bodies of the condemned were sometimes dismembered, and body parts were displayed at intersections and other points frequented by passersby to serve as a warning. In some cases, particularly later in the eighteenth century, the remains of offenders were used for medical dissection. The destruction of bodies may have been intended to prevent the reuniting of body and soul and thereby to prevent resurrection.[23] How often such actions were taken is unknown.

RACE, REGION AND CAPITAL PUNISHMENT

The available evidence suggests that colonial use of capital punishment was not as harsh as it has sometimes been made out to have been. Certainly the death penalty was used less frequently in the colonial and revolutionary period than it would be in later years. Viewed in relation to population, however, rates of execution were higher than they would be in the future. Execution rates tended to decline across the seventeenth and eighteenth centuries, but they remained higher at the close of the period than they would be in later years. While differences between colonial and more recent use of the death penalty are clear, racial and regional patterns emerged that would persist far into the future. One of these involved the regional distribution of capital punishment. In the seventeenth century, most executions took place in New England. During the period 1696–1785, more executions occurred in the Southern colonies than in any other region, while the smallest number took place in New England, a pattern that would persist and become more pronounced in following years.

A further lasting change involved racial differences in the use of the death penalty. In the seventeenth century, most of those put to death, around 60%, were white. African Americans made up only about 7% of the total, but as their number grew, so also did the number put to death. During the period 1696–1785, slightly more African Americans than whites were put to death, and the disparity would have been greater had it not been for the unusually large number of whites executed during the revolutionary years. These ethnic and regional changes also were reflected in the execution of women. Information on the gender of those executed is not complete, but based on available data it appears that women constituted a larger percentage of those executed in the colonial and revolutionary years than in later years. It appears as well that most of the women put to death in the eighteenth century were white and executed in New England. In the eighteenth century, in contrast, most were executed in the South and were African American.

These changes in the regional and ethnic distribution of capital punishment might be seen as a product of growth of the African American population and its increasing concentration in the Southern and Border regions. That is part of the explanation. As discussed earlier, however, beginning virtually with their first importation into the British colonies, people of African descent were executed at higher rates than whites, and the disparity was pervasive. These differences and their magnitude can be seen by examining the ratio of African American to white rates of execution per 100,000 population in Table 2.5. As can be seen, with few exceptions African Americans were executed at rates higher than whites, often many times higher, in most regions and time periods. If we were to shift our focus to the level of individual colonies, then the pattern would persist with only a few more exceptions.

The table also suggests what might be taken at first glance as an anomaly. Contrary to what might have been expected, the disparity between African American and white rates of execution appears in general smallest in the Border colonies, next smallest in the South, larger in the Middle Atlantic region, and largest in New England. Exceptions appear, of course, but the general pattern is clear. Rather than

Table 2.5. Ratio of African American to white rates of execution by region, 1636–1785*

	1636–45	1646–55	1656–65	1666–75	1676–85	1686–95	1696–1705	1706–15
New England	—	—	—	11.4	57.9	3.5	4.9	43.0
Mid-Atlantic	4.2	—	—	—	—	16.7	14.5	—
South	—	—	—	—	—	—	1.9	—
Border	—	—	7.6	2.3	—	—	3.2	1.2

	1716–25	1726–35	1736–45	1746–55	1756–65	1766–75	1776–85
New England	4.4	9.9	12.7	39.0	33.7	8.1	—
Mid-Atlantic	6.8	8.7	28.5	5.6	1.7	4.2	0.8
South	1.8	24.8	4.8	6.8	15.5	5.0	7.3
Border	0.6	2.8	9.5	3.6	7.9	5.5	2.4

Note: *Dashes indicate that no executions of members of one or both ethnic groups were carried out during the period.

an anomaly, this pattern suggests something of an irony. During the colonial and revolutionary years, only a comparatively small number of whites and a much smaller number of African Americans were executed in New England. In New England, however, the African American population was small, and the execution of even small numbers of African Americans produced high rates of execution. The execution of larger numbers of whites produced only substantially lower rates of execution, but the striking feature of the table is the near consistency of the discrepancy between African American and white execution rates.

Still other racial disparities in the use of capital punishment were present. We know that in the colonial period what amounted to separate justice systems appeared that made African Americans—and, it is likely, Native Americans as well—more vulnerable to execution than whites. African Americans were more frequently executed for such crimes as arson, poisoning, and, of course, slave revolt than whites. African Americans were tried by white juries; they usually did not have the benefit of counsel and could not testify against whites. Extreme methods of execution may have been used only rarely, but it appears that they were used more frequently for African Americans than for whites. The available data suggest that few whites were burned or broken on the wheel. These methods were used more frequently for African Americans, usually for slave revolt, and the pattern was characteristic of both the British colonies and Louisiana. In the latter colony, however, breaking on the wheel was used more frequently than burning as a penalty for slave revolt.

Chapter 3

The Early Republic, 1786–1865

In the late eighteenth century and the early decades of the nineteenth the United States was marked by widespread and intensive efforts to reform and perfect society, its institutions, and the practices and behavior of its members. Diverse motives underlay and colored these efforts. Religious precepts and biblical injunctions were certainly among them. The values and ideas of the Enlightenment, drawn upon to justify revolution and independence and to construct and explain a new constitutional order, raised questions concerning other institutions and practices. At the same time pragmatic concerns for the adequacy and efficiency of existing institutions and practices as means to meet the concrete needs of society and government also provoked efforts to bring about change. The consequences were efforts to achieve sweeping reform of society that continued through much of the nineteenth century.

The criminal justice system was one of the targets of reformers, and their efforts extended to the use and legitimacy of capital punishment. Many of the same intellectual currents underlay efforts to curb the use of the death penalty, modify its administration, or abolish it entirely. Scriptural text could be found to support opposition to the death penalty, just as it could be found to justify the institution. Enlightenment doctrines could be seen as questioning the rectitude and wisdom of the deliberate infliction of death. More immediate practical matters, however, were probably of at least equal importance in stimulating efforts to modify or abolish capital punishment. Among these were growing doubts as to the efficacy of the death penalty as a means to achieve the ends of deterrence and punishment. From this perspective the goal of reform of the death penalty was as much, or more, to deter and punish more effectively than to serve humanitarian or other more abstract goals.

47

Efforts to reform and modify the criminal justice system were not evenly distributed across the regions of the nation. During these years economic development continued and further increased the differentiation of the regions that began in the colonial years. The Northeastern regions abolished slavery. The agricultural sector remained dominant, but the regional economies became increasingly diverse and interdependent with the rapid growth of business and commerce, transportation, and the early phases of industrialization. The greater interdependence characteristic of the Northeastern economy and society worked to place a premium on the nonviolent resolution of conflicts, and in these regions efforts to reform the criminal justice system tended to be strongest and were carried farthest.

In the South and Border regions, agriculture also continued to dominate economic life, but if anything, its dominance increased during the period. As a consequence, these regions lacked the economic and social diversity and interdependance that was a growing characteristic of the Northeast. By most accounts the South and parts of the Border were the most violent areas of the nation. Here the tradition of "honor" often required violent resolution of conflict. In both regions slavery—an institution based on violence or the threat of violence—remained a primary source of labor. Efforts to modify and reform the criminal justice system were least strong here and in some respects tended to look in different directions.

Whatever the underlying reasons, capital punishment did undergo change. This chapter is concerned with change in the use of capital punishment in practice and does not attempt to rehearse efforts to reform the death penalty or to catalog the successes and failures of these efforts. The chapter is particularly concerned with change in the incidence of capital punishment, with change in the offenses that led to execution, and, to a lesser extent, with change in the administration of the death penalty and in the methods of execution employed. In all of these respects regional, racial, and ethnic differences and similarities that appeared in the colonial period continued and became more pronounced. The regions examined in this chapter are the older ones of the nation: the South, the Border region, and the three regions of the Northeast—New England, the Middle Atlantic, and the Old Northwest (the East North Central region).[1]

FREQUENCY OF EXECUTION

The number of executions increased during the period 1786–1865, as chapter 1 indicates and as might be expected given population growth. From the founding of the first permanent English colony through 1785, a period of almost 180 years, over 2,400 people were legally put to death, most of them in the eighteenth century. During the following eighty years the number executed rose to over 4,500, and the actual number during both periods was probably greater. Change in the number executed was not evenly distributed. The New England and Middle Atlantic regions most nearly follow patterns suggested by studies of efforts to reform, modify, and restrict the use of the death penalty. As Table 3.1 indicates, fewer executions occurred in New England and the Middle Atlantic states than during the Colonial and Revolutionary periods. Even if the newly settled states and territories of the East North Central region are combined with the two older regions, the total number executed in the Northeast during these years (approximately 830) was well below the number put to death in the Colonial and Revolutionary periods (roughly 1,000). In contrast, the number put to death in the Southern and Border states and territories was more than double that of the Colonial and Revolutionary periods. The number executed in the South alone was almost triple that of the earlier years (see Table 3.2). In this respect, the regions followed a pattern that appeared in the eighteenth century.

Table 3.1 gives the total number of known executions in the three Northeastern regions during each ten-year period from 1786 through 1865. (The periods are defined in preceding chapters.) The number put to death in New England during the closing years of the period was smaller than during the earlier years, although the trend is at best irregular. The Middle Atlantic region follows no clear trend. In both regions the number of executions during the period 1786–1795 was unusually large, just as it was during the preceding ten years (see Table 2.3). In both periods the large numbers put to death probably reflected the Revolutionary period and its troubled aftermath.

The number put to death in the East North Central region, in contrast to the older regions of the Northeast, was marked by a relatively regular rising trend, as would probably be predicted given the growth of the regional population. The settlement of the Old Northwest began in the Colonial period as settlers moved west from the colonies along the Atlantic seaboard and from what would become Canada. In the early years of the nineteenth century the population of the region increased rapidly. The Census of 1800 gives only 45,000 population in Ohio Territory and an additional 6,000 in Indiana Territory, probably undercounts in both cases. By 1860 the population of the five states of the region had grown to nearly seven million. The number put to death did increase as expected, but not as rapidly as the population.

In the Northeastern regions whites constituted the great majority, almost 70%, of those executed. In these regions African Americans were only a minority (approximately 13%) of those put to death, and all but five of them were executed in New England and the Middle

Table 3.1. Number of executions by region and ethnic group: The Northeast, 1786–1865

	1786–95	1796–1805	1806–15	1816–25	1826–35	1836–45	1846–55	1856–65	Total
New England									
African American	5	6	1	4	4	0	0	2	22
White	10	7	12	15	11	8	9	11	83
Native American	2	0	1	1	2	0	0	0	6
Hispanic	0	0	0	0	6	0	0	0	6
Unknown	12	1	1	6	2	1	2	2	27
Total	29	14	15	26	25	9	11	15	144
Mid-Atlantic									
African American	19	13	4	6	12	12	6	6	78
White	40	18	77	37	24	35	55	46	332
Native American	1	2	1	2	0	2	0	0	8
Hispanic	0	0	1	0	2	0	1	0	4
Unknown	46	6	6	1	2	8	9	5	83
Total	106	39	89	46	41	56	71	57	505
East North Central									
African American	0	0	0	2	0	1	1	1	5
White	1	4	11	17	14	40	26	39	152
Native American	0	1	2	7	1	2	1	0	14
Unknown	0	0	1	0	0	2	0	7	10
Total	1	5	14	26	15	45	28	47	181
Grand total	136	58	118	98	81	110	110	119	830

Atlantic states. The number of African Americans executed declined in New England and followed no clear trend in the Middle Atlantic region. In both regions the number of whites executed fluctuated irregularly without an apparent trend. Small numbers of members of other ethnic groups also were executed, as Table 3.1 indicates. Most of the Native Americans were executed in developing states and territories, particularly western New York, Ohio, and Michigan as whites penetrated this area. Of the small number of Hispanics put to death, six were executed, five on the same day, for piracy in Boston in 1835. Even combined with those of unknown ethnicity, members of ethnic groups other than African Americans and whites made up only a small minority of those put to death.

The Border region, like the Old Northwest, was marked by a consistent rising trend in the number put to death across the period (see Table 3.2). In the South, the number of executions dropped during the three decades beginning in 1786 and then steadily rose during the remainder of the period. The trend in both regions is distorted by the sharp increase in the number executed during the period 1856–1865. The number of African Americans executed increased compared to the preceding ten years, but the increase was far more pronounced among whites. In the South the number of whites put to death was more than five times the number executed during the preceding ten-year period. In the Border region the increase was almost fourfold.

The sharp increase disproportionately reflects the Civil War and its accompanying turbulence and dislocation. Substantial numbers were executed by the Union and Confederate armies in the field and by state and local authorities for desertion and other military and civil offenses.[2] Compared to the preceding ten years, the number of whites put to death increased in all Southern and Border states. The increases were most pronounced in Virginia. There the number of whites put to death increased on the order of fifteenfold, reflecting, it is likely, the extensive military action carried out in that state. This was, of course, an unusual period in American history, marked by an aberrant number of executions.[3] To the degree that the data include executions carried out by the Union Army operating in Southern states, they work to overstate the use of the death penalty by Southern and Border authorities and to understate the use by Northern authorities. For these reasons, in the comparisons and discussions of trends here and later we exclude this ten-year period from consideration.

Even disregarding the spike in the number of executions during the period 1856–1865, the use of the death penalty was far more common in the South and, to a lesser degree, in the Border states than in the rest of the nation. During most of the ten-year periods, summarized in Table 3.2, approximately two thirds of all executions occurred in the

South. If the Border states are included, the proportion often approaches four fifths. Taken in total, during the period 1786–1855, more than 66% of all executions occurred in the South and almost 80% in the South and the Border states in combination. As will be recognized, the Southern population never amounted to 60% of the national population, and the two regions in combination never accounted for four fifths of the national total. The undercount of the actual number of executions is probably greater for the South and the Border region than for the other three regions. It is probable, therefore, that the South and the Border regions account for an even larger share of all executions in the nation than these proportions indicate.

The racial and ethnic characteristics of the executed also reflected trends that began in the eighteenth century. Over half of those put to death in the five regions were African Americans; only about 40% were white. This disproportion was largely a product of the use of the death penalty in the slave states, particularly in the South. In the South and the Border regions the number of both African Americans and whites put to death rose irregularly across the period, as Table 3.2 indicates. African Americans, however, consistently made up the large majority of those executed. During most ten-year periods at least two thirds of those put to death in the South were African Americans, and the proportion sometimes exceeded 80%. The concluding and beginning years of the period are the exception. In the Border region African Americans usually accounted for more than half of those executed, with the concluding years of the period also the major exception. Members of other ethnic groups, of course, also were subjected to the death penalty, but their numbers were comparatively small, as Table 3.2 indicates. Most of the Native Americans put to death in the South were executed in Georgia and in states and territories undergoing settlement and development, as in Alabama, Arkansas, and Louisiana. A small number of Hispanics were executed in Louisiana, Texas, Virginia, and Alabama.

The regional and ethnic distribution of capital punishment, shown in Tables 3.1 and 3.2, is particularly noteworthy. Most executions during the period, over 80%, were carried out in the South, and most of those executed in the South were African American slaves—both patterns had emerged in the eighteenth century. Of all African Americans executed in the five regions, over 80% were put to death in the South, and if the Border states are included, the percentage rises to over 90%. As indicated earlier, this regional distribution cannot be explained by the regional distribution of the national population. It might be tempting to dismiss the large number of African Americans executed in the South as a reflection of the distribution of the African American population. The African American population was concentrated disproportionately in the South and to a lesser degree in the Border states, and the dispropor-

Table 3.2. Number of executions by region and racial and ethnic groups: South and Border, 1786–1865

	1786–95	1796–1805	1806–15	1816–25	1826–35	1836–45	1846–55	1856–65	Total
South									
African American	152	186	91	176	204	286	375	446	1,916
White	87	28	42	61	73	86	67	348	792
Native American	0	0	5	2	11	10	3	1	32
Asian	0	0	0	0	0	1	0	0	1
Hispanic	0	0	0	2	9	0	5	3	19
Unknown	3	0	0	2	2	6	9	19	41
Total	242	214	138	243	299	389	459	817	2,801
Border									
African American	17	20	26	24	30	43	52	69	281
White	12	6	19	29	24	33	40	159	322
Native American	1	1	0	0	0	0	0	1	3
Asian	0	0	0	0	0	1	0	0	1
Hispanic	0	1	0	0	0	0	0	0	1
Unknown	0	2	2	4	6	5	4	7	30
Total	30	30	47	57	60	82	96	236	638
Grand total	272	244	185	300	359	471	555	1,053	3,439

tion tended to increase across the period. Viewed in this way, it is not surprising that more African Americans were executed in the South and the Border region than in the regions of the Northeast.

The evidence indicates, however, that this interpretation provides at most a partial explanation. With the exception of the period 1856–1865, African Americans made up two thirds or a greater majority of those executed in the South and approximately half of those put to death in the Border states. During the entire period, however, African Americans never accounted for as much as 45% of the Southern population, and they made up an even smaller proportion of the population of the Border region. It is true that during most or part of the period, African Americans outnumbered whites in South Carolina, Mississippi, Louisiana, and, briefly, Florida. In particular counties and areas within states, African Americans also outnumbered whites, sometimes by substantial margins. But in the two regions whites were never in the minority and African Americans never in the majority, although African Americans consistently constituted a larger proportion of those put to death than of the regional population.

It appears that only a small number of women were executed during these years, on the order of 5% or 6% of those put to death.[4] These executions were marked by the same racial distribution as the use of capital punishment more generally, but in more extreme form. Between 75% and 80% of the women put to death were African Americans; less than 15% were white. Most of the women put to death were executed in the South. The available data indicate that of the women executed in that region, more than nine out of ten were African Americans. African Americans also were disproportionately represented among the women put to death in the Middle Atlantic and Border states. African Americans made up almost half of the women executed in the former region, and about three fourths of those executed in the latter. Two women were executed in the Old Northwest—one was white, the other African American.

RATES OF EXECUTION

The number put to death increased during the early republic, just as the population increased. The national population expanded from nearly four million in 1790 to over thirty-one million in 1860. While the rate of growth varied from one region to another, all regions experienced a substantial population increase. The African American population also increased in all regions, but the proportion of African Americans in the Northeastern and Border regions declined. In the South, the proportion increased.

The use of capital punishment did not increase commensurately with the increase in either the African American or white population in any of the five regions. Table 3.3 gives the average number of executions each year per 100,000 population for African Americans and whites in the three Northeastern regions, the South, and the Border region. (The population of other racial and ethnic groups is unknown.) White rates of execution declined in all five regions if the 1856–1865 period is excluded. The decline was not entirely consistent and was certainly not precipitous, but the general tendency is clear. By the latter years, whites were executed at lower rates in the Northeast than in the South or the Border states. In the Northeastern regions, African American rates of execution also declined across the period, although aside from the twenty years when no African Americans were executed in New England, they were executed at rates consistently higher than whites. In the South and the Border region, African American execution rates dropped during the early years of the period but were roughly stable from 1816 onward. As in the Northeast, African Americans also were executed in the South and Border states at rates substantially higher than whites.

The ratio of African American to white rates of execution (Table 3.4) shows these differences more clearly. As the ratios indicate, African American rates of execution in all five regions were greater, often many times greater, than white rates. The only exceptions are New England and the Old Northwest during periods when no African Americans are recorded as executed. What is striking about the data in the table is the differences in the ratios between the regions. During most periods the ratios for the Northeastern regions were substantially higher than for the South or the Border region. The number of executions in the Northeastern regions was small compared to the South, and few of those executed were African Americans. Of the twenty-five executions in New England during the period 1826–1835, for example, only four were of African Americans, 16% of the total. According to the Census of 1830, however, African Americans made up only a little over 1% of the New England population, and the African American rate of execution was approximately twenty times that of whites. The same pattern was present in the other regions of the Northeast, usually in less extreme form. There were many more executions of both African American and whites in the South. The execution rates for both groups tended to be higher and the discrepancies between them smaller.

By the early years of the nineteenth century slavery had been abolished in all of the states of the Northeast, but even in these states African Americans continued to suffer a wide range of disadvantages, not the least of them before the law and in the courts. They could not serve on juries and were barred in most states from giving testimony against whites. In some unknown, but probably large, number of cases this meant that, effectively, African Americans could not testify on their

Table 3.3. Rates of execution per 100,000 of African American and white population by region, 1786–1865*

	1786–95	1796–1805	1806–15	1816–25	1826–35	1836–45	1846–55	1856–65
New England								
African Americans	2.94	3.16	0.48	1.82	1.82	0.00	0.00	0.95
Whites	0.10	0.06	0.08	0.09	0.09	0.04	0.04	0.04
Mid-Atlantic								
African Americans	3.80	2.03	0.49	0.67	1.15	1.00	0.47	0.46
Whites	0.44	0.13	0.40	0.14	0.07	0.08	0.10	0.06
East North Central								
African Americans	0.00	0.00	0.00	2.86	0.00	0.34	0.24	0.18
Whites	0.00	0.80	0.41	0.22	0.10	0.14	0.07	0.06
South								
African Americans	2.76	2.58	0.94	1.40	1.23	1.37	1.40	1.32
Whites	0.94	0.24	0.31	0.38	0.39	0.32	0.20	0.76
Border								
African Americans	1.21	1.02	0.87	0.61	0.57	0.69	0.69	0.82
Whites	0.34	0.11	0.22	0.25	0.16	0.17	0.15	0.46

Note: *Population of states that abolished capital punishment in the period; Michigan (1846), Rhode Island (1852), and Wisconsin (1853) are not included in the calculation of regional rates of execution.

Table 3.4. Ratios of African American to white rates of execution per 100,000 population by region, 1786–1865*

	1786–95	1796–1805	1806–15	1816–25	1826–35	1836–45	1846–55	1856–65
New England	29.4	52.7	6.0	20.2	20.2	0.0	0.0	23.8
Mid-Atlantic	8.6	15.6	1.2	4.9	16.4	12.5	4.7	7.7
East North Central	0.0	0.0	0.0	13.0	0.0	2.4	3.4	3.0
South	2.9	10.8	3.0	3.2	3.1	4.3	7.0	1.7
Border	3.6	9.3	4.0	2.4	3.6	4.1	4.6	1.8

Note: *Population of states which abolished capital punishment in this period; Michigan (1846), Rhode Island (1852), and Wisconsin (1853) are not included in the calculation of regional rates of execution.

own behalf. Because of their economic status it is likely as well that they were more frequently unrepresented by counsel than whites.[5] We cannot say that these disadvantages account for the entire disparity in rates of execution between African Americans and whites. Clearly, however, that factor accounts for some proportion, probably large, of that disparity.

Executions carried out by the Union Army during the Civil War were marked by the same racial discrepancy. In 1864 African Americans made up only a small minority of the Union Army, 3% or 4% at the most, but approximately 13% of the soldiers executed by the army were African Americans. In 1865 the number of African American soldiers was probably greater but still only a small minority. However, 41% of the soldiers executed that year were African Americans, far in excess of their representation in the Union Army.[6]

Many of the same racial patterns appear at the level of individual states and territories, but with exceptions and inconsistencies. Viewed in relation to population, Massachusetts and, to a lesser degree, Connecticut tended to make heavier use of capital punishment than did the rest of New England. On the other hand, rates of execution in these two states usually were lower than in the three states of the Middle Atlantic. Although comparatively few African Americans were executed, none in particular states during some time periods, disparities between African American and white rates of execution were present in all of the New England and Middle Atlantic states.

Disparities between African American and white rates of execution per 100,000 also were not entirely consistent across all time periods and Southern states and territories. A state by state and time period by time period comparison indicates that in the large majority of states and time periods African American rates of execution exceeded white rates. In about one fifth of the comparisons, however, the white rates exceeded those of African Americans. The differences often were small and not consistent for any state or time period. The same comparison for the Border states and territories indicates that with only two exceptions African American execution rates per 100,000 population were higher than those of whites. Disparities between African American rates of execution were not consistently present in all states, territories, and time periods, but they were a dominant characteristic of the use of the death penalty in the early Republic.

REFORM OF CAPITAL PUNISHMENT

During the latter eighteenth century and the early decades of the nineteenth capital punishment underwent significant change. The territory of Michigan ended capital punishment in 1846, with the inconsequential exception of treason. Rhode Island abolished the institution in 1852 and Wisconsin in 1853.[7] While no other states or territories went so far as to abolish capital punishment, more modest changes were frequent and of considerable importance. Capital offenses were redefined, methods of execution changed, as did the manner in which capital punishment was administered, sentencing became less rigid, and the advent of prisons provided a viable alternative to the death penalty. Some of these changes had begun earlier in the Colonial period, but they were carried farther in the years that followed. While change in these and other respects occurred, the extent and nature of change also varied from one part of the nation to another and from one group to the next. As a consequence, change in the use of the death penalty also worked to accentuate regional and racial differences that had appeared much earlier.

Scholarly explanations for efforts to reform capital punishment have varied somewhat over time. An older view stressed intellectual currents, changing values, and ideals as factors underlying these efforts.[8] The death penalty was seen as inhumane and not in keeping with progress toward a more civilized society and government. Social processes and an unjust society must share the blame, it was argued, for offenses committed by individuals. The ideal of equality meant that inequalities characteristic of the criminal justice system must be rectified. Religious precepts dictated concentration upon rehabilitation and reform of offenders rather than solely upon punishment and deterrence. A more equal and more humane criminal justice system that respected the rights and the intrinsic value of offenders as human beings was seen as dictated by evolving democratic principles.

More recent scholarship has placed relatively heavier emphasis on practical and utilitarian factors as the bases for reforming efforts. From this perspective, reforming capital punishment did not necessarily mean abolition; it also could mean devising an approach to capital punishment that better served the purposes of deterrence and punishment. The large number of capital offenses was seen as a liability in the criminal justice process. Grand juries often were unwilling to indict and petty juries unwilling to convict for offenses for which the death penalty was mandatory but seemed excessive or when the circumstances of the offense seemed to dictate a lesser penalty. The consequence was that actual offenders went unpunished. Similarly, prosecutors and magistrates settled for lesser offenses when conviction seemed unlikely if the death penalty was the consequence. Even when convictions did occur, pardons and commutations were common when officials, the public, or supporters of the convicted saw death as an excessive penalty or not in accordance with the character of the offender or the circumstances of the offense. Under these conditions the death penalty could not be seen as a certain consequence of capital offense and was not, therefore, an effective deterrent for serious offenses. The restriction and the modification of the death penalty were seen as necessary to provide more effective deterrence and punishment.[9]

CAPITAL OFFENSES

A major change of the period involved the redefinition of capital offenses. In the eighteenth century, as noted earlier, a wide variety of offenses carried the death penalty, although it is probable that for many of these offenses the death penalty was rarely invoked. The death penalty was imposed for various forms of robbery and theft and for other crimes against property. It was probably for these latter offenses particularly that death seemed an excessive punishment. In the Northeast during the 1790s and the years that followed, the death penalty was increasingly reserved for crimes that involved the death of a victim. Pennsylvania was the first to take this step when in 1794 it abolished the death penalty for all offenses except those that involved homicide. In the years that followed other Northeastern states followed suit and tended to restrict the death penalty to lethal offenses. In most of these states and territories there were exceptions. Some rape and first-degree arson cases were exceptions, as were various military and political crimes such as treason and desertion. In at least one state bestiality and sodomy remained capital offenses.[10] There were other exceptions throughout the Northeast, but the general trend was clear. Nonlethal offenses increasingly resulted in a prison rather than a death sentence. By the early years of the nineteenth century many states also differentiated between degrees of capital offenses, including homicide, which effectively reduced the offenses subject to the death penalty.[11]

The consequences of redefinition are suggested by the data in Table 3.5. The table gives for the period 1786–1855 the percentage of known executions of African Americans and whites for offenses that did not involve the death of a victim.[12] To allow better assessment of the evidence, the table also gives the percentage of known executions for which the offense charged is not available. As can be seen, the number of executions for which the offense is unknown is troublesomely large, particularly for the earlier years and the South and Border regions.

Changes in the offenses charged are most clear in the Middle Atlantic states. Executions of both whites and African Americans for nonlethal offenses declined sharply after the Revolution and fell to a small minority in the pre-Civil War years. Executions for such offenses also declined in New England, but there the decline came primarily in the 1840s and 1850s. The Old Northwest is omitted from the table. The available data indicate only two executions for nonlethal offenses as these states and territories also limited the death penalty to offenses

Table 3.5. Percentage of African Americans and whites executed for nonlethal and unknown crimes: New England, Mid-Atlantic, South, and Border, 1786–1855*

	1786–95	1796–1805	1806–15	1816–25	1826–35	1836–45	1846–55	Total
New England								
African American								
Non-Lethal	60.0	50.0	100.0	50.0	100.0	0.0	0.0	13
Offense Unknown	0.0	16.7	0.0	0.0	0.0	0.0	0.0	1
White								
Non-Lethal	40.0	14.3	16.7	46.7	18.2	37.5	0.0	25
Offense Unknown	30.0	0.0	33.3	0.0	0.0	12.5	0.0	13
Mid-Atlantic								
African American								
Non-Lethal	63.2	0.0	0.0	16.7	0.0	0.0	0.0	13
Offense Unknown	31.6	23.1	0.0	16.7	25.0	25.0	0.0	16
White								
Non-Lethal	30.0	5.6	7.7	0.0	3.8	0.0	1.8	21
Offense Unknown	27.5	33.3	66.7	2.7	3.8	22.9	7.1	83
South								
African American								
Non-Lethal	38.2	50.0	37.4	46.0	23.0	26.6	10.7	429
Offense Unknown	34.2	21.0	35.2	17.0	41.2	52.8	67.7	642
White								
Nonlethal	16.1	7.1	16.7	23.8	9.8	7.0	9.7	59
Offense Unknown	74.7	82.1	64.3	27.0	25.6	59.3	40.3	233

continued on next page

Table 3.5. (Continued)

	1786–95	1796–1805	1806–15	1816–25	1826–35	1836–45	1846–55	Total
				African American				
Border								
Nonlethal	5.9	0.0	15.4	25.0	3.3	18.6	19.2	30
Offense Unknown	82.4	85.0	38.5	41.7	23.3	39.5	34.6	93
				White				
Nonlethal	16.7	0.0	10.5	6.9	0.0	0.0	5.0	8
Offense Unknown	50.0	83.3	52.6	37.9	29.2	41.2	30.0	65

Note: *Twenty-three Native Americans and four Hispanics were executed in these years, all for lethal offenses, except one Native American, whose offense is unknown.

that involved a death. In the Northeastern states, in short, by the Civil War years execution for nonlethal offenses was rare.

The Southern and Border states and territories also moved to reduce the number of capital offenses and to limit the death penalty to lethal offenses, but with major differences. In the Southern and Border regions there was little effort to abolish capital punishment. While the number of nonlethal capital offenses was reduced, in many states and territories a number of such offenses remained capital, although they apparently rarely if ever led to execution. Of greater importance in some respects, in the Southern and Border regions the redefinition of capital crime might well be described as involving a "for whites only" element. The number of capital offenses was reduced for whites, but if anything the number was increased where African Americans were concerned. As an example, in Virginia in the 1850s, according to George M. Stroud, whites could be executed for four offenses—murder, treason, and two classes of arson; African Americans could be executed for sixty-eight. It is likely that similar—if sometimes not as extreme—differences existed in the other slave states. Slave rebellion was a capital crime that was primarily, but not exclusively, relevant to African Americans. A few whites also were executed for this offense. Various other nonlethal offenses carried the death penalty, only if committed by slaves or, in some cases, only if committed by African Americans whether slave or free. In some states rape was defined as a capital offense, only if committed by an African American male against a white woman, not if committed by a white male. In any event, it was difficult if not impossible to convict whites for offenses against African Americans. As in other regions, African Americans could not serve on juries or testify against whites.[13]

The available data reflect these racial discrepancies. Leaving aside the period 1856–1865, it does appear that the percentage of whites executed for nonlethal offenses did tend to decline, albeit irregularly, in both the South and the Border region (Table 3.5). In the South it appears that execution of African Americans for such offenses also tended to decline. No such trend is apparent in the execution of African Americans in the Border region; if anything, the available data suggest the opposite pattern. Whatever the trend, in both regions during most periods African Americans were more frequently executed for nonlethal offenses than were whites, and the differences were usually of substantial magnitude. The available data indicate that in the South during the period 1786–1855 some fifty-nine whites were executed for nonlethal crimes as compared to over 400 African Americans, 186 of them for slave revolt. There is no evidence that a white man was ever executed for rape or attempted rape during these years; over ninety African American men were. At least thirty-six African Americans were executed in the South for attempted murder compared to one white. A similar pattern characterized the Border states, although in less exaggerated form: eight whites were executed for nonlethal offenses compared to at least thirty African Americans. Here again, there is no indication that a white was ever executed for rape or attempted rape. At least eighteen African Americans were executed for these offenses.

Viewed at the state level, the differences were sometimes even more marked. In Virginia, for example, from 1786 through 1855, some 200 African Americans were executed for nonlethal offenses compared to four whites. Of the African Americans, approximately thirty-six were executed for slave revolt. In Louisiana the available data indicate that only three whites were executed for nonlethal offenses compared to eighty-eight African Americans, eighty of them for slave revolt. Again, the data are limited. Information on the offenses charged is available for less than half of the known executions in the South and the Border states during the period.

ADMINISTRATION OF THE DEATH PENALTY

Other aspects of capital punishment also underwent change. Methods of execution changed in at least limited ways, and the practice of holding executions in public came under attack and was modified. In neither case, however, is the exact extent or consequences of change completely clear, but it does appear that in both cases change had the effect of sharpening differences between the regions of the nation and in the treatment of particular racial groups.

Hanging came to be by far the most common method of execution in the early nineteenth century, with shooting a distant second. This was, of course, a trend that had begun much earlier but was carried farther in the nineteenth century. Execution by burning did occur in at least some Southern and Border states, including Georgia, North and South Carolina, and Tennessee. It is possible that other extreme methods of execution also were used. How often and under what circumstances is unclear. The secondary literature indicates that executions of African Americans for slave rebellion and sometimes other offenses were frequently carried out in ways calculated to frighten other slaves and deter them from committing similar offenses. According to some of these accounts torture was sometimes used to extract confessions and to identify other offenders. Some accounts also indicate that the heads and bodies of African American offenders were publicly displayed for purposes of deterrence.[14]

These accounts, however, are not always specific in indicating the frequency with which these methods and practices were used. It also is unclear how often their use followed trial, conviction, and formal sentencing or, on the other hand, how often they occurred without any form of legal process and amounted to no more than lynchings. We do not know how often extreme methods of execution were used in the earlier nineteenth century, but they were used, and the evidence strongly suggests that they were used more frequently in the slave states and territories than in the Northeast.[15]

Efforts to end public executions, it appears, marked an important change in attitudes toward capital punishment.[16] Public executions attracted spectators numbering in the thousands and sometimes the tens of thousands. How often crowds of this size actually assembled is not, of course, a matter of record. However frequent or infrequent, crowds this large were remarkable indeed, given that in 1830, for example, around 90% of the national population lived in rural areas or small towns and villages with under 2,500 inhabitants.[17]

In an earlier day, crowds of this magnitude would have been seen by many as evidence that public executions were having desired effects. Public hangings would have been seen as giving the citizenry—man, woman, and child—an opportunity to participate in the just punishment of an offender, to be warned that serious offenses had serious consequences, and to rejoice in the imminent salvation of a repentant sinner if, that is, the offender repented as apparently he or she usually did. As the nineteenth century wore on, crowds at public hangings came to be seen as threatening and as hazards to public order, as composed largely of the "lesser sort," attracted for entertainment and titillation rather than edification, and as given to raucous, unruly, and drunken behavior that was not in keeping with the solemnity of the occasion or with legitimate standards of decorum.

Recent scholarship has seen this change in attitude toward public executions as not primarily the product of change in the behavior of spectators, but instead as in large measure a reflection of the sensitivities of an emerging middle class that regarded itself as superior to the "ordinary sort," that sought to adhere to and impose different standards of behavior, and disapproved of public executions. The response was to shift the conduct of executions to more private circumstances. By 1860 the Northeastern states had shifted executions to prisons or jail yards or into the prisons or jails themselves. Mississippi, Alabama, Delaware, and Georgia also shifted to private executions. In the other Southern and Border states and territories, executions continued to be public.[18] Here again, the slave states and territories, in the main, followed a course that tended to set them apart from the rest of the nation.

The shift to "private" executions was a less sweeping change than it may appear. Such executions were usually private only in the technical sense of the word. In many cases more or less large numbers of witnesses and special deputies were appointed to attend executions. The number of spectators was reduced, but apparently in many cases only from thousands to hundreds. Those of position, the "well connected," gained admittance. Critics contended that the deterrence effect of public executions was thereby lost, and charged, with a measure of class snobbery of their own, that executions were now closed to the very people who needed deterrence but open to those who did not.

Changes in the administration of the death penalty in these years were certainly not earthshaking. It can be argued, however, that they marked the beginning of a long-term process that fundamentally changed the function and justification for capital punishment. That process worked to shift the death penalty "out of sight" and, therefore, increasingly "out of mind." The death penalty became something of an abstraction. Its function as a deterrent to serious crime was thereby diminished, and because it was carried out in secret, it could be continued and supported with little thought to its gravity or to its actual role in national life.[19]

Chapter 4

The South and the Border, 1866–1945

Just as the Civil War disrupted other aspects of national life, it also had an impact on the use of capital punishment. In immediate terms the impact was felt primarily in the South and the Border states. As Chapter 1 indicated, the war years were marked by a sharp surge in the number put to death. This surge was largely a reflection of executions carried out in the South, although not always by Southern authorities. The Reconstruction period, in contrast, was marked by an abrupt drop to levels below the prewar years, and again this drop was primarily due to change in the Southern and Border states. The decline in the use of the death penalty in these regions was not voluntary as far as many whites were concerned, and it was certainly not permanent. With the end of Reconstruction, the number executed in these regions rose to levels above those of the antebellum years.

In tracing change in the legal use of the death penalty in the Southern and Border regions, this chapter also touches briefly on change in the legal and institutional context of capital punishment. Changes that had begun earlier in American history also continued in the latter nineteenth and early twentieth centuries. In general, change in the former slave states followed the patterns of the Northeast. For the most part, however, changes in these states came later and were not carried as far. Lynching and the legal use of the death penalty also were linked in both practice and attitudinal terms and were sometimes indistinguishable.

THE SOUTH

For the South, the elimination of slavery ended both an economic and labor system and a racial control system. To better appreciate the latter point it may be useful to reflect briefly on the nature of slavery. Slavery meant that every white—man, woman, and child—was superior to all slaves. Even the most derelict white was by law and custom superior to all slaves. Slavery meant white power. As Lawrence M. Friedman puts it, "The concrete form of this power was the right to administer punishment or 'correction.' In plain English, it was the power to beat, to hit, to flog, to whip, to inflict quick and dirty punishment, on the spot and to the point."[1] That newly freed slaves felt resentment and that some wished for revenge, even violent revenge, would not be surprising. Whether or not, or to what degree, former slaves wished for violent revenge is unknown, but undoubtedly many whites believed that they did. White fear was compounded by the fact that all but a few former slaves were abysmally poor with little or nothing to lose and much to gain. That these white fears were probably in large measure groundless is immaterial. Fear helps explain white willingness to resort to virtually any measure that would maintain control and supremacy over a subject population.

For many whites abolition meant that newly freed African Americans constituted not only a potential source of competition and an economic and political threat but also a possible danger to life and limb. The legal system had always supplemented slavery as a means to control a subject population. After the war, heavier weight was placed upon the legal system. The evidence of capital punishment indicates that Northern control, or the threat of Northern control, during Reconstruction limited the use of legal mechanisms to control and regiment the newly freed African American population. With the end of Reconstruction larger reliance could be placed on legal processes for these purposes. Before, during, and after Reconstruction, lynching and other forms of terrorism aimed largely but not exclusively at African Americans provided a violent supplement to the legal system. The legal use of the death penalty, lynching, and terrorism of other forms were all elements in the process of disenfranchising and segregating African Americans and imposing the other restrictions that have come to be known as "Jim Crow."

During the ten-year period 1866–1875, roughly the Reconstruction period, the legal use of the death penalty dropped sharply in the South. Only about 333 executions are known to have occurred during these years. Leaving aside the unusually large number of executions in the region from 1856 through 1865, this compares to approximately 450 executions during the period 1846–1855 and 380 during the preceding ten years (see Table 3.3). Again disregarding the unusually high number of executions during the period 1856–1865, it appears that African Americans and whites both benefited from the reduced use of the death penalty during the Reconstruction years. The reduction, however, was somewhat greater for African Americans than for whites.

Following Reconstruction the use of the death penalty rose across the South. During the ten years after 1875, more than 600 legal executions were carried out in the Southern states, almost twice the number in the Reconstruction years. The numbers grew. Between the end of the Civil War and 1945, more than 5,000 were executed in the Southern states, an average of about five executions per month, and this does not take into account lynching.

Most of those put to death were African Americans (Table 4.1). Taken in total, almost four out of five legally executed in the South during the period were African Americans; less than one out of five was white. High points in the number of African Americans executed came during the period 1896–1915, when approximately 79% of those executed were African Americans, and this again does not take into account lynching. During the following years African Americans declined slightly as a percentage of those executed, reflecting, perhaps in part, the relative decline of African Americans as a proportion of the Southern population.[2] But at the end of the period more than seven out of ten put to death were African Americans. High points in the number of whites executed came in the period 1926–1945. Even in these years, however, African Americans outnumbered whites among those put to death by more than three to one. The pattern at the level of individual states was consistent with the regional pattern. In all Southern states in all ten-year time periods, from 1866 through 1945, the number of African Americans executed exceeded the number of whites. In these, as in earlier years, although a minority of the regional population and of the population of most individual states, African Americans constituted the large majority of those legally put to death.

Members of other ethnic groups also were executed, as Table 4.1 indicates. All of the known executions of Hispanic Americans took place in Texas. Most of the Native Americans were executed during the earlier years of the period, and almost all of them in Arkansas, probably reflecting the early stages of development of the area and its proximity to what was then Indian territory. Particularly during the early years, the ethnicity of significant numbers is unknown. It appears that only about 1% of those executed were women, approximately three out of four of them African American.

As would be expected, viewed in relation to population, the use of capital punishment followed a different pattern. Both African American and white average annual rates of execution per 100,000 population tended to decline, particularly if the low rates of the Reconstruction period are disregarded (Figure 4.1).[3] White rates per 100,000 population declined modestly and somewhat inconsistently after the decade beginning in 1876.[4] African American rates were relatively stable prior to 1916 and dropped thereafter, although the decline was slight. Thus

Table 4.1. Number of executions by racial and ethnic groups: The South, 1866–1945

	1866–75	1876–85	1886–95	1896–1905	1906–15	1916–25	1926–35	1936–45	Total
African American	221	442	496	628	620	367	487	537	3,798
White	44	92	96	104	117	87	146	170	856
Native American	12	18	13	8	1	1	2	3	58
Hispanic	8	10	9	10	9	6	9	12	73
Unknown	48	54	38	37	43	14	6	6	246
Total	333	616	652	787	790	475	650	728	5,031

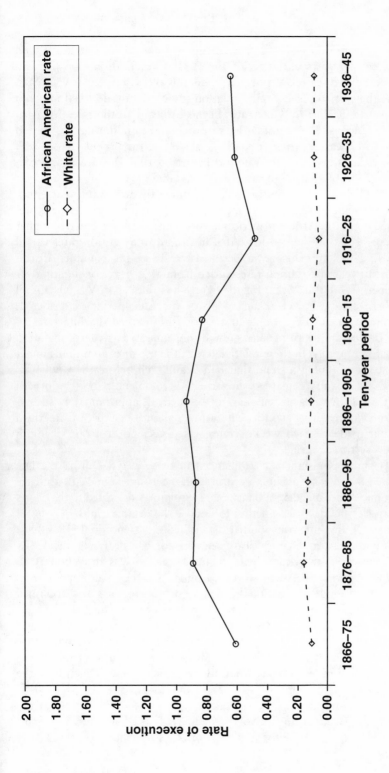

Figure 4.1 Average annual rates of execution of African American and white population: The South, 1866–1945

the long-term decline in the use of capital punishment continued, and in the closing years of the period the rates of execution of both African Americans and whites were below the levels of the pre-Civil War years. While the rates of execution in relation to population declined for both groups, the decline in white rates began earlier than the rates for African Americans. For whites, the rate of execution during the period 1936–1945 was approximately 55% of that of the period 1876–1885. For African Americans, the rate for the period 1936–1945 was approximately 70% of that of the period 1876–1895.

While rates of execution changed modestly across the years from 1866 through 1945, one characteristic use of the death penalty remained constant: African Americans were consistently executed at higher rates per 100,000 than whites. African American execution rates varied from state to state. During the period 1876–1885, for example, African American yearly execution rates varied from an average of slightly over 2.25 per 100,000 in Arkansas to slightly less than .5 in Virginia. In all Southern states, however, during all of the time periods considered, African American execution rates consistently exceeded white rates.

Use of the death penalty grew during these years, but population grew more rapidly. In these relative terms, the use of capital punishment declined, continuing a trend that had begun well before the Civil War. The death penalty remained, however, a prominent part of Southern life. During the closing ten years of the period, approximately six executions occurred per month. On average, about one African American was put to death each week; whites were executed at a rate of about one every three weeks.

Capital punishment also changed in other ways. During the late nineteenth and early twentieth centuries in most states the death sentence for homicide became discretionary. State legislatures delegated to the courts or to juries the decision whether to impose the death penalty or a lesser sentence. If anything, the Southern states led this trend. In 1918, twelve states retained a mandatory death sentence for first-degree homicide. By 1915, however, the death sentence for homicide was discretionary in every Southern state except North Carolina.[5] On the other hand, during the years around the turn of the century, a number of states abolished capital punishment, at least temporarily. No Southern state did so.[6]

It also is likely that the South during these years diverged from a long-term trend in the history of capital punishment in the United States. Beginning as early as the mid-eighteenth century, the death penalty was increasingly limited to crimes that involved the death of a victim. In the Northeast, by the time of the Civil War, as chapter 2 indicated, it appears that the death penalty was rarely imposed for crimes that did not involve a death. In the South, the execution of African Americans and, less clearly, whites for nonlethal offenses may have increased after

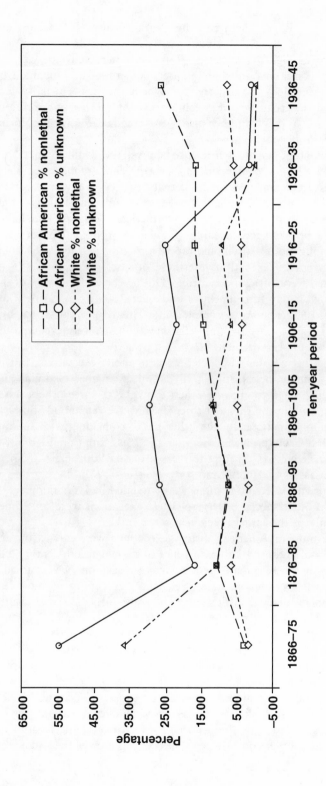

Figure 4.2 African American and white executions for nonlethal and unknown offenses as a percentage of total executions: The South, 1866–1945

the Civil War, as Figure 4.2 shows.[7] Rape and attempted rape were by far the most common nonlethal offenses, sometimes accompanied by another offense such as burglary, for which the death penalty was imposed, and the frequency of execution for these offenses appears to have increased. A small number also were executed for various forms of theft and robbery.

Unfortunately, as the figure also shows, the available data are incomplete. At the end of the period, when the data are most complete, whites were rarely executed for nonlethal offenses. For whites capital offenses had more nearly been redefined to include only offenses that involved the death of a victim. African Americans, on the other hand, continued to be executed in larger numbers for nonlethal offenses, particularly for rape and attempted rape. During the period 1866–1945, there were over 500 executions for these offenses; more than 475 of those executed were African Americans. During the last ten years of the period approximately fifteen whites and over 130 African Americans were executed for rape and attempted rape. In the last thirty years of the period at least twenty-two, all African Amerians, were executed for some form of robbery or theft.

The Southern states also acted to end public executions, but at later dates than in the Northeast. By 1860, Alabama, Georgia, and Mississippi had acted to end the practice; by 1900, three others states had done so; and during the next three decades the remaining Southern states took similar action. On the other hand, coinciding with the imposition of Jim Crow practices, Georgia and Mississippi briefly reintroduced public executions during the years around 1900.[8] Here again, it is difficult to assess the significance of these steps. As in the Northeast, supposedly private executions often were attended by large numbers of witnesses and other special observers. These executions were sometimes "private" only in the largely technical sense of the word.

During most of American history executions were carried out locally under local authority. In the last half of the nineteenth century and the first half of the twentieth the conduct of executions was gradually shifted from the local to the state level, where executions usually were carried out in state penal institutions. The consequences of this change are unclear. However, it may have made appeals, commutations, and stays of execution more likely. In some areas this change also may have prevented an occasional lynching by an impatient mob. It is probable as well that the shift in the conduct of executions to the state level worked to reduce the incidence of public executions. Many of the small towns of the period lacked the facilities to conduct executions in private. In state penitentiaries executions could more easily be conducted without providing a public spectacle. For the historian, the change in the location of executions had another consequence. The centralization of the conduct of executions meant the centralization and improvement of record keeping. As a result, in the various states more complete and reliable data are available for the years after centralization than for preceding years.

Centralization came more slowly in the South than in the Northeastern and Western states. By 1905, twenty-three states, none of them in the South, had shifted the conduct of executions to the state level. Eight Southern states did so between 1906 and 1925. Louisiana and Mississippi continued to carry out executions at the local level into the 1950s.[9] A probable consequence is that public executions remained more common longer in the South than in the rest of the nation. Change in the technology of capital punishment also contributed to increased privacy in the conduct of executions. Eight Southern states replaced hanging with electrocution at the time of centralization. Louisiana and Mississippi managed to both shift to the new technology and preserve local executions through the expediency of a portable electric chair and generator.[10] In the absence of centralization, information bearing upon use of the death penalty also continued to be less reliable and complete for the South than for the Northern and Western states.

THE BORDER STATES

As we have defined it, the Border region was diverse, and if anything, diversity increased as the nineteenth and early twentieth centuries passed. At the time of the Civil War, slavery was legal in all of the Border states and the District of Columbia. West Virginia, of course, was a part of Virginia until 1863. The region was, in general, less dependent upon slave labor and had a smaller African American population than the South, although the various states that comprised the region also differed from one another in both respects.

The end of slavery posed some of the same issues for the Border states as for the South, and the response was similar. As in the South, the use of the death penalty rose sharply during the Civil War years, and the increase was greatest for whites. During the ten years following the Civil War, the number put to death fell to approximately the level of the period 1846–1855. In those years slightly over 100 executions were carried out in the region; roughly the same number were executed from 1866–1875 (cf. Tables 3.2 and 4.2). Thereafter, the use of the death penalty increased, and both African Americans and whites felt the increase. By 1945, over 1,200 executions had been carried out in the region compared to almost 700 during the preceding eighty years, an increase of approximately 70%. As in the South, high points in the number of both African Americans and whites put to death came in the years centering on 1900, as Table 4.2 indicates. No clear trend is apparent thereafter. The numbers executed dropped in the periods immediately

Table 4.2 Number of executions by racial and ethnic groups: The Border, 1866–1945

	1866–75	1876–85	1886–95	1896–1905	1906–15	1916–25	1926–35	1936–45	Total
African American	55	72	99	117	93	71	96	116	719
White	37	56	51	69	37	39	60	79	428
Native American	0	0	0	1	0	0	0	0	1
Unknown	13	13	19	19	5	2	3	0	74
Total	105	141	169	206	135	112	159	195	1,222

following, but in the ten-year period 1936–1945, approximately as many African Americans and whites were put to death as at the turn of the century—slightly more in the case of whites. Virtually all of those executed in the Border states were either African American or white. No Hispanic or Asian Americans and only a single Native American are recorded as having been executed during these years. The ethnicity of about 5% is unknown.

As in the South, African Americans consistently exceeded whites among those put to death, although the differences were smaller in the Border region. The differences tended to grow as the period passed. In the earlier years about five out of ten of those executed were African Americans; less than four out of ten were white. In the period 1906–1915, African Americans accounted for almost seven out of ten executed. Consistently in the following years, roughly six out of every ten put to death were African Americans. Few women were executed in the Border region during these years; we know of only five, four of them African American.

No pronounced trends are apparent when the use of the death penalty is viewed in relation to population. As Figure 4.3 indicates, white rates were marked by an irregular and almost imperceptible downward trend across the period. At the end of the period white execution rates were slightly lower than at the beginning. The rates at which African Americans were executed rose during the nineteenth century to their highest levels at the turn of the century, coinciding with white efforts to institutionalize segregation, disenfranchisement, and other Jim Crow practices. Thereafter, execution rates dropped, but even at the end of the period African Americans were executed at a rate that was higher than at the beginning. African American rates of execution were, of course, consistently higher than white rates. Across the period African American rates range from eleven to seventeen times those of whites, with the largest differences in the middle and closing years. As in the South, African American execution rates were consistently higher than white rates in all Border states and time periods.

Rates of execution in the Border states tended to be lower than in the South, as a comparison of Figures 4.1 and 4.3 will show. The annual average number of whites executed per 100,000 population was consistently lower in the Border states, although the differences were sometimes small. African American rates present a more mixed picture. During the earlier years of the period African Americans were put to death in the Border region at rates roughly the same as in the South. In the latter years of the period African Americans were executed at rates higher than in the South.

In the Border states the timing and extent of redefinition of capital crime and the change in the administration and conduct of executions were similar to the South. In one respect efforts to restrict the use of

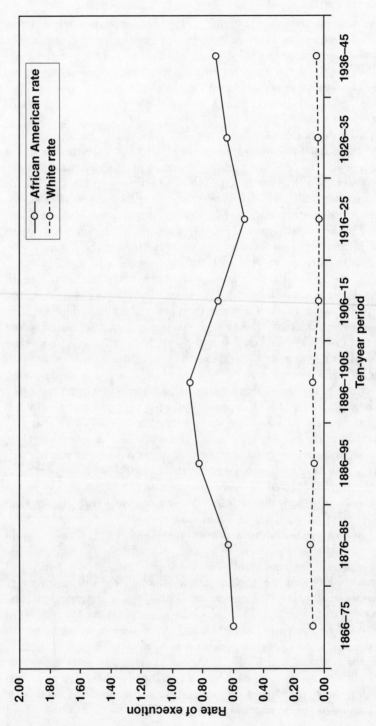

Figure 4.3 Average annual rates of execution of African American and white population: The Border, 1866–1945

capital punishment were carried farther in the Border states than in the South. No Southern state abolished capital punishment, but two Border states, Tennessee (in 1915) and Missouri (in 1917), did.[11] Abolition, however, was brief and of limited significance. The change to discretionary sentencing for first-degree homicide was probably of greater importance. That change was completed in the Border region by the end of the period of concern here.[12]

It appears that in the Border region, as in the South, the use of the death penalty may have diverged from the long-term national trend toward limiting capital punishment to offenses that involved the death of a victim, although the divergence was relatively small (Figure 4.4). In the Border states the relevant data are more complete than for the South, justifying somewhat greater confidence in the apparent trend. Across the entire period, most whites were executed on charges that involved the death of a victim.[13] At the end of the period the percentage of whites executed for nonlethal offenses increased sharply. In most cases the offense charged was rape. The number executed for nonlethal offenses was increased by the execution of six German nationals charged with espionage in Washington, D.C. in 1942.[14] African Americans were more frequently executed on charges that involved nonlethal offenses, in all but a few cases of rape or attempted rape. Across the period approximately 18% of African Americans put to death were charged with these offenses.

As in the South, the Border states replaced public with at least semiprivate executions at later dates than the Northeast. Delaware did so before 1860, and West Virginia apparently ended public executions when the conduct of the death penalty was centralized in 1899 and moved to the state prison. By 1900 the remaining Border states also had moved executions to more private circumstances.[15] As in other areas, how private these executions actually were, and how often attendance actually was restricted, is subject to considerable doubt. The last public hanging conducted without restricting the number of spectators is said to have been that of Rainey Bethea, charged with rape, carried out in Owensboro, Kentucky, on May 21, 1936, with an estimated 10,000 to 20,000 in attendance. Food and drink were available for purchase.[16]

Like the South, the Border states were relatively slow to relinquish local control over the conduct of executions. Prior to 1910, only a single Border state, West Virginia, had shifted executions to the state level. Kentucky did so in 1911, Tennessee in 1916, Maryland in 1923, and Missouri in 1938. Delaware did not shift to state control before 1945.[17] Some, but not all, Border states replaced hanging with electrocution as the means of execution—Tennessee in 1909, Kentucky in 1911, and Washington, D.C., in 1928. Change was not complete. Missouri adopted lethal gas in 1938, and the remaining Border states continued to

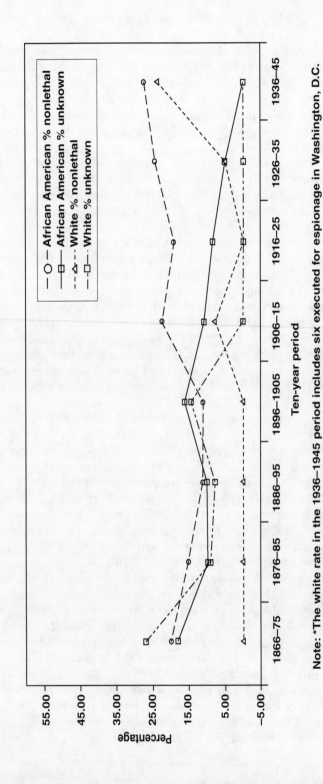

Note: *The white rate in the 1936–1945 period includes six executed for espionage in Washington, D.C. Without these six, the rate of execution would be 16.5

Figure 4.4 African American and white executions for nonlethal and unknown offenses as a percentage of total executions: The Border, 1866–1945*

use the gallows until after World War II. Kentucky reinstated public hanging for rape in 1920 and repealed the statute in 1938.[18]

THE DEATH PENALTY OUTSIDE THE LAW

In the Southern and the Border states following the Civil War and into the twentieth century the frequent legal use of the death penalty coincided with frequent lynching. Lynching was, of course, a criminal act, but in much of the nation it was rarely treated as a crime. Perpetrators were rarely prosecuted and even more rarely convicted and punished. Lynching was accepted and enjoyed the tolerance, if not always the unqualified approval, of government and many leading citizens.

It appears that many believed, or claimed to believe, that lynching was as legitimate as any other form of execution and was justified by such honored principles as the right of revolution, popular sovereignty, and simple self-protection. As a member of the North Carolina Supreme Court explained, "The cause of lynching is not a spirit of lawlessness. As a rule the men who participate in it wish ardently to enforce justice. Whenever society has lost confidence in the promptness and certainty of punishment by the courts, then whenever an offense sufficiently flagrant is committed society will protect itself by lynching."[19]

While lynching was sometimes justified on the grounds that legal authorities failed to act or acted too slowly, the entire judicial systems of the Southern and Border states were biased against African Americans charged with serious offenses. African Americans often had only ineffective council or none at all. Juries were composed of white males, and the same men who participated in or accepted lynchings made up the bulk of jury pools. Outcomes of trials were sometimes announced with the assurance that the sentence would be death, and scaffolds were constructed before the beginning of trials. On some occasions, the entire proceedings from the opening of trial through conviction, sentencing, and execution required only a few hours and were conducted under intimidating conditions. Here again, the distinction between lynching and the legal imposition of the death penalty was less than sharp.[20]

As in the case of legal executions, no definitive inventory or official record of deaths by lynching exists. However, several recent studies and older compilations, although not entirely consistent with each other, provide at least a reasonable approximation of the incidence, timing, and geographical distribution of lynching. *The Negro Year Book* for 1952 provides a useful national perspective on lynching from 1882 through 1951. According to the *Year Book*, 4,730 lynchings took place during these years, 3,973 in the Southern and Border states, almost 85% of them African Americans.[21] There is disagreement concerning whether this count and other early compilations, such as the annual summary published in the *Chicago Tribune*, which also begins with 1882, understate or overstate the number of lynchings that actually occurred.[22] In any event, the numbers alone cannot fully convey the meaning of lynching.

Lynching did not, of course, begin in 1882. It also occurred prior to the Civil War, particularly in the South, the Border region, and the Far West, and it took place in the South and the Border states during the Civil War and Reconstruction. In this sense the available compilations greatly understate the number of lynchings that actually took place. There is evidence that during Reconstruction the incidence of lynching in these states may have been at least comparable to that of later years. George C. Wright indicates that a third of all lynchings in Kentucky after the Civil War took place during the nine years from 1865 through 1874.[23] It may be that the change in the character of lynching after Reconstruction is part of the explanation for the greater attention that it received in the later nineteenth and early twentieth centuries. During Reconstruction lynchings probably tended to be disproportionately covert actions carried out in relative secrecy because of the fear of attracting intervention by Northern authorities. After Reconstruction, when Northern intervention was less likely, lynchings often were carried out as ritualized spectacles designed to attract crowds and publicity and intended to terrorize African Americans as well any others who might sympathize with them.

Richard Maxwell Brown has summarized the components of this form of lynching: advance notice and publicity that a lynching was to occur so that a crowd would be attracted; the lynching itself as a mass spectacle, with large numbers in attendance; the burning, torturing, and mutilating of the victim; taking, distributing and selling body parts of the victim as souvenirs and preparing and selling postcards—although the perpetrators were known, any investigative report usually simply described them as "persons unknown."[24] How many lynchings actually conformed to these characteristics and included all components is unknown. There were enough, however, to attract widespread attention throughout the former slave states and in the rest of the United States as well as in other nations.

While death, whether imposed by lynch mobs or executioners, was a centerpiece in the effort to preserve white supremacy and restore the economic, social, and political arrangements of the antebellum slave states, that effort had other elements as well. Richard Maxwell Brown lists twenty-five riots in towns and cities of the South and the Border states between 1866 and 1921. These, it appears, often took the form of white mobs attacking African American businesses, families, and neighborhoods and sometimes involved pitched battles.[25] African Americans were sometimes driven from their lands, or lands that they sharecropped, and were

deprived of their homes and possessions.[26] It may be that relatively pros-
perous African Americans were most often the targets of this form of
terrorism. How often such actions took place is unknown.

While complete and systematic information bearing on the depre-
dations committed against African American during these years is not
available, it is possible to gain an approximate view of the geographic
and temporal distribution of lynching. Based on the *1952 Negro Year
Book* it appears that approximately 60% of lynchings between 1882
and 1951 occurred in the late nineteenth century. Lynching continued
throughout the first half of the twentieth century but with declining
frequency. The predominance of the South also is clear. According to
this tabulation, almost 70% of all lynchings during these years took
place in the South, and another 14% occurred in the Border states,
particularly in Kentucky, Missouri, and Tennessee. Approximately 73%
of those lynched in the nation were African Americans. In the South,
African Americans accounted for 84% of those lynched. The imbalance
was somewhat less extreme in the Border region, where about 74% of
lynching victims were African Americans.[27]

Table 4.3 gives the approximate number lynched in the South for
ten-year periods, from 1886 through 1925.[28] During the entire forty-
year period slightly more were legally executed (approximately 2,705)
than were lynched (2,621). During the period 1886–1895 more were
lynched (approximately 929) than were legally executed (652). The
disparity between African Americans and whites and the prominence in
Southern life of the death penalty, legally and illegally imposed, also are
apparent. During the forty-year period, nearly ten times as many African Americans were lynched as whites, and in one ten-year period
(1906–1915) the number of African Americans lynched was twenty-
three times the number of whites. The pattern also was consistent at the
state level. In all Southern states and all time periods, more African
Americans were lynched than whites.

The total number lynched and legally executed, including members of all racial and ethnic groups and those of unknown ethnicity,
between 1886 and 1925 also is given in Table 4.3. During these forty
years, on average, over eleven individuals were lynched or legally put to
death each month. In the first ten years the average was a little over
thirteen each month, and the number declined in the following periods.
Across the forty-year period African Americans were lynched and executed at an average rate of over nine each month; whites averaged just
over one each month. Virtually all of those lynched in the South were
either African Americans or whites. However, thirty-two Hispanics also
were lynched, most of them in Texas.

In the Border states during these years nearly 70% of all lynchings
occurred in the twenty years between 1886 and 1905 at the height of

Table 4.3. Number of lynchings and legal executions by racial and ethnic groups: The South and Border, 1886–1925

SOUTH

	1886–95*	1896–1905	1906–15	1916–25	Total
Lynched					
African American	751	683	515	376	2,325
White	149	43	22	19	233
Hispanic	6	2	26	—	34
Unknown	23	4	—	2	29
Total	929	732	563	397	2,621
Lynched and Executed					
African American	1,247	1,311	1,135	743	4,436
White	245	147	139	106	637
Native American	14	8	1	1	24
Hispanic	15	12	35	6	68
Unknown	61	41	43	16	161
Total	1,582	1,519	1,353	872	5,326

BORDER

	1886–95	1896–1905	1906–15	1916–25	Total
Lynched					
African American	100	116	71	29	316
White	14	30	7	5	56
Native American	10	0	0	0	10
Unknown	0	3	0	0	3
Total	124	149	78	34	385
Lynched and Executed**					
African American	199	233	164	100	696
White	119	99	44	44	306
Unknown	19	22	5	2	48
Total	337	354***	213	146	1050

Note: *One Native American lynched
Note: **No Native Americans, Hispanics or Asians lynched
Note: ***One Native American executed

efforts to establish white supremacy, impose complete segregation, and disenfranchise African Americans. The discrepancy between the numbers of African Americans and whites lynched was smaller in the Border states than in the South. Even so, across the entire period and during all four of the ten-year periods, the number of African Americans lynched was greater than five times the number of whites, and during one time period ten times the number of whites. As in the South the pattern was consistent across the individual states. In all of the Border states, to the degree lynching occurred, African Americans consistently outnumbered whites among those lynched. The death penalty, legally or illegally imposed, was a less prominent fact of life in the Border region than in the South. During the first twenty years of the period an average of approximately three lynchings and executions occurred each month. African American lynchings averaged almost two each month, whites less than one.

The number of both African Americans and whites lynched in the Border region was smaller than in the South (Figure 4.5), and the same relationship appears when the number lynched is converted to the average number lynched each year per 100,000 population (Figure 4.6). The high point of lynching in the South occurred in the period 1886–1895, when African Americans were lynched at approximately 1.32 per 100,000. The high point in the Border region was reached ten years later, when the African American rate was .83 per 100,000 population. In the following years the rate of lynching declined in both regions, slightly more rapidly in the Border states than in the South. During the period 1916–1925, African Americans were lynched in the South at a rate of a little over twice that of the Border states.

The discrepancy between African American lynching rates was greater in the Border region than in the South. In the South, African Americans were lynched at rates per 100,000 ranging from approximately seven to almost forty times that of whites. In the Border region the comparable range was from approximately twenty-five times that of whites to seventy-three times. Similar discrepancies appear in the case of combined lynching and execution rates, also given in Figures 4.5 and 4.6. In the South, during the period 1886–1896, African Americans were lynched and executed at an average rate of 2.19 per 100,000, and at the end of the period at a rate slightly less than one (.98). In the Border region the comparable rates were 1.66 and .75. During the initial ten years of the period, the combined execution and lynching rates for whites in the South and the Border region were respectively, .32 and .09; at the end of the period, the white rates were .07 and .04. In the Border states, African Americans were lynched and executed at rates ranging from fourteen to twenty-five times that of whites; in the South, the range was from seven to twenty-five times that of whites.

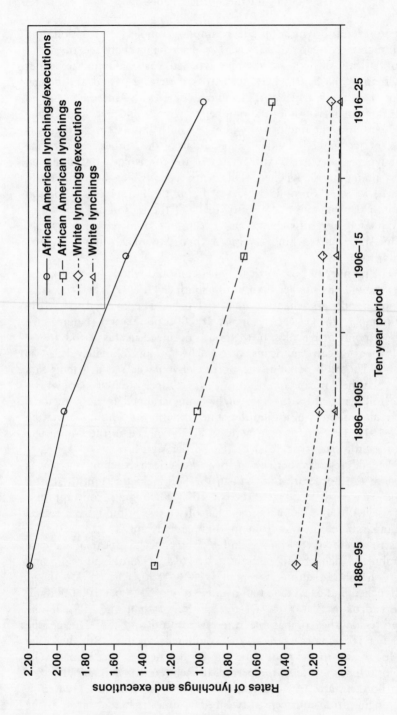

Figure 4.5 Average annual rates of lynchings and of lynchings and executions of African Americans and whites: The South, 1886–1925

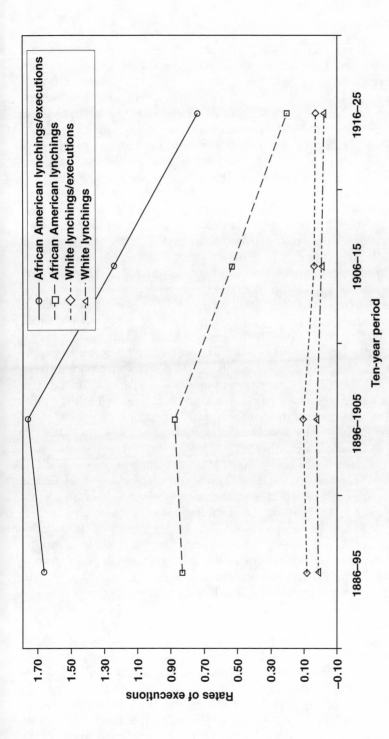

Figure 4.6 Average annual rates of lynchings and of lynchings and executions per 100,000 population for African Americans and whites: The Border, 1886–1925

Rates of lynching and execution per 100,000 population varied from one Southern state to another. During the four time periods, Florida, Mississippi, Arkansas, and Louisiana, not always in that order, usually had the highest rates of lynching for both African Americans and whites. African Americans were lynched at the lowest rates in relation to population in North and South Carolina and Virginia, and again, not always in that order. These same states and sometimes Alabama and Georgia had the lowest white lynching rates, although the pattern was not consistent. During the period 1885–1896, African American lynching and execution rates in the South tended to be closely related. Those states with the highest African American lynching rates also tended to have the highest African American execution rates. In the following years, the relationship declined, and in the last period (1916–1925) the rates were effectively unrelated.

Lynching rates varied even more widely among the Border states than in the South. African Americans were lynched at the highest rates in West Virginia. The state had a relatively small number of lynchings, but the African American population also was comparatively small. West Virginia was followed in terms of rates of African Americans lynched per 100,000 by Kentucky, Tennessee, and Missouri, where the African American population was larger. There were no reported lynchings in the District of Columbia and only one, an African American, in Delaware. Eighteen were lynched in Maryland, seventeen of them African Americans. As in the South, African Americans were consistently lynched in the Border states in larger numbers and at higher rates per 100,000 population than whites.

Lynching began before the 1880s, although most of the available tabulations and studies begin with these years. The exception is George C. Wright's study of lynching in Kentucky, which deals with the period 1865–1940 and includes a list of the victims of lynching during these years. That list is summarized in Table 4.4 for the period 1866–1925. It appears that in Kentucky the number and rate of lynching in relation to the population were higher during the Reconstruction period than in later years. Wright suggests, moreover, that the actual number lynched during these early years was probably significantly larger than indicated by his tabulation.[29]

There is, of course, no reason to believe that Kentucky was representative of other Southern and Border states. However, rather fragmentary evidence provided by Richard Maxwell Brown suggests that in Texas deaths through vigilante lynchings also began well before the 1880s. Although the dating of vigilante deaths is imprecise, it appears that in Texas as many as 70% of these deaths came before the 1880s.[30] Other unsystematic evidence also indicates that lynching occurred with some unknown frequency prior to the 1880s in the other states of the

Table 4.4. Number and rate of lynchings of African Americans and whites per 100,000 population: Kentucky, 1866–1925

	1866–75	1876–85	1886–95	1896–1905	1906–15	1916–25	Total
				NUMBER			
African American	86	24	69	40	27	8	254
White	24	20	28	10	4	1	87
				RATE			
African American	3.87	0.89	2.57	1.40	1.03	0.34	
White	0.22	0.15	0.18	0.01	0.22	0.00	

South and the Border.[31] In these terms it is highly likely that the available compilations seriously understate the actual incidence of lynching in the post-Civil War years and suggest as well that lynching was temporally more confined than was in fact the case.

From the eighteenth century to the mid-twentieth, the use of the death penalty in the United States declined in relation to population, as chapter 1 indicated. In the South and the Border states in the post-Civil War years, both African Americans and whites were executed at rates per 100,000 below those of the earlier nineteenth century. Where whites were concerned, rates of execution tended to decline further across the period 1866–1945. Where African Americans were concerned, the decline was much fainter if, indeed, it was present at all. If lynching is taken into account, and the rates of lynching and legal executions per 100,000 population combined, then the rates of use of the death penalty appear higher than those of the pre-Civil War years. Lynching effectively cancelled out any decline in the legal use of the death penalty, and of course, the toll of lynching, like legal use of the death penalty, fell most heavily upon African Americans. In the later eighteenth century and the early nineteenth, the use of extreme methods of execution was discontinued in the Northeast and diminished in the South and Border states. In the latter two regions, lynching restored the use of such methods with a vengeance.

In the latter nineteenth century and into the twentieth, lynchings and legal executions were frequent events in the Southern and, to a lesser degree, Border states. The death penalty was a prominent fact of life in another respect as well. In much of the South and the Border region, executions were public events. Some states did attempt to end public executions, but even in these states significant numbers of witnesses and other spectators were allowed to observe. After the end of Reconstruction, lynchings usually were public events. Lynching was carried out by mobs of lesser or greater size and was intended to terrorize, warn, and intimidate African Americans in particular but also whites and others whose behaviors or other characteristics were deemed objectionable. Since punishment rarely occurred, there was little need or reason for secrecy and greater reason for publicity. In keeping with the goals of terrorizing and intimidating, lynching was carried out with brutality, and sometimes, exactly how often is unknown, it involved torture, mutilation, burning, and the sale and distribution of pictures and body parts as souvenirs. It appears as well that legal executions were often, perhaps usually, carried out in public and sometimes became public spectacles. Death by lynching and legal execution, in other words, was a highly visible aspect of life in these states.

After the Civil War, legal execution in the South and the Border states was largely limited to offenses that involved the death of a victim and to rape and attempted rape. There were no such limitations where lynching was concerned. Murder was more commonly given as a reason when whites were lynched than in the case of African Americans. Murder and attempted murder also were among the most common reasons given for lynching African Americans, but African Americans also were lynched for numerous other supposed reasons. Presumed offenses against white women, including rape and attempted rape but also a number of lesser and often trivial offenses, were among the most common of these other reasons. But African Americans also were lynched for such diverse reasons as voting for the wrong political party, giving testimony against whites, arguing with whites, indolence, being related to persons presumed guilty of various offenses, and the list could be considerably extended.[32] Lynching, in short, effectively negated restrictions on the legal use of the death penalty and made the death penalty an almost commonplace event. In these terms, the South and parts of the Border region lived up to their violent reputation.

Chapter 5

The Northeast, 1866–1945

During the years after the Civil War, as in earlier years, the regions of
the nation differed in their use of the death penalty. The most obvious
difference was in the sheer number executed. Approximately 2,500
executions took place in the fourteen Northeastern states between 1866
and 1945. With almost half of the national population, these states
accounted for approximately one fourth of all executions during the
period. In contrast, over 5,000 executions occurred in the ten Southern
states, slightly less than 50% of the total for the nation. Only a little
over one fifth of the national population resided in these states. Efforts
to modify and restrict the use of the death penalty also began earlier
and were carried farther in the states of the Northeast than in the
Southern states. The Northeastern regions also included the most urban
states of the nation as well as most of the larger cities.

While these are striking and important differences, there also were
similarities between the three regions. These similarities reinforce the
obvious conclusion that the pattern of executions during these years in
the Northeast as well as in the South and in the Border states was
intimately related to the presence of diverse ethnic groups, particularly,
but by no means exclusively, African Americans and whites. The point
is reinforced by an examination of the Western states and territories in
the following chapter. The late nineteenth century and the early twentieth were marked by the large-scale migration of African Americans
from the South and Border states to the Northeast, especially to the
larger cities. As the African American population increased in the
Northeast, the number of African Americans executed also increased, as
might have been predicted. Less predictably, the rate at which African
Americans were executed in relation to the population also increased,
sometimes to levels above those of the South or the Border region. In
the Northeast, as in the Southern and Border states, African Americans

were executed in numbers far out of proportion to their representation in the population.

This chapter traces the use of the death penalty, both legal use and lynching, in the New England, Middle Atlantic, and East North Central regions from the end of the Civil War through 1945. In doing so, it examines the differences and similarities both between these regions and with the Southern and Border states. At the same time changes in the institutional context of the death penalty are touched upon.

INSTITUTIONAL CHANGE

In the Northeast the institution of capital punishment underwent considerable change. Most of the Northeastern states shifted the conduct of executions from the local level to state facilities at relatively early dates. By 1901, all of the New England states had either abolished capital punishment or shifted its conduct to the state level. Maine and Vermont shifted to the state level in 1864, New Hampshire in 1869, and Connecticut and Massachusetts in 1894 and 1901, respectively. Centralization in the Middle Atlantic states came somewhat later. The change was made in New York in 1890, New Jersey in 1907, and Pennsylvania in 1915. The conduct of executions was centralized at the state level in Ohio in 1895 and Indiana in 1897. Illinois left executions to be carried out under local jurisdictions until 1928.[1] The death penalty was abolished in Michigan and Wisconsin before centralization. As indicated earlier, centralization meant better and more consistent record keeping. As a consequence, the available data support more detailed discussion for the years after centralization than for earlier years or for the Southern and Border regions.

It is reasonable to surmise that centralization also meant that executions could be carried out in more private circumstances than was often possible at the local level. Efforts to end public executions had begun well before the Civil War. *The Prisoners Friend* reported in 1849 that "Fifteen states have passed laws respecting the execution of the terrible penalty which removes the gallows from the highway to the jail yard!"[2] Removal to the jail yard, however, was apparently often not enough to preserve privacy. Large numbers of "witnesses" and special deputies were sometimes invited to observe executions, thus defeating the objective of privacy. Of greater importance, even larger numbers of uninvited spectators were sometimes able to observe from nearby trees, fences, and the roofs and windows of neighboring buildings.[3] As a consequence, executions could remain both an offensive spectacle for some critics and a potential source of public disorder. The facilities of state penitentiaries, in contrast, made at least a relatively greater degree of privacy possible.

Capital punishment was changed in other ways as well. One state joined Michigan, Rhode Island, and Wisconsin by abolishing the institution. Maine abolished capital punishment in 1876, restored it in 1883, and abolished it again in 1887, this time permanently. During much of the period, in short, over a quarter of the Northeastern states did not use the death penalty. The death penalty was made discretionary in homicide cases during the period, although in most cases at later dates than in the Southern and Border states.[4] Virtually all of those put to death in the Northeastern states were charged with offenses that involved a death. Only three are recorded as having been charged with rape and attempted rape, two of them African Americans.[5] Numbers this small raise a question of whether they reflect any more than random error in data processing or collection. These matters to the side, it is clear that execution for rape and attempted rape or other nonlethal offenses was less frequent in the Northeast than in the Southern and Border states.

In the late nineteenth and early twentieth centuries hanging was replaced by electrocution in nine out of the ten Northeastern states that retained capital punishment. New York, the first to do so, adopted the electric chair in 1890; Illinois (1929) and Connecticut (1937) were the last. New Hampshire continued to use hanging. (Lethal gas was never used in the Northeastern states during the period.) Electrocution was adopted as a more humane method of execution than hanging and was hoped to be both painless and instantaneous.[6] Definitive evidence on the latter questions is, of course, lacking. Change in the technology of the death penalty also contributed to the end of public executions. The number of witnesses and others who could observe an electrocution was necessarily small.

FREQUENCY OF EXECUTION

The evidence indicates that both the legal and illegal use of capital punishment was less frequent in the Northeastern regions than in the Southern and Border states. Lynching did occur in the Northeast, but less frequently than in the regions to the South or, as discussed in the following chapter, in the states and territories of the West, although the Northeastern regions varied widely in both the legal and illegal use of the death penalty. Taken in total, moreover, the evidence suggests that use of the death penalty was a less prominent part of life in the Northeast than in the Southern and Border states.

New England

If we look for differences between the Northeastern regions in the frequency of the use of the death penalty, New England stands out at the lower end of the distribution. Only about 195 executions took place in the New England states from 1866 through 1945, a smaller number than in any other region during the same period. This was in contrast to 144 executions in New England during the preceding eighty years, an increase of a little over one third. This was a relatively modest increase compared to other regions, and proportionately less than the increase in the New England population. As might be expected the majority of those executed were white. The available data indicate that six African Americans and five Asian Americans also were put to death, and the ethnicity of sixteen is unknown. The remaining 171 (88%) were white (Table 5.1). At least two of those put to death were white women charged with homicide. Across the period the number executed was marked by a slight, irregular rising trend, with the largest numbers put to death during the period 1906–1935. The secondary sources and compilations that we know of record a single lynching in New England, a white man lynched in Maine in 1907, with the reason given as rape.[7]

As Table 5.1 indicates, the number of whites executed during the period reached high points in the early years of the twentieth century and declined thereafter. Only a small number of African Americans were put to death, two in Connecticut, one in Maine, and three in Massachusetts, well under half the number executed in the preceding eighty years. No African Americans were executed during the twenty-year period from 1906 through 1925, and only one was during each of the other ten-year periods. Compared to the other regions of the nation, executions were rare events in New England. Across the period, an average of a little over two executions were carried out each year, and only in two ten-year periods did the average reach three each year. Even in some of the New England states that retained the death penalty, no executions were carried out during relatively long periods. It appears, as suggested earlier, that most of the executions that did occur took place in at least the relative privacy of state penal institutions.

Rates of execution of African American and whites per 100,000 population followed a different pattern. The rates given in Figure 5.1 are calculated for the two groups on the basis of the population of the states that continued to use capital punishment. If based on the entire population of the region, the rates would, of course, appear lower. The rate of execution of whites per 100,000 white population during these years was marked by a very faint, irregular decline, continuing the pattern that had begun in the eighteenth century. This long-term trend was interrupted by a slight short-term increase during the early years of the twentieth century.

The African American population of the New England death penalty states grew steadily across the period, from about 28,000 according to the 1870 Census, to approximately 90,000 in 1940. The rate of

Table 5.1. Number of executions by racial and ethnic groups: New England, 1866–1945

	1866–75	1876–85	1886–95	1896–1905	1906–15	1916–25	1926–35	1936–45	Total
African American	1	1	1	1	0	0	1	1	6
White	17	22	12	17	33	26	24	20	171
Native American	0	0	0	0	0	0	0	0	0
Asian	0	0	0	0	3	0	2	0	5
Hispanic	0	0	0	0	0	0	0	0	0
Other	0	0	0	0	0	0	1	0	1
Unknown	1	1	3	2	0	0	3	2	12
Total	19	24	16	20	36	26	31	23	195

growth was relatively slow, and in 1940 African Americans still made up only slightly more than 1% of the population of these states. (An increase in the African American population is shown in proportional terms in Figure 5.1). Despite population growth, however, the number of African Americans put to death remained stable, and the rate of execution per 100,000 population continued to decline, as it had in earlier years. As will be seen, this was a different pattern than in the other regions of the Northeast. In New England, as in other regions of the Northeast, African American execution rates were consistently higher than white rates, except for the twenty years when no African Americans were put to death.

It might be tempting to see these higher rates for African Americans as no more than a historical anomaly that merits no comment. Few African Americans were executed, only six in the region during the entire period. Here again, such small numbers raise the obvious possibility of random error. Certainly the execution of an African American was a rare event in New England during these years, and the high rate of African Americans executed might be seen as essentially spurious. On the other hand, the African American population of the New England states also was very small. The execution for murder, rape, and robbery of a single African American in Maine in 1869 might be treated as being of no more than anecdotal interest. However, the African American population of Maine in 1870 was only about 2,000, and that of the entire region was roughly 33,000. The single African American executed in Maine meant an average annual execution rate of five per 100,000. These contrasts explain the high rates of execution of African Americans. Whatever else is to be said, it appears that even in New England, where the death penalty was used rarely in comparison to other regions, African Americans were put to death at a higher rate than whites, and in numbers in excess of their representation in the population.

These same issues and questions arise in the case of executions of Asians. Three Asians charged with homicide are recorded as having been executed in Massachusetts on the same day in 1888. Two more, also charged with homicide, were executed in Connecticut on the same day in 1927. Judging from the names, all were probably Chinese. While almost as many Asian Americans (five) as African Americans (six) were executed in New England in this period, the Asian American population was much smaller and average annual rate of execution much higher.

In the use of capital punishment, New England appears quite different than the Southern and Border states and, as will be seen, to a somewhat lesser degree different from the other regions of the nation as well. Indeed, on the basis of the available data and the record of continued modification and restriction of the use of the death penalty, it

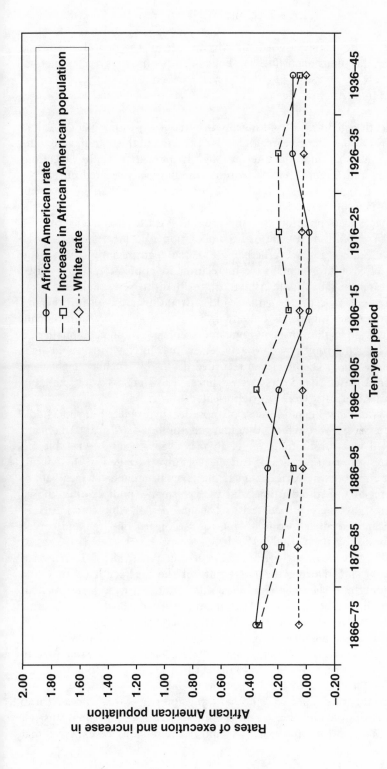

Figure 5.1 Average annual rates of execution of African Americans and whites and proportional increase in African American population: New England, 1866–1945

might be reasonably argued that by the end of the period considered here capital punishment in New England was on its way to extinction.

The Middle Atlantic Region

The death penalty was used much more frequently in the Middle Atlantic states during these years, and those executed in the region were more diverse in racial and ethnic terms. Slightly more than 1,600 executions in these states, more than three times the number executed during the preceding eighty years and about eight times more than in New England. The difference between the regions is not surprising, given the differences in population size and growth. As discussed later, however, rates of execution in relation to population also were higher in the Middle Atlantic region. Whether use of the death penalty is viewed in terms of absolute numbers or in relation to population, it was used more often in the Middle Atlantic states than in New England. A few lynchings also occurred in the Middle Atlantic states. As in other regions the exact number is unknown, but it was almost certainly small, although larger than in New England. According to one compilation, a single lynching took place in New Jersey, two in New York, and eight in Pennsylvania. Of the eleven recorded deaths by lynching, eight were African Americans and three were whites.[8] The numbers were small, but African Americans were overrepresented.

As in New England, most of those legally executed in the Middle Atlantic states were white, although the number of African Americans executed was substantially larger than in New England. As Table 5.2 indicates, approximately one out of every five executed in the Middle Atlantic region was African American. A small number of members of other racial and ethnic groups and an even smaller number of unknown ethnicity also were put to death. The number of whites and African Americans executed rose following the Reconstruction era and surged sharply during the period 1916–1935.

That the number of African Americans put to death increased is not surprising. During the latter part of the nineteenth century and continuing into the twentieth, large numbers of African Americans left the South and Border states, and many settled in the Middle Atlantic region. During these years the African American population of the region underwent an almost tenfold increase, from approximately 131,000 in 1860 to almost 1.3 million in 1940. Despite this increase, African Americans remained a small segment of the regional population, less than 5% according to the Census of 1940.

It might be expected, all other things the same, that as the African American population increased, the number of African Americans put to death also would increase. It would not necessarily be expected that

Table 5.2. Number of executions by racial and ethnic groups: The Middle Atlantic, 1866–1945

	1866–75	1876–85	1886–95	1896–1905	1906–15	1916–25	1926–35	1936–45	Total
African American	16	12	19	54	57	71	64	51	344
White	73	100	91	116	211	210	209	131	1,141
Native American	0	0	1	0	0	0	0	1	2
Asian	0	0	1	0	4	3	2	3	13
Hispanic	2	0	0	0	0	4	2	5	13
Unknown	12	10	14	31	10	6	0	9	92
Total	103	122	126	201	282	294	277	200	1,605

the rate of execution of African Americans in relation to population also would increase. In the Middle Atlantic states the average number of African Americans put to death each year per 100,000 population had followed a very irregular declining trend since the eighteenth century. That long-term decline was interrupted during the Reconstruction years and then rose sharply to a peak in the years surrounding the turn of the century (Figure 5.2). The peak in African American execution rates coincided with a sharp increase in African American migration to the Middle Atlantic states. Between the censuses of 1890 and 1900, the African American population of these states increased by almost 45% (shown in proportions in Figure 5.2). The African American population also increased in the following years. Between the censuses of 1920 and 1930, the increase was over 75%.[9] Surprisingly, in some respects, the rate at which African Americans were executed did not increase but declined steadily after the turn of the century to its lowest point during the period 1936–1945.

In the Middle Atlantic region, whites were executed at a higher rate in relation to population, usually about double, than in New England. From the 1840s onward, in the Middle Atlantic region white average annual rates of execution fluctuated within a very narrow range, from approximately .03 to .06 per 100,000. The period 1905–1935, widely believed at the time to be marked by high levels of criminal violence, saw a short-term, almost imperceptible rise (Figure 5.2). White rates of execution in relation to population differed markedly from those of African Americans, as Figure 5.2 also indicates. White rates were, of course, more stable and consistently lower. During one ten-year period, African American rates exceeded white rates by more than twenty times. Thereafter, the rates converged, but even at the end of the period African Americans were still executed at a rate eight times that of whites. African American execution rates were higher than white rates in all states across the period.

The East North Central Region

Executions were less common in the East North Central region than in the Middle Atlantic region but more common than in New England. From 1866 through 1945, approximately 721 executions took place in the East North Central states. This compares to about 180 during the preceding years. The increase is explained, at least in part, by the greater population during the latter period than in earlier years. The number of executions during the latter period takes on a somewhat different meaning when it is recalled that the executions took place in three states— Illinois, Indiana, and Ohio. As indicated earlier, Michigan and Wisconsin

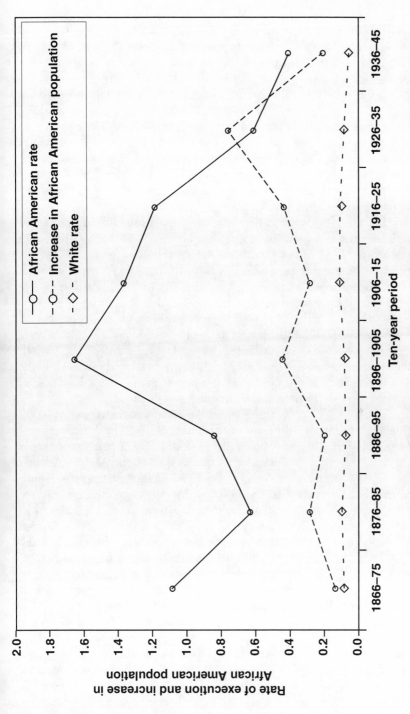

Figure 5.2 Average annual rates of execution of African Americans and whites and proportional increase in African American population: Middle Atlantic, 1866–1945

had abolished capital punishment before the Civil War. As Table 5.3 indicates, almost 66% of those executed were white. African Americans accounted for approximately 26%. At least two Native Americans, an Asian, four Hispanics, and fifty of unknown ethnicity also were executed. Growth in the number of whites put to death was quite irregular. The largest number put to death, in terms of the way we have summarized the data, occurred in the period 1926–1935, with almost 25% of the total for the eighty-year period. The number of whites executed dropped during the next ten-year period. The number of African Americans put to death grew more regularly. The largest number of African Americans was executed in the period 1916–1935, and the number also declined in the following period.

Between 1860 and 1940, the white population of the three capital punishment states grew by approximately 225%. (That of the entire region grew by a little over 270% during the same period.)[10] The increase in the number of whites put to death barely kept pace with the population increase, as Figure 5.3 indicates. A modest short-term bulge in the rate of the execution of whites can be observed during the period 1916–1925, when the rates rose from .02 during the preceding period to .05 per 100,000, and then to .07 in the period 1926–1935. Thereafter, the rates dropped to earlier levels. During most of the period, whites were executed in the East North Central states at rates below the Middle Atlantic region, but somewhat higher than in New England, as a comparison of Figures 5.1, 5.2, and 5.3 will show.

The average number of African Americans executed per 100,000 population followed a different but familiar pattern. The African American population also grew during the period, but at a much more rapid rate than the white population. As in the case of the Middle Atlantic states, large numbers of African Americans migrated from the South and the Border regions to the Old Northwest. Migration to the three capital punishment states, all of them adjacent to slave states, was particularly large. During the first sixty years of the period, African American rates of execution per 100,000 population increased in the capital punishment states as the African American population increased, not necessarily the expected relationship, and the largest increases in execution rates sometimes coincided with sharp increases in the African American population. Between the censuses of 1860 and 1870, the African American population of these states more than doubled, from approximately 55,000 to 117,000, and the rate of execution of African Americans rose from approximately .18 to .34 per 100,000. The African American population of the region grew by 60%, shown as a proportion in Figure 5.3, between the censuses of 1910 and 1920, and execution rates rose from .8 to 1.0 per 100,000. Thereafter, execution rates declined, although the African American population continued to grow.

Table 5.3. Number of executions by racial and ethnic groups: The East North Central, 1866–1945

	1866–75	1876–85	1886–95	1896–1905	1906–15	1916–25	1926–35	1936–45	Total
African American	4	9	9	21	21	45	52	29	190
White	39	59	46	47	27	72	109	75	474
Native American	1	0	0	0	0	0	1	0	2
Asian	0	0	0	0	0	0	0	1	1
Hispanic	0	0	0	0	0	1	3	0	4
Unknown	7	8	6	6	2	8	9	4	50
Total	51	76	61	74	50	126	174	109	721

While they migrated in substantial numbers to the capital punishment states (Illinois, Indiana, and Ohio), African Americans remained a small proportion of the total population. They more than doubled in number between 1860 and 1870, but they still made up less than 2% of the 1870 population. Although the African American population of the three states in 1940 was about fifteen times that of 1860, African Americans still accounted for less than 5% of the total population in 1940.[11] Even so, nearly 30% of those executed between 1926 and 1935 were African Americans. As Figure 5.3 shows, African American rates of execution in the three states consistently exceeded white rates, often by very substantial margins. During the years around 1910, the average number of African Americans executed per 100,000 population was over thirty-five times greater than that for whites. The average number of African Americans executed per 100,000 never fell below six times the average for whites. No African Americans were executed in Indiana during the period 1876–1885, but with that exception African Americans were executed in all states and time periods at rates many times greater than whites.

Lynching also occurred in the Old Northwest during these years, although it is unclear whether lynching was tolerated and sanctioned to the same degree as in the Southern and Border states. But whatever the degree of tolerance, it is clear that lynching was part of the context for the legal use of the death penalty. As in the case of the other regions, the exact number of lynching deaths is unknown and will probably never be known. *The Negro Year Book,* however, places the number at 121 during the period 1882–1951, many more than in the Middle Atlantic states, and certainly more than in New England, but substantially fewer than in either the South or Border states. If we accept this secondary source, as we have elsewhere, as a reasonable approximation of the actual number lynched, then several points emerge. Most lynchings occurred in states that retained capital punishment, thirty-four in Illinois, forty-seven in Indiana, and twenty-six in Ohio. In contrast, few took place in the states that had abolished the death penalty, only eight in Michigan and six in Wisconsin.[12] Clearly, in the East North Central region, absence of the death penalty was not accompanied by greater lynching.

According to *The Negro Year Book*, the majority (almost 60%) of those lynched in the East North Central states were whites rather than African Americans, and in this respect the region differed from both the Southern and Border states. The distribution, however, was not consistent from one state to the other. In Illinois and Ohio, a majority of those lynched were African Americans.[13] Moreover, the regional distribution takes on a somewhat different significance when it is recalled that in only one state of the Old Northwest, Ohio, according to the Census of 1920, did the African American population exceed 3% of the total state

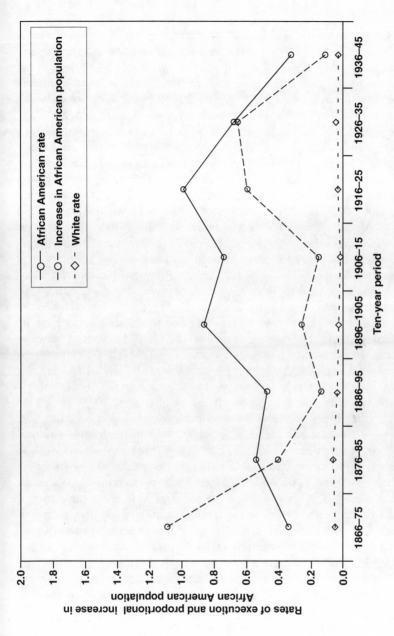

Figure 5.3 Average annual rates of execution of African Americans and whites and proportional increase in African American population: East North Central, 1866–1945

population. The African American population in all of these states was even smaller in earlier years. Even in 1940, in no state did the African American population exceed 5% of the total population. The point is, of course, that African Americans were lynched in Illinois, Indiana, and Ohio in numbers far in excess of their representation in the state populations.

These disparities appear more clearly and in more extreme form when lynching is related to population, as was done in examining the Southern and Border states. The average number of African Americans and whites lynched per 100,000 population is given in Figure 5.4 for ten-year periods, from 1886 through 1925. The difference between African American and white lynching rates is apparent. White lynching rates were consistently low throughout the period. During the period 1916–1925, African Americans were lynched at an average rate of forty times that of whites. During one ten-year period, 1886–1895, moreover, African American average lynching rates were higher than rates of legal execution (cf. Figure 5.3). In the following years, African American lynching rates declined, but even at their lowest, in terms of available data, during the period 1916–1925 they remained higher than those of whites. Figure 5.4 also gives the combined rates of lynching and legal execution in relation to the population. Here again, of course, the sharp discrepancy between African American and white rates is readily apparent. The execution rates of African Americans during the period 1886–1925 tended to increase, and the combined rates of lynching and legal execution for African Americans remained consistently higher than that of whites.[14]

In the three Northeastern regions, African American execution rates were substantially higher than white rates. In the Middle Atlantic and East North Central regions, the pattern was consistent; in New England, the pattern also was consistent, except for the years 1906 through 1925, when no African Americans were executed. A measure of care is needed in interpreting these differences. In all of the censuses from 1870 through 1940, the population was undercounted, although probably by declining proportions in those of the twentieth century, and the magnitude of the undercount varied from one group to another. As Richard H. Steckel succinctly puts it in his discussion of the quality of data from national censuses, "The poor, the unskilled, ethnic minorities, the very young, residents of large cities, and residents of frontier areas are more likely to have been uncounted."[15] African Americans, of course, shared more than one of these characteristics.

The magnitude of difference between African American and white execution rates usually was quite large. In New England, African American rates of execution ranged from almost three to almost eight times that of white rates. In the Middle Atlantic states, the range was from over six to almost twenty-one times, and in the capital punishment states of the East North Central region from almost eight to thirty-five

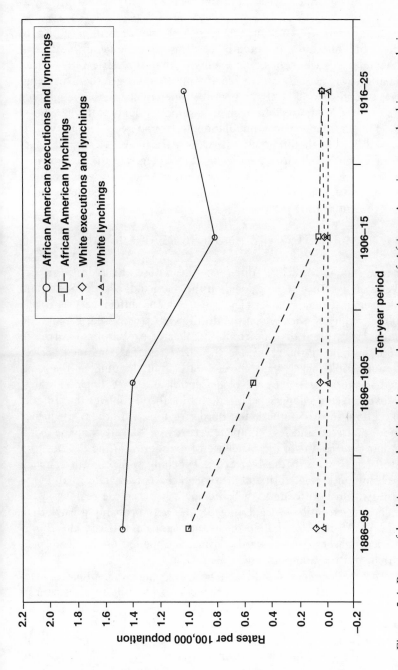

Figure 5.4 Rates of lynchings and of lynchings and executions of African Americans and white population: East North Central, 1886–1925

times. Put differently, to reduce African American rates of execution to the level of white rates, it would be necessary to imagine, in the case of the Middle Atlantic states, for example, that the African American population was actually six to twenty-one times larger than that enumerated in the censuses of the period. Undercounts of this magnitude are, to say the least, unlikely. Such an assumption ignores the likelihood that segments of the white population were undercounted as well. It may well be that the differences between African American and white rates of execution discussed earlier tend to exaggerate the actual rates. Even so, there can be little doubt that African Americans were executed in all states of the Northeast at significantly higher rates than whites across the entire time period.

RACE, ETHNICITY, AND THE DEATH PENALTY

It is easy enough to identify differences in the use of the death penalty between the Northeastern regions, on the one hand, and the South and Border regions, on the other. The most obvious difference was in the absolute frequency with which the death penalty was used. From 1866 through 1945, more than twice the number of executions occurred in the South than in the three Northeastern regions combined. Fewer executions took place in the Border states, but the number there exceeded the total of the East North Central and New England states. Moreover, given the longer persistence of local control over the conduct of executions in the Southern and Border regions, with the consequence of more scattered and less complete records, it is likely that the available data underestimate the incidence of executions in these states to a greater degree than in the Northeast. Lynching was, of course, much more common in the South and in some of the Border states than in the Northeast. On both counts, the differences between the regions in the incidence of executions—legal and illegal—were probably greater than it appears. All three of the Northeastern regions, moreover, moved farther and at earlier dates toward constraining the use of the death penalty than did the Southern and Border states.

These differences should not, however, mask the similarities between the regions and important elements of continuity in American history. The latter nineteenth century and the earlier years of the twentieth can only be described as a time of crisis in the relations between racial and ethnic groups in the United States and, more generally, in national values and the law. Actions taken by whites in the South and the Border states directed against African Americans—disenfranchisement, lynching and other forms of terrorism, and the institutionalization of Jim Crow, among them—are often stressed in this regard.

The Northeast and, as discussed in the following chapter, the Western territories and states had their own tensions concerning relations between racial and ethnic groups. Similar forms of oppression and suppression of African Americans also were present in the Northeast. Richard Maxwell Brown lists eleven major race riots between 1900 and 1943 in such Northern cities as Akron, Ohio, Chicago, New York, Philadelphia, Detroit, and East St. Louis, Illinois.[16] Doubtlessly there were other lesser altercations. The African American population of the cities was increasingly ghettoized and subjected to forms of discrimination which, though perhaps more subtle and less oppressive than the Jim Crow practices of the South and the Border regions, nevertheless sharply constrained opportunities and rights.

The disparity between African American and white execution rates observed earlier is a further point of resemblance between the Northeastern regions, on the one hand, and the South and the Border regions, on the other. In the Northeast, during the latter nineteenth and earlier twentieth centuries, the law and criminal justice system discriminated against African Americans just as it had in earlier years, although perhaps in diminishing degrees in some states and jurisdictions. Economic factors undoubtedly also played a role, including access to legal counsel. It is impossible to assign relative importance to the characteristics of the law and criminal justice system in explaining the disparities in execution rates, since other factors, including, it is likely, differences in rates of violent crime, also were involved.

Ethnic tensions were not limited to the relations between whites and African Americans. Tension also existed between white population groups. In the late nineteenth and early twentieth centuries, large numbers of Eastern and Southern Europeans migrated to the Northeast and to a lesser degree other areas of the nation. These newcomers and their offspring encountered suspicion and hostility on the part of more established groups of whites, including some who were themselves members or the offspring of earlier waves of immigrants who also had encountered hostility from older-stock whites.

The early years of the twentieth century were marked by an increase in crime and violence, or at least the perception of an increase, including a rise in homicides.[17] Certainly accounts of the post-World War I years and the 1920s into the 1930s usually emphasize the growth of organized crime and high levels of violent crime. As discussed earlier these years also were marked by an increase in the number of whites executed in the Northeast (Tables 5.1, 5.2, and 5.3) and by a much fainter increase in white rates of execution (Figures 5.1, 5.2, and 5.3).

In the view of many Americans the newcomers from Southern and Eastern Europe were largely responsible for the crime and violence of the time.[18] Whatever is to be made of this view, the roster of whites put to death in the Northeast includes a disproportionate number of Southern and Eastern European-appearing names. On the basis of names it seems that during the period 1906–1935 in the New England states that retained capital punishment, over 55% of whites put to death were probably of Eastern or Southern European origin or descent. Over 45% of those put to death in the Middle Atlantic states and over 30% of those executed in the three capital punishment states of the East North Central region had Eastern- or Southern European-appearing names. Assigning ethnicity on the basis of names is, of course, a highly unreliable process, but it is at least noteworthy that in the 1920 U.S. Census the "foreign-stock" population of Southern and Eastern European origin accounted for only 20% of the population of the New England capital punishment states, 27% of the Middle Atlantic states, and 16% of the East North Central states with capital punishment, well below their representation among those executed in the three regions.

The disproportion appears equally striking if we focus upon a single group, Italian Americans, and upon the seven Northeastern states, which in 1920 were most heavily represented. Arguably, names provide at least a marginally more reliable means to identify this group than other groups. Since the available data do not include the place of birth of those put to death, Table 5.4 gives the execution rates per 100,000 population for Italian Americans, calculated in two different ways. The first uses the Census count of Italian Americans born in Italy as the denominator. The second uses the Census count of "foreign-stock" Italian Americans—those born in Italy, plus those born in the United States, with at least one parent born in Italy—as the denominator.[19] For comparison, the table also gives the rates for "native-stock" whites using the Census tabulation of whites born in the United States, with both parents also born in the United States as the denominator, and those executed whose names do not appear to be of Southern or Eastern European origin as the numerator.[20] The latter calculation, of course, overestimates the execution rates for native-stock whites. At least some of the whites whose names do not appear to be of Eastern or Southern European origin probably were foreign born or had one or both parents of foreign birth. For comparison, the table also gives execution rates for African Americans.

As Table 5.4 shows, whether calculated on the basis of the foreign born or by combining the foreign born with the native born of foreign parentage, the Italian American execution rates appear higher, often substantially higher, than the rates for other whites. In the two periods after 1916, rates calculated using the Italian foreign-stock population as the denominator are more nearly comparable to the native-stock rates but are also, with one exception, higher. Calculated on the basis of the

Table 5.4. Rates of execution of Italian Americans compared to African Americans and native-born whites of native-born parents in seven Northeastern states, 1906–1935

	1906–15	1916–25	1926–35
Massachusetts			
African Americans	0.00	0.19	0.00
Italian Foreign Born	0.12	0.09	0.40
Italian Foreign Stock	0.10	0.04	0.25
Native White/Native Parents	0.07	0.04	0.07
Connecticut			
African Americans	0.00	0.00	0.30
Italian Foreign Born	1.23	1.37	0.23
Italian Foreign Stock	0.78	0.65	0.14
Native White/Native Parents	0.13	0.40	0.02
New Jersey			
African Americans	0.34	0.24	0.31
Italian Foreign Born	1.21	0.64	1.05
Italian Foreign Stock	0.73	0.29	0.39
Native White/Native Parents	0.10	0.15	0.08
New York			
African Americans	0.51	0.65	0.53
Italian Foreign Born	1.02	0.51	0.67
Italian Foreign Stock	0.65	0.25	0.45
Native White/Native Parents	0.14	0.13	0.11

	1906–15	1916–25	1926–35
Pennsylvania			
African Americans	2.00	0.74	0.30
Italian Foreign Born	1.94	1.39	0.53
Italian Foreign Stock	1.27	0.66	0.31
Native White/Native Parents	0.07	0.09	0.07
Illinois			
African Americans	0.77	0.55	0.21
Italian Foreign Born	0.00	1.17	0.72
Italian Foreign Stock	0.00	0.56	0.50
Native White/Native Parents	0.03	0.08	0.09
Ohio			
African Americans	1.51	0.87	0.50
Italian Foreign Born	0.48	2.14	0.98
Italian Foreign Stock	0.32	1.09	0.64
Native White/Native Parents	0.04	0.12	0.07

foreign born in all three periods, the rates for Italian Americans are at least several times the rates for the native stock. The comparison to African Americans is striking. Outside of New England, the Italian American execution rates are frequently higher than those for African Americans. If we take these calculations at face value, it appears that in some regions and time periods Italian Americans were more likely to be executed than African Americans.

It is likely that the legal system of the latter nineteenth and early twentieth centuries placed Italian Americans at a disadvantage, just as it did other immigrant groups at the time and in earlier years. Cultural and linguistic differences, and the fact that immigrant groups were disproportionately poor, virtually guaranteed as much. It also is the case that at the time these groups were seen as marked by high rates of crime and violence, a view that is perpetuated in much of the popular literature and films of our own time. Here again, the lack of systematic information on crime rates precludes assigning relative weights to the various factors that undoubtedly combined to produce disparities in execution rates.

Disparities in the use of the death penalty were present in the regions of the Northeast, just as in the Southern and Border states. It also is clear that the death penalty was used more frequently in the latter regions than in the former. Regional differences are much less clear when population is taken into account. Table 5.5 compares the regions using the ratios of the rates of execution per 100,000 population in the Northeastern regions to the rates for the South for African Americans and whites. The same comparisons are made for the Border region.

Viewed in this way, rates of execution in the South and Border regions do not appear consistently higher than in the Northeast. In this comparison New England again stands out. African American execution rates in New England were consistently lower than in either the South or Border regions. The differences also are present but are less consistent for whites. White execution rates rose in New England in comparison to the South during the period 1906–1925 and exceeded rates in the Border states during these years. The three capital punishment states of the East North Central region followed a somewhat different pattern. In the late nineteenth and early twentieth centuries, African American execution rates were well below those of the South or Border regions. With increased migration of African Americans, however, execution rates in these states rose to levels above those of both the Southern and Border regions. As in New England, white execution rates in the East North Central states rose to higher levels in comparison to the South and to levels higher than in the Border region during the period 1916–1936. These years usually are treated as characterized by their high rates of violent crime.

Table 5.5. Ratio of rates of execution in the Northeast to rates of execution in the South and Border, 1866–1945

	1866–75	1876–85	1886–95	1896–1905	1906–15	1916–25	1926–35	1936–45
				African American				
New England/South	0.58	0.34	0.32	0.22	0.00	0.00	0.20	0.18
Middle Atlantic/South	1.77	0.71	0.96	1.77	1.64	2.45	0.99	0.63
East North Central/South	0.56	0.61	0.55	0.93	0.90	2.08	1.13	0.53
				White				
New England/South	0.48	0.38	0.25	0.35	0.63	0.73	0.40	0.31
Middle Atlantic/South	0.82	0.61	0.56	0.70	1.12	1.62	0.92	0.55
East North Central/South	0.52	0.46	0.37	0.38	0.21	0.82	0.72	0.48
				African American				
New England/Border	0.60	0.48	0.34	0.23	0.00	0.00	0.19	0.16
Middle Atlantic/Border	1.81	1.00	1.02	1.87	1.93	2.23	0.94	0.56
East North Central/Border	0.57	0.86	0.58	0.99	1.06	1.89	1.07	0.47
				White				
New England/Border	0.69	0.65	0.47	0.48	1.63	1.16	0.70	0.45
Middle Atlantic/Border	1.18	1.06	1.05	0.95	2.87	2.59	1.59	0.80
East North Central/Border	0.76	0.79	0.69	0.52	0.54	1.30	1.24	0.69

Execution rates in the Middle Atlantic states followed a still different pattern. During most of the periods into which we have grouped the data, African American execution rates equaled or exceeded those of the South and Border regions. Only in the closing years of the period did African American rates in these states fall below those of the South and Border regions. White execution rates in the Middle Atlantic region rose to levels above those of the South during the period 1916–1925, resembling the pattern of the other two Northeastern regions, and consistently equaled or exceeded those of the Border region.

The comparisons in Table 5.5 are clouded by several considerations and must be viewed with reservations. African American execution rates in the South and in some of the Border states during the Reconstruction years probably were artificially depressed by the presence or threat of Northern control. It is likely as well that the incidence of executions is underestimated to a greater degree for the South and Border regions than for the Northeast. It also is likely that execution rates in the Middle Atlantic and East North Central states are inflated by underenumeration of the African American population in the censuses of the earlier parts of the twentieth century. However, it would be necessary to assume that the African American population of the Middle Atlantic states, for example, was almost two and half (2.45) times that recorded by the 1920 Census to reduce execution rates in that region to the South's level. An undercount of that magnitude is, of course, unlikely. In any event, the assumption waives the possibility that African Americans also were undercounted in the South. It is necessary to conclude, therefore, that during some periods African Americans were legally executed at higher rates than in the South, although the margin of difference is unknown.

These comparisons, however, do not take into account lynching. In the South and some of the Border states, the combined death toll from lynching and the legal use of the death penalty was substantially higher than that of legal executions taken alone. Table 5.6 gives the ratio of the combined rates of legal and illegal executions for the Middle Atlantic and East North Central states to the equivalent rates for the Southern and Border states during the four time periods for which lynching information is available. African American lynching and execution rates in the Middle Atlantic states, as can be seen, were somewhat below the Southern rates for three of the four time periods but were higher during the final period. The Middle Atlantic rates were greater than the Border rates during two of the periods. The East North Central states followed a somewhat similar pattern. The rate for the capital punishment states in this region was lower than the Southern rates in all four periods and exceeded the Border rates only in the period 1916–1925.

Table 5.6. Ratio of rates of executions and lynchings per 100,000 population in the Middle Atlantic and East North Central to rates of executions and lynchings in the South and Border, 1886–1925

	1886–95	1896–1905	1906–15	1916–25
African American				
Middle Atlantic/South	0.46	0.86	0.90	1.21
East North Central/South	0.68	0.72	0.54	1.07
White				
Middle Atlantic/South	0.23	0.50	0.82	1.34
East North Central/South	0.09	0.12	0.07	0.24
African American				
Middle Atlantic/Border	0.61	0.96	1.09	1.58
East North Central/Border	0.89	0.80	0.66	1.40
White				
Middle Atlantic/Border	0.83	0.68	2.41	2.35
East North Central/Border	0.33	0.16	0.17	0.42

The combined rates of execution and lynching for whites in the Middle Atlantic states also exceeded those of the South in the period 1916–1925 and exceeded the combined Border rates in the period 1906–1925. White lynching and execution rates combined in the East North Central region were consistently lower than in both the South and Border states during the entire period.

It is easy enough to recognize differences in use of the death penalty between the Southern and, to a lesser degree, the Border states, on the one hand, and the Northeastern states, on the other. When population is considered, along with questions of possible Census undercounts, other shortcomings of available data, and how lynching is to be treated, significant ambiguities appear. Despite such ambiguities, one difference in the use of the death penalty seems incontestable. That is the nearly pervasive difference between African American rates of execution compared to white rates and perhaps, differences in rates of execution between various European stock-ethnic groups. An examination of the Western states suggests equally striking ethnic differences.

Chapter 6

The Western Regions, 1836–1945

Violence is often seen as a hallmark of the development of the Western United States. The West was characterized by the intersection of ethnic groups: whites on the one hand, and on the other, the indigenous Native American population and, depending on time and place, Asian, Hispanic, and African Americans as well as various European national groups. Cattle ranching, mining, lumbering, maritime pursuits, and railroad construction tended to attract a disproportionately male and youthful population. Stable family life was frequently the exception rather than the rule, other social and political institutions were underdeveloped, and isolation and hardship were often basic characteristics of life. These were all conditions that were conducive to high levels of violence and disorder.[1] Other areas of actual and potential conflict included large-scale cattle ranchers opposing homesteaders, farmers and smaller-scale ranchers, business versus labor, cattle ranchers against sheepherders, and ever-present racial and ethnic tensions.

Scholars have, however, questioned both the degree and pervasive character of Western violence and have suggested that the West was no more violent than other areas of the nation. It has been pointed out that scholars have tended to describe characteristics of the West that might seem conducive to violence but have seldom documented or compared the actual extent of Western violence with that of other areas of the nation.[2] Recent work has demonstrated that homicide rates in some areas of the West exceeded those of Boston, New York, and Philadelphia.[3] Nonetheless, it remains possible that violence in the West was less pervasive than it was sometimes made out to be. Similarly, it remains unclear how the West compares to other areas of the nation in addition to the Northeastern cities.

An examination of the use of capital punishment cannot reconcile questions concerning the relative incidence of Western violence compared to other areas of the nation. As indicated at several points earlier, the incidence of capital punishment is at best an imperfect indicator of the incidence of homicide or other capital offenses or of violence more generally. On the other hand, if the circumstances of the Old West were conducive to high levels of violence then it would be reasonable to expect that they also would lead to greater use of capital punishment than in more settled areas with more usual demographic and institutional characteristics. The incidence of homicide and other capital offenses would have been higher and the propensity to use capital punishment in response would have been greater.

This chapter is concerned with the states and territories of the West North Central, Mountain, and Pacific regions during the period 1836–1945.[4] As in preceding chapters the frequency with which the death penalty was employed in these regions is examined both in terms of the number executed and in relation to population. To these ends, the chapter compares the legal use of the death penalty in the Western regions with the use in other regions of the nation. It also briefly examines and compares extralegal use of the death penalty by vigilantes and lynch mobs.

USE OF THE DEATH PENALTY

The death penalty was used less frequently in the West North Central territories and states than in the other two Western regions. From the late 1830s through 1945, approximately 366 legal executions were carried out in this region, compared to almost 470 in the Mountain region and nearly 790 in the Pacific Coast territories and states. These differences cannot be fully explained by differences in population. During the entire period the Mountain region had the smallest population of the three regions.

Table 6.1 summarizes the number of executions in each region from 1836 through 1945 in the same fashion as in preceding chapters.[5] When summarized in this way, it is clear that as the population increased, the number of executions also tended to increase. The trend is by no means consistent. In the West North Central region, the use of the death penalty peaked in the period 1856–1865 as a consequence of a single event, which is discussed later. The use peaked again in the period 1886–1895 and remained at lower levels during later years. In the Mountain region legal use of the death penalty reached high points in the latter nineteenth century and remained relatively constant thereafter. In the Pacific Coast region, the rising trend in the number of executions was most pronounced in the twentieth century. It appears that in all three regions relatively heavy use was made of capital punishment during the earlier years of settlement when population was sparse.

Table 6.1 Number of executions by regions and racial and ethnic groups: The West, 1836–1945

	1836–45	1846–55	1856–65	1866–75	1876–85	1886–95	1896–1905	1906–15	1916–25	1926–35	1936–45	Total
West North Central												
African American	0	0	0	0	1	5	8	14	15	11	5	59
White	4	0	19	7	7	29	16	5	17	30	47	181
Native American	9	4	41	3	14	25	16	0	1	1	1	115
Unknown and Other	0	0	1	0	1	2	4	2	0	0	1	11
Total	13	4	61	10	23	61	44	21	33	42	54	366
Mountain												
African American	0	0	0	1	4	7	2	3	8	4	9	38
White	0	4	19	14	41	30	38	23	29	36	37	271
Native American	0	4	1	1	5	9	0	4	1	1	1	27
Asian	0	0	0	0	3	0	0	2	2	4	0	11
Hispanic	0	1	4	2	6	8	20	11	23	9	3	87
Unknown and Other	0	0	3	2	6	8	4	3	2	2	6	36
Total	0	9	27	20	65	62	64	46	65	56	56	470
Pacific												
African American	0	0	4	1	2	1	3	3	7	12	18	51
White	0	34	41	18	31	41	65	57	50	87	82	506
Native American	2	15	8	11	16	2	2	3	1	1	1	62
Asian	0	0	3	3	9	10	12	3	9	11	6	66
Hispanic	5	10	5	7	5	4	6	3	12	8	7	72
Unknown and Other	1	1	3	1	3	1	5	3	3	3	6	30
Total	8	60	64	41	66	59	93	72	82	122	120	787
Grand total	21	73	152	71	154	182	201	139	180	220	230	1,623

The use of the death penalty reflected the racial and ethnic diversity of the regions, as Table 6.1 suggests. In the Pacific and Mountain regions a majority of those put to death, on the order of six out of ten, were white, but in both regions significant numbers of Native Americans, Hispanics, and Asians, most of them Chinese, as well as African Americans also were among the executed. The ethnic and racial distribution of those put to death reflected the diversity within the regions. All but a few of the Asians were executed in California. As might be expected, most of the Hispanic Americans were executed in California, Arizona, New Mexico, and Colorado, where the Hispanic population was largest. Executions of Native Americans and African Americans were more evenly distributed across the Mountain and Pacific regions, although the largest number was executed in California.

Executions in the West North Central region were much less diverse in racial and ethnic terms than in the other Western regions. Approximately half of those executed in the region were white, with Native Americans the second largest group, followed by African Americans. This sort of summary, however, gives an erroneous impression of the racial diversity of executions in the region. A single episode in Minnesota in 1862 accounts for almost one third of the Native Americans put to death in the region. In that year a military court sentenced 303 Santee Sioux to death for murder and other crimes. President Lincoln pardoned all but thirty-eight, who were publicly hanged from a single scaffold on the day after Christmas at Mankato, Minnesota, often said to have been the largest mass execution in the history of the United States.[6] Some sixty-five additional Native Americans were executed in the closing decades of the nineteenth century in Oklahoma, Indian territory until 1889. Almost all (over 90%) of the known executions of Native Americans in the West North Central region, in other words, took place in Minnesota and Oklahoma.

Executions of members of the several racial and ethnic groups follow predictable patterns (see Table 6.1). Most of the African Americans were put to death relatively late in the period as they migrated to the Western states. In the West North Central region, actually Minnesota and Oklahoma, most of the executions of Native Americans took place during the early stages of settlement, recalling that Oklahoma was still a frontier area in the latter nineteenth century and into the twentieth. Most of the executions of Native Americans in the Mountain and Pacific regions also took place during the early stages of settlement. In these regions executions of Hispanic Americans occurred disproportionately in the first three decades of the twentieth century. Nearly all executions of Asians took place in the Pacific region during the late nineteenth and earlier twentieth centuries. The large majority of these executions were in California.

It is probable, of course, that the number of members of all ethnic groups that were executed was actually greater than indicated in Table 6.1. It is possible that the underestimate is relatively greatest in the case of Native Americans. The number executed obviously does not take into account those killed in the many skirmishes and battles of the period. That number also may not include an unknown number of Native Americans put to death by troops in the field, either summarily or after military trial. Military trials were sometimes brief, and the convicted were executed either the same or the following day. In these terms both the inadequacy of source material and problems of definition introduce uncertainties as to the actual number of Native Americans legally put to death.[7]

In the Western regions the gender distribution of the executed was, if anything, even more skewed than in the older regions of the nation. Ten women, less than 1% of the total number executed, are recorded as having been executed in the three regions. The ten include two Hispanics, one African American, six whites, and one woman of unknown ethnicity. As in the older regions, the death penalty in the West was almost completely restricted to men.

Calculation and comparison of rates of execution in relation to population involve a number of difficulties. One is the variation in Western rates of population growth. Growth was often particularly rapid during the early years of settlement. California is an example. The federal Census of 1850, the first that included California, gives the population as 93,000. A decade later, according to the 1860 Census, the population of the state had more than quadrupled to over 380,000, and much of the increase probably occurred in the years immediately following 1850.[8] California may be an extreme example, but other states and territories, including Oregon and Washington, were marked by similar increases. In these terms the procedures used in calculating the rates of execution, shown in Table 6.2, probably underestimate the population during the early years and, consequently, overestimate the actual rates of execution of whites.

With these reservations in mind, rates of execution per 100,000 population follow a predictable pattern. White rates appear high during the early years, particularly for the Mountain and Pacific regions, and decline in following years. It is likely that the rates for the early years are in part a product of misestimation, as indicated earlier, and the declining trend may have been less precipitous than it appears. African American rates also follow a predictable pattern. In all three regions, as in the older regions of the nation, African Americans were executed at substantially higher rates—often ten or more times higher—than whites. No African Americans are recorded as having been executed in the West North Central region during the first forty years of the period (see Table 6.2). The rates

Table 6.2 Rates of executions by racial and ethnic groups: The West, 1836–1945

	1836–45	1846–55	1856–65	1866–75	1876–85	1886–95	1896–1905	1906–15	1916–25	1926–35	1936–45
West North Central											
African American	—	—	—	—	0.18	0.52	0.61	0.87	0.83	0.54	0.19
White	0.93	—	0.19	0.03	0.02	0.05	0.02	0.01	0.03	0.05	0.06
Native American	—	—	—	—	—	—	—	—	—	0.10	0.15
Mountain											
African American	—	—	—	8.56	13.33	5.83	1.18	1.36	2.67	1.29	2.43
White	—	0.68	1.40	0.53	0.77	0.34	0.37	0.13	0.16	0.13	0.10
Native American	—	—	—	—	—	—	—	0.53	—	0.10	0.08
Asian	—	—	—	—	1.89	—	—	1.30	1.30	2.44	—
Pacific											
African American	—	4.19	10.00	2.50	3.33	0.71	2.00	1.00	1.46	1.32	1.34
White	—	—	1.33	0.41	0.36	0.26	0.30	0.15	0.11	0.12	0.09
Native American	—	—	—	—	—	—	—	0.92	—	0.57	0.58
Asian	—	—	0.86	0.57	1.02	1.15	1.54	0.29	0.70	0.56	0.31

reached high points, however, during the period 1906–1925. These were, of course, years of heavy African American migration to the region. In the West North Central region, as in the Middle Atlantic and East North Central regions, increased migration of African Americans was followed by an increase in both the number and rates per 100,000 population at which they were executed.

The two other Western regions followed a similar pattern, but in more extreme form. African Americans were executed at much higher rates in these regions than in the West North Central region. In the Pacific Coast states, African American execution rates remained at high levels—consistently over one per 100,000—throughout the first half of the twentieth century. In the Mountain states during these years execution rates for African Americans were even higher, sometimes approaching three per 100,000. As will be recalled in Table 6.1, however, only a small number of African Americans were executed in the two regions.

As Table 6.2 shows, rates of execution for both African Americans and whites were consistently lower in the West North Central region than in either the Mountain or Pacific regions. The rates for the former region, however, require qualification. Several states in the West North Central region permanently or temporarily abolished capital punishment during the period, discussed later. To the degree possible, the rates in Table 6.2 are based on only those states that retained capital punishment. Rates of execution for the West North Central region also are complicated by the inclusion of Oklahoma in the region. During the period, almost half of all executions in the region took place in Oklahoma. Almost 70% of all African Americans executed in the West North Central region were put to death in Oklahoma. However, until the closing years of the period, African American execution rates were not consistently higher in Oklahoma than in other states and territories in the region. The African American population of Oklahoma was also larger than that of the other states and territories. Even so, the inclusion of Oklahoma has a heavy influence on regional rates, particularly the rates for African Americans and whites.

Calculation and comparison of execution rates for other ethnic groups involve additional difficulties, largely due to inconsistent enumeration and to the distribution of these groups within the regions. As noted in chapter 1, historical censuses did not distinguish between Hispanics and other whites. In calculating rates of execution in relation to population, we have necessarily combined the Hispanic and white categories included in the Espy collection.[9] The Chinese and Japanese population was enumerated separately beginning with the 1860 Census. The Espy collection, however, does not distinguish between Chinese and Japanese or other Asian groups, although it is probable that most of those executed during the earlier years were Chinese. Native Americans were enumerated beginning in 1860, excluding, however, those living on reservations and in Indian territory. In the 1910 and 1930 censuses and those thereafter, efforts were made to achieve a more complete enumeration, and the Native American population appears significantly larger in those years than in 1920 or the years prior to 1910. Given these characteristics of the data, it seemed appropriate to restrict calculation of rates of execution of Native Americans to the data for 1910, 1930, and 1940. To the degree population data are available, it appears that with few exceptions Asians and Native Americans were executed at higher rates than whites.[10]

The Asian and Hispanic populations were not evenly distributed across the West but tended to be concentrated in particular states and territories. As a consequence, rates of execution calculated at the regional level may be misleading. Limited information bearing upon the Hispanic population also is available. For the 1930 Census, people of Mexican descent were inadvertently tabulated separately from other whites. It is reasonable to assume that in the Western regions the Hispanic American category used in the Espy collection is disproportionately composed of people of Mexican derivation.[11] In Table 6.3 the available data are used to calculate rates of execution for Asians, Hispanics, and Native Americans for those territories and states and time periods for which population data are available and members of these groups were executed. For comparison, white rates of execution also are included in the table.

While the table provides only limited information, it appears that with three exceptions, members of these racial and ethnic groups, such as African Americans, were executed at higher rates in relation to population than whites. Asian American execution rates appear particularly high in comparison to whites and other ethnic groups. Exceptions to the generalization appear somewhat more frequent with Native Americans. It will be recalled, of course, that in the twentieth century when relevant population data are available, much of the Native American population lived on reservations, where they were subject to a different justice system, and contact with whites was reduced.

These execution rates, as those of African Americans, present a familiar problem of interpretation. As Table 6.1 indicates, the number of African, Asian, Hispanic, and Native Americans executed in the Western regions was relatively small. Their numbers also were small, and they were not evenly distributed across the various territories and states. As in the older regions of the Northeast, relatively few executions translated into very high average annual rates of execution in relation to population. Washington State is an example. The 1928 execution of a single individual of Mexican derivation out of a population of 562 yields the high rate given in Table 6.3.[12]

Table 6.3 Rates of executions of Asians, Mexicans, Native Americans, and whites by state and ethnic groups: The West, 1856–1945

	1856–65	1866–75	1876–85	1886–95	1896–1905	1906–15	1916–25	1926–35	1936–45
Oklahoma									
Native American								0.1	0.2
White								0.1	0.0
Arizona									
Native American									0.2
Asian								16.3	
Mexican								0.3	
White								0.2	0.3
Colorado									
Mexican								0.7	
White								0.2	
Idaho									
Asian			3.0						
White			1.4						
Montana									
Asian			5.7			3.5			
White			2.3			0.1			
Nevada									
Native American						7.6			
Asian			1.9				6.9		
Mexican								3.2	
White			0.7			0.3	0.0	0.6	

continued on next page

Table 6.3 (continued)

	1856–65	1866–75	1876–85	1886–95	1896–1905	1906–15	1916–25	1926–35	1936–45
New Mexico									
Mexican								0.2	
White								0.0	
Wyoming									
Native American						5.4		5.4	
Asian							6.9		
White						0.1	0.1	0.1	
California									
Native American	0.9				1.6	1.8		0.5	
Asian		0.2	1.1	1.1		0.3	0.9	0.6	
Mexican								0.2	
White	1.1	0.5	0.3	0.3	0.3	0.1	0.1	0.1	
Oregon									
Asian			1.1	2.1					
White			0.5	0.3					
Washington									
Native American		85.5							0.9
Asian					3.2	0.6		0.4	
Mexican								17.8	
White				0.1		0.1		0.1	0.1

The average annual execution rates given in Tables 6.2 and 6.3 lend credence to the view that the Pacific and Mountain regions of the West were marked by a high degree of violence. After the early years the death penalty was used less frequently in relation to population in the West North Central region, even when Oklahoma is included, than in the other two regions. The questionable nature of data for population in the early years makes the generalization somewhat less persuasive for the Pacific and Mountain regions. However, even if we were to double the population base used in calculating execution rates for the Pacific region—probably the region of greatest distortion—the resulting rates would still appear high compared both to later years in the region and to the older regions of the nation at the time. Although the evidence is limited, it appears as well that the death penalty was used more frequently in relation to population where other ethnic groups were concerned than in the case of whites.

VIGILANTES AND LYNCH MOBS

In the nineteenth-century and early-twentieth-century West, frequent legal use of the death penalty was accompanied by frequent lynchings. During the early years of Western development, lynching often was carried out by more or less well-organized "committees of vigilance." The actions of vigilantes have sometimes been seen as a product, perhaps justifiable, or at least inevitable, of the absence of a duly constituted authority in the politically undeveloped areas of the frontier West. Incarceration facilities were unavailable, so the argument goes, and the only alternative was lynch law. Prominent figures at the local, territorial, and state levels, as well as the national level, endorsed vigilante actions. Leading citizens often provided the core and leadership of committees of vigilance, and on occasion law enforcement officers participated in vigilante actions. Vigilante "executions" were sometimes distinguished from other lynchings by the greater degree of organization involved and by the use of some of the trappings of legal procedure—appointment of defense and prosecuting attorneys, a judge and jury, and the conduct of a "trial."[13] It is clear, however, that vigilante actions sometimes reflected other motives—conflicting economic interests and political rivalries among them—rather than the simple maintenance of law and order.

It is clear as well that vigilante lynchings and other forms of vigilante violence often took place where law enforcement mechanisms were established and functioning and where courts, jails, and prisons were readily available. Indeed, mob and vigilante violence can be seen as a rejection of formal and established legal and judicial procedures. As Michael J. Pfeifer puts it:

Postbellum mobs did not respond to an *absence* of law but rather to a *style* of criminal justice that was careful and deliberative, ostensibly impersonal and neutral, in which the rights of the defendant, the reform of the criminal, and humanitarian considerations were factored in beyond the demands of communal opinion.[14]

During some time periods and in some areas, there were more deaths at the hands of vigilantes than legal executions. Richard Maxwell Brown has compiled a list of the vigilante organizations (over 180) that were active in the three Western regions and the number of individuals killed. Not all of these groups carried out lynchings, but many of them did. According to Brown's compilation, these groups accounted for approximately 410 deaths from the 1830s until 1885. Some 476 were legally executed during the same period. The Mountain states and territories led the other two regions in the number (221) of vigilante lynchings compared to legal executions (121). Approximately 100 of these occurred in Montana alone, with Idaho and Wyoming a distant second and third. In the West North Central region vigilantes lynched seventy-six during these years—most of them in Iowa, Kansas, and Nebraska. Approximately 122 were legally executed. Around 113 lynchings by organized vigilante groups took place in the Pacific region, most of them (106) in California, compared to legal executions (243).[15]

These numbers are more striking if we take into consideration the population of those states and territories with the largest number of vigilante killings. According to Brown's tabulation, of the approximately 110 killed by vigilantes in California from 1851 through 1897, eighty-two were lynched during the period 1851–1858.[16] As suggested earlier, the California population grew rapidly across the 1850s. A crude estimate of the state population in 1855 would be approximately 237,000, obtained by averaging the populations reported by the 1850 and 1860 Censuses. Using that population base, it appears that vigilantes "executed" at an average rate of approximately 4.4 per 100,000 per year from 1851–1858. During this same period, more than sixty Californians were legally executed. In these terms the combined extra legal and legal execution rate amounted to an average of approximately 7.5 per 100,000 per year.

Elsewhere the vigilante death toll was even more extreme. Of the thirty-five lynched by vigilantes in Idaho between 1862 and 1874, thirty-three were lynched in the period 1862–1866. Three also were legally executed in 1866. In Wyoming, vigilantes lynched thirty-one from 1868 through 1892, twenty-six of them in 1868 and 1869. Montana's 101 vigilante deaths were temporally more widely distributed. However, thirty took place from 1863 through 1866, and thirty-five more occurred in

1884. The Census did not tabulate the population of the three territories separately in 1860, but the 1870 Census gives the approximate population of Idaho as 15,000, Wyoming as 9,000, and Montana as 21,000. With these population bases, vigilante death rates for Idaho and Montana were on the order of forty-five per 100,000, for Wyoming almost 145 per 100,000, and for Montana in 1884, using the average of the 1880 and 1890 population as the base, almost forty per 100,000.

It is difficult to know what to make of death rates of this magnitude. An unavoidable response is to feel that elements of exaggeration are somehow involved. In fact, of course, vigilante actions tended to be episodic in nature and usually, but not always, limited to specific time periods and areas. If the state and territorial lynching rates given earlier were averaged over ten-year periods, as we have done for other regions, then they would appear much lower. As examples, if the thirty-three lynched in Idaho from 1862 through 1866 were averaged and related to the population in 1870, then the rate would be approximately twenty-two per 100,000 population. The thirty lynched in Montana in 1884 would yield a rate of almost nine per 100,000, and the twenty-six lynched in Wyoming in 1868 and 1869 a rate of over twenty-eight per 100,000.

While lower, these are still very high rates. These rates also refer, however, to lynchings carried out by more or less well-organized groups. Lynchings, however, did not always involve organized groups. Brown also describes "instant vigilantism." In most of the Western states and territories, vigilante groups apparently sometimes found formal organization, appointing attorneys, judges, and juries and conducting "trials," too time consuming, and thus they proceeded to the main event without delay or interruption.[17]

Writing in the mid-1880s, Hubert Howe Bancroft, the historian of early California and the West, described this form of vigilante action, which he called "mobocracy," with evident approval:

> Notwithstanding the strength and dignity given to justice by the calmer but no less determined [vigilante] tribunals of the larger cities, mobocracy was still the almost universal remedy throughout the mining and agricultural districts. Much machinery was out of place where there were no jails, and there was a directness about the business most refreshing when a criminal was caught, tried, and executed all within an hour. Nor was it always convenient or possible to organize; hence justice continued to be administered in various localities in the form of mobocracy.[18]

How common this form of vigilante "justice" was in comparison to the more organized form is unknown. However, Brown finds evidence of

101 of the more organized lynchings in California during the period 1851–1878. During the same period "instant vigilantism" accounted for seventy-nine deaths.[19] Clearly, vigilante actions, whether carried out by organized groups or the "mobocracy," took a heavy but an unknown toll in the early West.

Vigilantes, in whatever form, were largely phenomena of the middle nineteenth century, when the Western regions were undergoing rapid settlement and economic development. Lynching continued in the Western regions into at least the first half of the twentieth century and perhaps longer, although the numbers lynched declined, and lynch mobs were less frequently distinguished by the term *vigilante*. *The Negro Year Book* provides at least an approximate view of the distribution and incidence of lynching in these states and territories from 1882 through 1951. It gives the total number of lynchings during these years as 682, with the largest number, 304, in the West North Central states and territories. Of the lynchings in these states, however, 122 were in Oklahoma. The Mountain states were a close second, with 288, and according to this tabulation, only ninety took place in the Pacific states. Most of those lynched were whites. Seventeen African Americans are listed as lynched in the Mountain states and territories and four in the Pacific region. Of course, the African American population of these regions also was small. In contrast, seventy-three are given as lynched in the West North Central region, where the African American population was considerably larger. Of the African American lynchings in this region, more than half took place in Oklahoma.[20]

A further and more detailed approximation of the incidence and distribution of lynching in these regions, albeit for a shorter time period, can be assembled and related to population by drawing upon the compilations and sources used in earlier chapters, although these sources are not completely consistent with the *Negro Year Book*.[21] Table 6.4 shows for the three regions the approximate number lynched and their ethnicity during each ten-year period, from 1886 through 1925. Lynching was more prevalent in the Border states and, of course, in the South during these years than in any of the three Western regions. The differences, however, may not be quite as expected. The majority (over 70%) of those lynched in the Western regions were white. More whites were lynched in the West North Central (approximately 137) and the Mountain states (about 114) than in the Border (fifty-six) or the East North Central states (twenty-nine). If the sources are accepted, then more whites also were lynched in the West North Central and Mountain states taken in combination (358) than in the South (233). These comparisons may be surprising, given the population of the several regions. The white population of the West North Central region (in 1890) was smaller than that of the Border region and approximately half that of

Table 6.4 Number of lynchings by racial and ethnic groups: The West, 1886–1925

	1886–95	1896–1905	1906–15	1916–25
West North Central				
African American	14	10	24	15
White	100	23	9	5
Native American	10	4	—	—
Asian	—	—	—	—
Hispanic				
Total	124	37	33	20
Mountain				
African American	1	6	1	3
White	85	21	3	5
Native American	1	1	—	—
Asian	—	1	—	—
Hispanic	10	3	3	—
Total	97	32	7	8
Pacific				
African American	1	1	—	—
White	32	11	2	5
Native American	1	—	—	—
Asian	3	1	—	—
Hispanic	1	—	—	—
Total	38	13	2	5

the East North Central region. The white population of the Mountain states was about one tenth that of the East North Central states and a fifth of the Border region. The white population of both the Western and Mountain regions was slightly smaller than that of the South.

It appears that only a small number of members of other racial and ethnic groups was lynched. Most African American lynchings, about four fifths, took place in the West North Central region, and during the period 1906–1925 more African Americans were lynched than whites. The differences between the West North Central and the other Western regions in this respect are in some degree deceptive. Both the African American and white populations of the West North Central region were larger than that of the other two regions, and some 60% of African American lynchings in the region took place in Oklahoma and another 17% in Kansas. In the other two regions, more members of other ethnic groups were executed than African Americans. If we accept the sources employed, then it also is apparent that in the three Western regions lynching was largely a phenomenon of the nineteenth century, and its incidence dropped sharply beginning in the 1890s, if not before.

Average rates of lynching per 100,000 population can be compared for African Americans, Asians, and whites (Table 6.5). Few Asians

Table 6.5 Rates of lynching and rates of lynching and executions of African Americans, Asians, and whites: The West, 1886–1925

	1886–95	1896–1905	1906–15	1916–25
		West North Central		
African American				
Lynched	1.44	0.76	1.49	0.83
Lynched/Executed	1.96	1.21	2.36	1.66
White				
Lynched	0.16	0.03	0.02	0.01
Lynched/Executed	0.20	0.05	0.03	0.04
Asian				
Lynched	—	—	—	—
Lynched/Executed	—	—	—	—
		Mountain		
African American				
Lynched	0.83	3.53	0.45	1.00
Lynched/Executed	6.67	4.71	1.82	3.67
White				
Lynched	0.08	0.02	0.002	0.002
Lynched/Executed	1.19	0.52	0.16	0.18
Asian				
Lynched	—	0.86	—	—
Lynched/Executed	—	—	1.30	1.30
		Pacific		
African American				
Lynched	0.71	0.67	—	—
Lynched/Executed	1.43	2.67	1.03	1.46
White				
Lynched	0.19	0.05	0.005	0.009
Lynched/Executed	0.44	0.35	0.15	0.12
Asian				
Lynched	0.35	0.13	—	—
Lynched/Executed	1.50	1.67	0.29	0.70

and only a slightly larger number of African Americans were lynched in the Western regions, but these groups also constituted small segments of the regional populations. Although the numbers are small, it appears that Asians were lynched, to the degree that they were lynched at all, at higher rates than whites. African American lynching rates are consistently higher than those of whites, often many times higher. With a single exception, the same patterns appear when lynching and execution rates are combined (see Table 6.5). Moreover, rates of lynching and the combined rates appear high for all three groups in all three regions. As will be seen in a later section, African American and white rates usually were at least equal to and often higher than the equivalent rates for the South. The Mountain states are particularly striking in this respect, but the other Western regions also were marked by rates of the legal and illegal use of the death penalty that rivaled those of the South.

INSTITUTIONAL CHANGE

In the Western regions, as in the Northeast, capital punishment underwent significant modification in the latter nineteenth and early twentieth centuries. Centralization of the conduct of executions to the state level, bringing with it improved record keeping and probably at least relatively more private executions, took place at an irregular pace in the Western states just as in the other states of the nation. Between 1893 and 1904, the three Pacific Coast states shifted jurisdiction to the state level. The process was slower and less regular in the other regions. Between 1890 and 1913, the change was made in Colorado, Idaho, Utah, Nevada, Arizona, Wyoming, and New Mexico. Centralization did not occur in New Mexico until 1913, and not in Montana until after 1945. Centralization in the West North Central states followed a more complicated pattern. Between 1894 and 1905, Iowa, Nebraska, and North Dakota centralized imposition of the death penalty. Oklahoma did so in 1911. In some of the West North Central states, centralization was not an issue, since few legal executions occurred. South Dakota did not centralize until 1947, but in that state capital punishment was abolished from 1915 to 1939, and there were no executions until 1947. In Minnesota capital punishment was abolished and never centralized to the state level. Centralization did not occur in Kansas until 1944, but between 1871 and 1942 there were no executions under state authority to raise the issue.

The available evidence indicates that in the Western regions after the 1860s the legal use of the death penalty was largely confined to offenses that involved the death of a victim. In the Pacific region in the middle years of the nineteenth century, executions were carried out for such offenses as horse stealing, robbery, and theft. By the mid-1870s, however, the death penalty was largely restricted to murder and other crimes involving the death of a victim. In the twentieth century there were several executions for attempted murder, and in 1936 four were executed for kidnapping, two of these cases involving prison breaks. The recorded legal executions in the Mountain states were all for offenses involving death or, in three cases, unknown offenses.

Most legal executions in the West North Central region were for murder often involving other crimes. The major exception was the execution in 1862 of thirty-eight Native Americans, discussed earlier. Five of those executed were charged with kidnapping; for twenty-three the charge was accessory to murder; and the rest were charged with murder. During the remainder of the period considered here executions in the West North Central region, with few exceptions, were for offenses involving death. The exceptions included eight executions for rape—six of the eight were African Americans, and two executions were for robbery and kidnapping. The latter executions all occurred after centralization.

Nothing approaching complete information is available concerning the alleged offenses that led to lynching. The limited evidence that is available indicates that between 1886 and the 1920s more than half of the known lynchings were for alleged offenses other than murder, including, most commonly, horse and cattle theft but also wife beating, "race prejudice," "by mistake," and numerous other supposed offenses. Vigilante lynchings were almost certainly for other offenses in addition to murder, although systematic evidence is not available. Hubert Howe Bancroft described over 100 lynchings carried out by the "mobocracy." Many of these were for robbery and horse, mule, and cattle stealing, but the most common justification for the lynchings described by Bancroft was murder. In short, while the legal use of the death penalty may have been largely limited to crimes involving death, other supposed offenses continued to result in lynchings well into the twentieth century.[22]

Capital punishment also was changed in other ways. Discretion in sentencing for murder was established in all of the West North Central states and territories, except Kansas, by 1893. Kansas did so when it reinstituted capital punishment in 1935. This modification came later in the Mountain and Pacific regions. It was instituted in Utah and Arizona in 1885, in Colorado, Montana, Idaho, Nevada, and Wyoming between 1901 and 1915, and New Mexico in 1939. The practice was instituted in California in 1874, Washington in 1909, and Oregon in 1920.[23]

Despite, or perhaps because of, a history of frequent legal and extralegal use of the death penalty considerable effort was made, particularly during the early twentieth century, to abolish capital punishment entirely. Nine of the Western states, fully half of the states in the three regions, abolished capital punishment for at least brief periods. In some cases abolition was not complete, and the penalty was retained for such particular offenses as treason or murder of a police officer or prison guard. Abolition was permanent only in Minnesota and North Dakota. The states and periods of abolition follow:

Iowa 1872–1878   Oregon 1914–1920
Colorado 1897–1901   North Dakota 1915–
Kansas 1907–1935   South Dakota 1915–1939
Minnesota 1911–   Arizona 1916–1918[24]
Washington 1913–1919

Abolition of capital punishment in the Western regions was more complicated than the list suggests. In Kansas, it appears, no executions were carried out under state authority from 1871 to 1942. Executions did occur in the state, but under military or federal authority. Colorado reinstated the death penalty in 1901 but did not carry out an execution until 1907. South Dakota reinstated capital punishment in 1939 but did not impose the death penalty again until 1947. No executions are recorded in Idaho from 1910 through 1923, or from 1927 through 1950, although capital punishment was not abolished during these years. Various other Western states also did not use the death penalty for more or less lengthy periods, even though capital punishment remained in force. Methods of execution underwent change as well. During the early years of the twentieth century two Western states replaced hanging with electrocution. In the late 1920s and the 1930s six states instituted execution by lethal gas. Nine states either retained hanging or abolished the death penalty entirely. In 1903, one state, Utah, gave the condemned person the choice between hanging and the firing squad.[25]

THE WEST AND THE NATION

Viewed in relation to population, the use of the death penalty tended to decline in all three Western regions from the mid-nineteenth century through the mid-twentieth. Rates were consistently lower in the West North Central region than in the Mountain and Pacific states and territories. Moreover, both African American and white execution rates appear higher in the latter regions than in the older regions of the nation. Lynching was prevalent in the West during the latter decades of the nineteenth century, but as in other regions, it declined thereafter. It also appears that in all three regions members of minority groups usually were executed at higher rates than whites. The Western regions can be compared to the rest of the nation in terms of the incidence of the legal and illegal use of the death penalty and, less satisfactorily, with the relative frequency of the execution of members of minority groups.

Table 6.6 gives the ratios of African and Asian American to white execution rates per 100,000 population for the eight regions of the nation. (It will be recalled that a number greater than one indicates that African or Asian American rates were greater than white rates, and a number less than 1 indicates the opposite.) The comparison begins with the 1866–1875 period and is limited to African American and white execution rates. In this way, possible distortions introduced by the Civil War spike in execution rates (discussed in Chapter 4) and by incomplete population enumerations in the early West are avoided. With the exception of Texas, too few members of minority groups other than African Americans and Asians were executed in the older regions of the nation during these years to allow meaningful comparison.

As can be seen, in all three Western regions African Americans were executed at higher rates than whites. Two other aspects of the table are particularly striking. One is the ubiquity of the pattern. In all regions of the nation African American rates of execution were, with few exceptions, higher than white rates. The only exceptions are periods when no African Americans were executed. The second is that the disparity between African American and white execution rates usually was greater in other regions than in the South. Only in New England did the differences tend to be smaller than in the South, and even there the pattern was not consistent. The lower rates for the South do not, of course, indicate less frequent use of the death penalty in that region. It is, rather, that in the use of the death penalty the South tended to be more evenhanded between African Americans and whites, although it was far from evenhanded.

The table also compares Asian American and white execution rates for those years and regions in which Asians were executed. The pattern is familiar. In the New England, Middle Atlantic, Mountain, and Pacific regions, Asian Americans were consistently executed at higher rates, usually much higher, than whites. In the other regions of the nation, only two Asian Americans were executed.[26]

The approach used in preparing the table has limitations. It does not take into account differences in the numbers put to death in the regions, and it does not reflect, therefore, the much larger numbers of executions in the South than in the other regions. We also know that outside of the South and Border states many more whites than African or Asian Americans were executed. However, when three "Tong Members" were executed in Massachusetts on the same day in 1909, the combined Chinese and Japanese population of the entire New England region was 3,359, according to the 1910 Census.[27] That number accounts for the high ratio that appears in the table. While it may be tempting to view some of the high ratios that appear in Table 6.6 as

Table 6.6 Ratio of African American and Asian American to white rates of execution per 100,000 population by region, 1866–1945

	1866–75	1876–85	1886–95	1896–1905	1906–15	1916–25	1926–35	1936–45
	African American to White							
New England	6.8	4.9	8.5	5.3	*	*	3.3	4.0
Mid-Atlantic	12.5	6.5	11.5	21.6	12.2	12.0	7.3	7.8
East N. Central	5.9	7.5	9.8	21.0	35.6	20.2	10.4	7.9
South	5.4	5.7	6.8	8.4	8.4	7.9	7.2	7.2
Border	7.8	6.9	11.8	11.0	18.2	14.2	12.4	11.5
West N. Central	*	10.1	11.6	22.1	84.1	26.7	10.7	3.1
Mountain	37.8	18.6	1.8	3.2	10.1	16.5	10.2	24.2
Pacific	6.1	9.2	2.8	6.6	6.8	12.8	11.1	14.4

Note: *No African Americans executed.

	1866–75	1876–85	1886–95	1896–1905	1906–15	1916–25	1926–35	1936–45
	Asian American to White							
New England	**	**	**	**	148.9	**	118.8	**
Mid-Atlantic	**	**	29.2	**	36.9	22.8	11.7	24.8
Mountain	**	**	2.6	**	9.6	8.1	18.8	**
Pacific	2.1	4.7	4.4	4.6	2.6	7.9	7.2	3.4

Note: **No Asians executed. Rates were not computed for one Asian executed in the East North Central region and one in the South.

only the artifactual products of small numbers, their consistency may suggest the need for second thoughts.

Lynching in the West during the period 1886–1925 also can be placed in national context. Both the prevalence and rates of lynching in relation to population were greater in the South and in the Border regions than in the Northeast. Rates of lynching per 100,000 population for African Americans usually were higher in the West North Central and Mountain states than in the South, and equal to or higher than in the Border region. Rates were lower in the Pacific states than in either the South or the Border states, as the ratios in Table 6.7 indicate. White lynching rates followed a somewhat different pattern. Compared to lynching rates in the South, white rates usually were higher in the Mountain states, consistently lower in the West North Central states, and usually approximately equal or higher in the Pacific region. During two of the four ten-year periods, no African Americans were lynched in the Pacific states. African American lynching rates usually were higher in the West North Central and Mountain regions compared to those in the Border states. White rates usually were higher in the Western regions than in the Border states.

The interregional ratios for the combined rates of lynching and legal execution are also given in Table 6.7. On the basis of these ratios it appears that in the Western regions African Americans were lynched and legally executed at higher rates than in the South during eight of the twelve ten-year periods considered. The pattern is somewhat more consistent when the combined rates for African American are compared to the Border states. The combined rates of lynching and legal execution for whites are consistently lower for the West North Central states compared to the South and consistently higher for the Pacific and Mountain states. The comparison to the Border states yields the same pattern, although the ratios are consistently higher.

These comparisons are for a limited period only. The evidence suggests that by 1886 lynching in the Western regions was already declining. It is certainly possible that a comparison would show even greater use of the death penalty, legally and illegally imposed, in the earlier nineteenth century in the West than in the South and Border states. Unfortunately such a comparison cannot be made on the basis of available data. Even so, the evidence that is available suggests that in the West the death penalty was legally and illegally employed at rates that were at least comparable to those of the South, higher than in the Border region, and, by inference, still higher than in the Northeastern region.

Simple numeric comparisons, however, are by no means entirely satisfying. Vigilantes are part of the lore of the Old West, and often a celebrated part. Western lynching often has been treated as somehow

Table 6.7 Ratio of rates of executed and lynched African Americans and whites in the Western, Southern, and Border regions, 1886–1925

	1886–95	1896–1905	1906–15	1916–25
	Lynching Rates			
African American				
West North Central/South	1.09	0.74	2.16	1.68
Mountain/South	0.63	3.47	0.66	2.02
Pacific/South	0.54	0.65	*	*
White				
West North Central/South	0.84	0.67	0.49	0.73
Mountain/South	4.52	3.46	0.63	1.24
Pacific/South	1.00	1.06	0.13	0.73
African American				
West North Central/Border	1.73	0.86	2.76	3.82
Mountain/Border	1.00	4.02	0.84	4.61
Pacific/Border	0.86	0.76	*	*
White				
West North Central/Border	8.28	0.84	2.53	1.90
Mountain/Border	44.34	4.34	3.23	3.23
Pacific/Border	9.79	1.33	0.66	1.91

Note: *No African Americans lynched in Pacific region

	1886–95	1896–1905	1906–15	1916–25
	Execution and Lynching Rates			
African American				
West North Central/South	0.89	0.62	1.55	1.70
Mountain/South	3.04	2.41	1.19	3.75
Pacific/South	0.65	1.36	0.68	1.49
White				
West North Central/South	0.64	0.32	0.21	0.54
Mountain/South	3.77	3.35	1.16	2.40
Pacific/South	1.41	2.24	1.11	1.67
African American				
West North Central/Border	1.18	0.69	1.89	2.21
Mountain/Border	4.03	2.67	1.46	4.90
Pacific/Border	0.86	1.51	0.82	1.95
White				
West North Central/Border	2.28	0.43	0.63	0.95
Mountain/Border	13.37	4.49	3.43	4.19
Pacific/Border	4.98	3.01	3.26	2.91

different and viewed more favorably than lynching in the former slave states. And there were differences. The torture, mutilation, burning, and sale of souvenirs that were central elements of lynching in the former slave states, it appears, were largely lacking in the West. There were exceptions, and it is possible that these elements have simply been overlooked in the Western case.[28] Many more were lynched, most of them African Americans, in the old slave states than in the West. On the other hand, lynching sometimes took a heavier toll on the small African American population of the West than on the larger numbers in the South and Border states. Moreover, if a reasonable count of wrongful deaths of Native Americans and of deaths through labor conflicts in the West, then violence in the former slave states might not appear as quite the unique aberration in American history that it is sometimes made out to be.

As in the South and Border states, lynch law in the West had its defenders and exponents among locally and nationally prominent figures, including, at times, Theodore Roosevelt.[29] Vigilantes and lynching have sometimes been treated as necessary steps in the establishment of law and order and the creation of the machinery of justice. In the West, however, lynching, whether by vigilantes or the "mobocracy," also could be an instrument of oppression and a form of terrorism. Whatever else is to be said, lynching had a finality about it that allowed no correction. That characteristic is tellingly depicted in the classic film *The Oxbow Incident* and summed up pungently by an epitaph in the Boothill outside Tombstone, Arizona: "Here lies George Johnson/Hanged by mistake 1882/He was right/We was wrong/But we strung him up/and now he's gone."

Table 6.8 provides a third comparison of the West with older regions of the nation. The table shows the ratios of African American and white execution rates in the Western regions with those of the South in the same fashion that the Northwestern regions were compared to the South and Border region in Table 5.6. As can be seen, African Americans were executed at lower rates in the West North Central region than in the South, except for the twenty-year period, from about 1905 through 1926. These were, of course, years of migration of African Americans into the West North Central states. In the other two regions African Americans were consistently executed at higher rates than in the Southern states, except for a single ten-year period. White execution rates follow a similar pattern. The West North Central rates were consistently lower than those of the South, although at the close of the period white rates rose in comparison to the South. White rates of execution in the Mountain and Pacific regions also were consistently higher than in the South, but with some convergence at the end of the period.

Table 6.8 Ratio of rates of African Americans and whites executed in the West to rates executed in the South and Middle Atlantic, 1866–1945

	1866–75	1876–85	1886–95	1896–1905	1906–15	1916–25	1926–35	1936–45
African American								
West North Central/South	—	0.20	0.60	0.65	1.05	1.73	0.89	0.30
Mountain/South	14.04	14.98	6.70	1.26	1.64	5.56	2.11	3.80
Pacific/South	4.10	3.74	0.82	2.13	1.20	3.04	2.16	2.09
White								
West North Central/South	0.27	0.13	0.38	0.18	0.10	0.50	0.56	0.67
Mountain/South	4.82	4.78	2.61	3.34	1.35	2.70	1.41	1.12
Pacific/South	3.73	2.25	2.00	2.73	1.50	1.83	1.33	1.00
African American								
West North Central/Mid-Atlantic	—	0.29	0.62	0.37	0.64	0.70	0.89	0.48
Mountain/Mid-Atlantic	7.93	21.16	6.94	0.71	1.00	2.26	2.11	6.08
Pacific/Mid-Atlantic	2.31	5.29	0.85	1.20	0.74	1.24	2.16	3.35
White								
West North Central/Mid-Atlantic	0.33	0.20	0.71	0.25	0.09	0.30	0.63	1.20
Mountain/Mid-Atlantic	7.93	7.70	4.86	4.63	1.18	1.60	1.63	2.00
Pacific/Mid-Atlantic	4.56	3.60	3.71	3.75	1.36	1.10	1.50	1.80

Table 6.8 also compares the Western regions to the Middle Atlantic states. Execution rates in the Middle Atlantic region tended to be higher than in the other regions of the Northeast. Here again, African American execution rates in the West North Central states appear consistently lower than in the Middle Atlantic states. In the other two Western regions, African American execution rates are consistently higher and, in fact, appear to increase in comparison to the Middle Atlantic states at the end of the period. White execution rates in the Mountain and Pacific regions also appear consistently higher than in the Middle Atlantic states. Only at the end of the period did white rates in the West North Central region exceed those of the Middle Atlantic region.

It appears that in the Western regions frontier conditions were associated with at least one form of violence—use of the death penalty, whether legally or illegally imposed—and probably other forms as well. The more extreme these conditions, the more frequently the death penalty tended to be used. With institutional development and shifts in demographic patterns, the use of the death penalty tended to decline. A suggestive indication of conditions characteristic of the Western regions is provided by the relative balance between the number of men and the number of women. The greater the imbalance, the younger the male population tends to be, and the greater the incidence of violence tends to be.[30] In the Western regions, the gender ratio, sometimes stated as the number of men per 100 women, varied widely, both from place to place and over time. In California in 1850 there were well over 1,000 men (approximately 1,200) for every 100 women. The national gender ratio in 1860 was approximately 105. As we have seen, in California in the 1850s both the execution and lynching rates were high. The average gender ratio in the West North Central region, the farming frontier, was approximately 126 in 1880 and 117 in 1890. In contrast, the average ratios for the Mountain and Pacific regions, which might be described as encompassing the cattle and mining frontiers, were in the neighborhood of 190 and 151, respectively, with corresponding differences in execution rates. By 1910 the average gender ratios had fallen to 114, 140, and 134 for the West North Central, Mountain, and Pacific states, respectively, and execution rates had fallen as well.

The gender ratio does not, of course, explain differences in the frequency of use of the death penalty. At most it provides a crude indication of the presence of conditions conducive to the frequent use of the death penalty. It is clear, however, that in the course of the twentieth century the Western regions tended to converge in their use of the death penalty with the other regions of the nation. In the Western regions the death penalty underwent much the same pattern of institutional change as in the Northeast regions. Efforts to abolish the death penalty in the late nineteenth and early twentieth centuries were seemingly more pervasive than in the older regions, although in most cases these efforts were only temporarily successful. Viewed in relation to population, the use of the death penalty declined in all of the Western regions. In the Pacific and Mountain states, however, rates of execution remained at comparatively high levels. Execution rates dropped most sharply in the West North Central region, and by 1945 these states had come to resemble the New England states in their use of the death penalty. In the West, as in the older regions, African Americans and probably members of other minority groups were more likely to be executed than whites.

Chapter 7

Social Perspectives

Little is known of the people legally put to death in the course of American history. A great deal is known of a few famous cases and of a sprinkling of others that for one reason or the other have caught the attention of historians, legal scholars, or an occasional novelist. It also is true that as the contemporary era is approached, more information is progressively available concerning those who have been put to death. But for the large majority of those executed in the more remote past, only bits and pieces of information are available. Limited systematic information is available bearing upon such characteristics of the executed as prior brushes with the law, economic condition, education, family background, marital status, age, and the like. Much less is known of those who were illegally put to death by lynch mobs and vigilantes. For most of those who were legally executed, only scant information is available concerning the specific circumstances surrounding the offenses with which they were charged, or the exact nature of the procedures followed from arrest through conviction and execution. A good bit is known, however, about how the legal system was supposed to operate; how it actually operated from one of a multitude of jurisdictions to another or from one case to the next is far less certain.

This chapter addresses two basic questions concerning those who were put to death in the course of American history. Phrased in somewhat rhetorical form, they are: Who were they? Why were they executed? Partial but reasonable answers to these questions can be developed by drawing upon available information, plausible inferences, and a measure of conjecture.

WHO WERE THE EXECUTED?

The very absence of information about the executed is itself suggestive. By and large these were people, it appears, of a sort that left few traces in the historical record. Even with the progressive bureaucratization of society, and the proliferation of record keeping that it has entailed, these were people who left little evidence of their passing. It is unlikely, however, that many of them were people of even modest wealth or position, who were viewed with respect in their communities, or whose execution was viewed with any widespread sense of loss. It is much more likely that they were held in low esteem and viewed with indifference, as threatening, and even with a measure of fear and hostility by the established segments of the dominant white population. For the most part, these were not people whose lives and personal characteristics attracted the interest of the authorities, newspapers, or other record keepers of the time, except perhaps as their deaths could serve as a warning, as an example of vengeful justice, or as a source of titillation. At best they were probably viewed as being essentially unimportant to society.

The limited evidence that is available, combined with reasonable inferences from the pattern of information that is not available, supports and modestly extends this view. That evidence also provides support for the further conclusion that the law and criminal justice system operated differently and more harshly in the case of some groups than in the case of others.

Race, Ethnicity, and Region

Most of those legally put to death during the period 1608–1945 were members of minority groups. The most consistently available data bearing on the personal characteristics of the executed are their ethnicity. Race and ethnicity are known in terms of broad categories for approximately 95% of those put to death. As chapter 1 indicates (see Table 1.1), by these definitions, slightly less than half of all those executed were African Americans, and a little over 5% were Native, Hispanic, and Asian Americans. We know, of course, that during much of American history large segments of the white majority have tended to regard members of minority groups, virtually by definition, as inferior and often as potential threats to society and good order.

Approximately half of all executions during these years took place in the South. Another 13% occurred in the Border region, as we have defined it. In other words, around six or seven out of every ten legal executions took place in the most rural regions of the nation. Substantial numbers of the executions in the other regions took place during the earlier years of settlement when most people lived in rural areas, villages, and small towns. The examination presented here is not of a sufficiently fine grade to demonstrate the point fully, but it appears clear that the use of the death penalty was, relative to population, employed more frequently in small-town and rural America than in more urban areas.

Nearly 75% of the African Americans who were executed were put to death in the South. Indeed, the modal execution in the United States during these years was of an African American male put to death in the South. Another 14% of all African Americans executed were put to death in the Border region. Put differently, more than eight out of every ten African Americans who were legally executed were put to death in a state where slavery was legal in 1860. And this refers only to legal executions. As we have seen, over 70% of all lynchings from 1882 through 1951 occurred in the South and Border states, and the victims were disproportionately African Americans. Over 90% of the African Americans lynched were lynched in a Southern or a Border state.[1] Obviously if legal executions and lynching were taken in combination, the use of the death penalty in the predominantly rural and small-town Southern and Border regions would appear much greater and the preponderance of African Americans much larger. Most of the African Americans put to death, whether legally or illegally, were slaves, former slaves, or the descendants of slaves, and they were regarded by much of the dominant white population as inferior, threatening, and in need of regimentation and control. This is not to say that African Americans were less likely to be executed in the other regions of the nation. In all regions and all time periods African Americans were executed at rates per 100,000 population that usually far exceeded white rates. In the Northeastern and Western regions African Americans often were executed at rates in excess of those of the South and the Border states. As the African American population of the Northeast and the West increased, the number put to death and the rate of execution per 100,000 population both increased. In terms of the use of capital punishment, African Americans were little better off in the Northern and Western regions than in the South and the Border.

Most African Americans were, however, executed in the South, followed by the Border states. African Americans constituted a larger proportion of the population of these regions than of the other regions, but in both regions they were a minority. The African American population never approached three quarters of the population of the South, or of any Southern state, although African Americans constituted three fourths of those executed. They never amounted to half of the population of the Border region or of any state in the region, but they accounted for more than half of those put to death.

A simple counterfactual example illustrates the magnitude of the disparity in the national use of capital punishment between African Americans and whites in a different way. During the period 1896–1905, approximately 510 whites were legally executed in the United States, an average of about one each week in the ten-year period.[2] However, if whites had been executed at the same rate per 100,000 population as

African Americans, then approximately 6,300 would have been put to death during the same period. This amounts to slightly over twelve each week, or a little less than two each day. How whites would have reacted to this level of execution can be pondered.

African Americans, of course, were not the only minority group with members among the executed. Members of other groups also were put to death. Population data are not consistently available for these groups, but it is likely that they also constituted a larger proportion of those put to death than of the population of the areas in which they were executed. Most Native Americans were executed during the early and often conflict-ridden years of settlement of the various regions, where they were regarded by many whites as substandard rivals for land and resources and as clear-and-present dangers. Most Asian and Hispanic Americans were executed in the Pacific and Mountain states and in Texas, where they constituted a small but often equally denigrated minority.

Although the evidence is shaky, it appears that minority groups of whites—particularly recent immigrants—distinguished by their national origins also may have been overrepresented among the executed. As indicated earlier an examination suggests that disproportionate numbers of those put to death in the Northeast during the earlier decades of the twentieth century were of Southern and Eastern European origins. At that time other whites also often regarded members of these groups as intrinsically inferior and potentially dangerous. Taken together, African, Asian, Hispanic, and Native Americans made up over half of those executed during the years prior to 1945. Whites, in contrast, constituted only about 40%. It is likely that if various recent immigrant groups of whites could be identified—the so-called "hyphenate Americans," compared to "old" or "native-stock" Americans—then the proportion of members of minority groups among the executed would appear much larger.

Status and Occupation

It is probably accurate to say that during most of American history the white majority of the population has tended to regard members of minority groups as being of low socioeconomic status, with all that implies in terms of lack of education, behavior, and the like. The version of the Espy collection to which we have access provides limited information bearing more directly upon the socioeconomic status of some 6,225 of those put to death from 1608 through 1945, over one third of the total.[3] This information bears upon the occupation of these individuals given in over 700 categories that were apparently used in the original sources. Strictly speaking, many of these categories, as "slave" and "convict," reflect status rather than occupation. Slaves, of course, were used in a variety of occupations, as field hands and house servants but also as skilled and industrial laborers. There is no reason to regard the individuals for whom this information is available as a representative sample of those put to death. It is possible that data for the entire group would lead to conclusions different from those supported by the characteristics of this subset. It also is the case that a number of the occupational and status categories used are marked by considerable ambiguity, as examples given later will suggest.

Even so, a few clear impressions result from examining these occupational and status categories. It appears that few of those put to death could be regarded as involved in higher-status pursuits. Only about seventy (approximately 1.1%) of those for whom data are available were professionals, even if the term is liberally defined. Another eighty (about 1.3%) were involved in or owned businesses of one sort or another, including cafes, dance halls, taverns, and stores, or they were horse traders and contractors. These groups, combined with those employed in what appear to be skilled trades (over 300, or 4.8%), a few in government employment and political office, law enforcement, and religion, who might be described as "white-collar" workers (approximately sixty-five, or about 1%), accounted for about 10% of those for whom at least limited information concerning occupation and status is available. Approximately 7% are designated as farmers, ranchers, and planters, although it is not clear that these were in every case landowners and not renters or sharecroppers. The size of their holdings, if any, is not given. In other words, less than 20% of those of known status or occupation could be called people of substance, even by the most liberal definition of the term.

At the opposite extreme are groups that probably would be seen as clearly being of lower status. Almost 1,800 (less than 14% of the 6,250 for whom information bearing upon occupation or status is available) were slaves, including nine bond servants. Over 2,000 unskilled laborers, farm and other workers, domestics, and other lower-status service workers made up another 32% of those executed. Others among the 6,250 were apparently involved in less legitimate activities. Approximately 1,000 (about 16%) were designated only by criminal pursuits and activities—as armed robber, army deserter, gang leader, gangster, convict and ex-convict, thief, and whiskey runner. Another small group of nearly ninety (about 1.5%) was made of individuals described by such terms as drifter, tramp, hobo, and gambler, who were not necessarily outside of the law at the time, but who were almost certainly regarded as less than respectable. Approximately 20% of the specific occupational categories given in the data collection are too ambiguous to allow classification in even the general categories used here.

All of this leaves us, however, with some 11,000 individuals for whom no information bearing directly upon occupation or status is available. But even here something can be said of the likely status of these individuals. Most of them were members of minority groups. Almost 50% were African American, less than 4% were Native American, almost 2% were Hispanic American, and less than 1% were Asian American. The ethnicity of another 8% is unknown. Slightly more than 35% were white. In this context, of course, white is not equated to higher status in any straightforward fashion. We know that some unknown number of these whites were first- and second-generation immigrants who also were regarded with considerable suspicion by many older-stock Americans. Of the individuals with Eastern and Southern European names, discussed earlier, about 60% were without a known occupation. It is likely as well that some of those whose occupation is unknown were simply unemployed. In 1979 and 1986, approximately 30% of the inmates of state prisons were not employed at the time of their arrest. It is at least reasonable to surmise that some of those put to death in earlier years also were unemployed.[4]

Data bearing upon the occupation and status of the executed are incomplete and marked by serious ambiguities. Even so, when these data are combined with information on ethnicity the picture that emerges does not suggest that any large proportion of the executed were people of even middling wealth, status, or position. The data suggest instead a group disproportionately composed of the poor, those without skills, and marginal people who existed on the fringes of established society. A different assumption is also plausible. Information on the occupation and status of more than half of those put to death is missing. It is reasonable to ask, however, that if any significant number of them had been substantial members of their communities and of even moderate status, is it likely that this information would have been overlooked by the record keepers of the times?

Age

We know that in the contemporary United States those convicted of violent crimes are disproportionately older adolescent and younger adult males.[5] Of course, not all of those put to death in the past were charged with violent offenses, although most of those executed from the early nineteenth century onward were charged with such offenses. It is reasonable, therefore, to suspect that those executed prior to 1945 also tended to be disproportionately younger men.

While reasonable, data to support the inference are far from complete. Information bearing upon their age when executed is available for about 30% of those put to death from 1608 through 1945. Availability of data, however, is subject to several biases. As might be expected, information on age is unavailable for about 97% of those put to death from 1608 through 1785, about 85% of those executed from 1786 through 1895, and about 42% of those executed from 1895 through 1945. Systematic information on age becomes progressively more complete in the twentieth century but remains lacking for many states even at the mid twentieth century. Other forms of bias also mar the available data. The age of whites who were put to death is more frequently available than that of African Americans or members of other minority groups, as perhaps would also be expected. Information on age is more frequently available for the Northeastern and Western states than for the South and Border states.

Lack of information on age is not a reflection of inadequate data collection but is probably primarily due to other considerations. For one, during much of American history many people did not know their age in any exact way. The point is probably particularly valid in the case of members of minority groups. African American slaves, for example, usually were not in a position to know their age, although their owners sometimes knew. Native Americans probably reckoned age in a different way than whites, and because of language differences they were often, like many Asian and Hispanic Americans, unable to communicate their age even if they knew it, or if anyone was interested. At a time when much of the population was illiterate, many whites were undoubtedly also ignorant of their age.

It appears as well that even if offenders knew their age, the local, state, and territorial authorities that convicted and executed them did not consistently collect and record that information. In general, information on age tends to become more consistently available with the shift of jurisdiction over the conduct of executions from the local to the state level. However, even after centralization, only fourteen states recorded that information more or less consistently. Oregon did not systematically record information on age during the period of concern here; Pennsylvania did not do so until 1943. Most of the Southern and Border states did not record the age of those executed until the 1920s or 1930s, and half of the states of the South never systematically recorded the age of the executed before 1945. Several of the Western states also were inconsistent in recording the age of those put to death.[6]

The data available suggest that those put to death were, on average, younger than the general population. The percentage of executed African Americans and white males fifteen to thirty-four years of age in the group whose age is known is shown in Table 7.1.[7] For comparison, the table also shows the same age distribution for the period 1896–1945 of the total African American and white male populations. (The number of members of other minority groups for whom age is known

Table 7.1 Percentage of African Americans and whites ages fifteen to thirty-four executed, percentage of African Americans and whites ages fifteen to thirty-four of total population, and percentage of African Americans and whites of unknown age, 1896–1945

	1896–1905	1906–15	1916–25	1926–45
African American				
Percentage executed ages 15–34	82.2	79.4	73.9	75.2
Percentage of population ages 15–34	35.5	35.7	33.7	35.3
Percentage executed of unknown age	85.0	77.2	74.8	49.7
White				
Percentage executed ages 15–34	61.6	65.6	72.5	66.4
Percentage of population ages 15–34	35.0	35.9	33.1	32.8
Percentage executed of unknown age	67.7	55.2	48.8	43.2

is too small to allow for a useful comparison.) As the table makes clear, those put to death tended to be disproportionately in the fifteen to thirty-four age range. During each ten-year period, between 1896 and 1945 (when data on age are more complete), African American males ages fifteen through thirty-four years were overrepresented among the executed by well over twice their proportion of the national population; whites also were overrepresented, but by a lesser margin. The available data suggest not only that those executed tended to be younger than the national population, but also that African Americans tended to be executed at younger ages than whites. It appears as well that the median age of the whites put to death was modestly greater (28.4 years) than that of African Americans (25.6). The evidence, however, should be accepted with caution. The data are less than satisfactory, and as the table suggests, the African American fifteen to thirty-four age group may have been slightly larger than the equivalent white age group.

The available data are compatible with the inference that those put to death were disproportionately younger males. The data are, however, incomplete and biased toward whites, the Northeast and the West, and the more recent past. On the basis of partial data, it also appears that those who were executed were disproportionately of lower socioeconomic status. Unfortunately, we have information on both age and status for only about 2,800 of those executed, approximately 800 African Americans and 1,800 whites. Most were put to death in the twentieth century prior to 1945 and in the Northeast and West.[8]

The characteristics of this group are about as would be expected. Roughly three fourths of African Americans and two thirds of whites were under age thirty-five. Two thirds of whites under age thirty-five are described as workers and laborers of some form, as criminals or convicts, or as involved in illicit pursuits. The younger African Americans are even more overwhelmingly of lower socioeconomic status. Over 85% fall into this general category. Over 60% are listed as laborers of one sort or the other; almost 20% are described as some form of criminal or convict, or as employed in illicit pursuits. A little less than 5% are listed as slaves. It would be easy to exaggerate the socioeconomic differences between the age groups. Using the same categories, a little over 45% of the older whites were of lower socioeconomic status. The differences between the African American age groups are even smaller. Again, using the same categories, over 75% of the older African Americans were of lower socioeconomic status.

On the basis of partial data, it appears that those who were executed were disproportionately members of minority groups, of lower socioeconomic status, and younger than the national population. Limited information from another source is generally in accordance with this view, but with some differences. From 1904, when the conduct of executions was centralized at the state level, through 1945, fifty-nine men, no women, were executed in the state of Washington. Fifty-eight were executed for murder, sometimes involving other crimes, and one for kidnapping. No executions were carried out from 1911 to 1921. The records maintained by the state include a somewhat broader range of information bearing upon the characteristics of the executed than is available for the national group discussed earlier. Those executed in Washington were somewhat older, on average, than the national group. They were, however, younger than the national population. The youngest was seventeen and the oldest sixty-three, but thirty-three (roughly 56% of the total) were thirty-four years of age or younger. On average, their occupational status also was somewhat higher than those executed in the entire nation. Even so, most of the group appear to have been employed in lower-status occupations. Twenty-two (approximately 37%) were occupied as laborers of some form, two (3.4%) were listed as being without occupations, and eight (13.6%) could probably best be described as involved in semi-skilled occupations, amounting in total to some 54% of those put to death.

In contrast, the group also included nine farmers and ranchers (15.3%), nine who appear to have been skilled laborers, and a single professional, a mining engineer. The remainder included two cooks, a barber, a decorator, a musician, and a salesman. The latter is listed as being without a formal education. The occupational categories are sometimes ambiguous. Whether the farmers and ranchers were landowners or in what quantity is not given, and one was only nineteen when put to death. Those executed in the Washington group appear, on average, to have been employed in higher-status occupations than the national group. Even so, the Washington group could hardly be described as being of high status.[9]

At first glance those executed in Washington also appear to differ from the national group in ethnic terms. The Washington group was overwhelmingly white. Fifty are listed as Caucasian, five as Black, two as Asian, one as Hispanic, and one as Native American (an Aleutian Islander). The numbers take on a somewhat different cast when it is noted that according to the censuses of 1900–1940, African Americans accounted for only about one half of 1% of the Washington State population. In contrast, they accounted for a little over 8% of those put to death, some sixteen times their representation in the state population. In this respect, Washington resembled the rest of the nation.

Other characteristics of the Washington group executed are of equal interest. Seventeen, almost 30%, had prior prison records. They were poorly educated. Forty (67%) had attended eight grades of school or less, and eight of those had never attended school. Over 80%, in other words, had an eighth-grade education or less. Nine (approximately 15%) had attended high school; three of these apparently had completed all twelve grades. One had completed college, and one had attended college for two years, about 3% of the total. The 1940 Census provides the earliest available data on the educational attainment of the national population. In that year, 10.3% of the population had attended at least some college, 26.2% had attended or completed high school, and 61.8% had eight grades of education or less.[10] Those executed in Washington later in the period were somewhat better educated than those executed earlier, as would be expected, but the group can only be described as being of limited education. In terms of marital status, thirty-one (about 52%) were single, and eleven (19%) were divorced, separated, or widowed. Seventeen (less than 30%) were married at the time of their execution.[11]

There is no reason to believe that those executed in Washington State were typical of the larger national group, discussed earlier. However, they did share some of the characteristics of the larger group, although in somewhat attenuated form. They were also disproportionately men of limited education. Many of them had not established family lives of their own or had been unsuccessful in doing so. A substantial number of them had already served prison sentences. Whether or to what degree it can be inferred that the total population of those put to death in the nation shared any of these characteristics is a matter for conjecture, but it is at least reasonable to assume that they did.

Town and Countryside

The temporal and regional distribution of executions suggests that viewed either in relation to population or in terms of raw numbers, most of those put to death before 1945 came from the small towns, villages, and rural areas of the nation. The proposition is, of course, almost a truism. During most of its history, the United States has been a predominately rural nation. The 1920 Census showed that for the first time in its history a majority of the nation's inhabitants resided in urban areas, defined by the Bureau of the Census as places of 2,500 population or larger. As late as 1940, however, according to the Census of that year, almost 60% of the national population lived in rural areas or in places of less than 10,000. In these terms, the national population in 1940 could still be described as predominately small town and rural in nature. Moreover, a long-term decline in the use of the death penalty— viewed in relation to population—coincided with a long-term increase in the urban segment of the national population. Whether a causal relation could be inferred is another matter.

At first glance, this distribution of executions may seem to conflict with a widely held view of American history that associates increasing levels of violence with increasing urbanization.[12] This apparent conflict can be explored somewhat farther, albeit still inconclusively, by comparing the degree of urbanization of the various states with rates of execution during three somewhat arbitrarily selected periods (1876–1885, 1916–1925, and 1936–1945). It should be recalled, however, that execution rates are at best an imperfect indicator of levels of violence or the incidence of capital crime. The states also differed widely in terms of the legal structures governing the use of the death penalty. The incidence of capital punishment reflected these and other differences as well as differences in levels of violence and the incidence of capital offenses.

The most urban regions during all three periods were those of the Northeast.[13] With few exceptions, these states also ranked at or below the median rate of executions for all states and territories of the nation.[14] During the three periods the predominately rural South ranked above the national median in rates of execution. The Border states followed no clear pattern, but the Mountain and Pacific states, also largely rural, usually ranked above the national median in rates of execution. The West North Central states were the exception. Although also predominately rural, these states during the three periods were below the national median, often well below, in rates of execution. The data, in other words, do not suggest that more urban areas had higher rates of execution. They suggest only that some more urban areas had lower rates of execution than some more rural areas.

Correlation of average rates of execution per 100,000 population, including all executions, with the percentage of urban population (defined as residence in places of over 2,500 population) for all states and territories, also provides no evidence that the more urban areas had higher rates of execution. The correlation for the ten years centering on 1880 is −.44, −.27, and −.29 for the periods centering on 1920 and 1940. If the West North Central states are removed, then the correlation is −.43, −.43, and −.41 for the three time periods. Viewed in this way, in other words, the more highly urban states tended to have lower rates of execution and the less urban states tended to have higher rates. While the statistical relationship is comparatively modest, it is in a direction opposite from what might have been expected if greater urbanization was associated with higher levels of violence.

Comparison of execution rates in major cities with rates for the states in which they were located also provides no indication that higher execution rates were associated with greater urbanization. Table 7.2 compares the execution rates during each time period for the ten largest cities in the nation in 1900 with the rates for the rest of each state, excluding the cities in question. The comparisons are imprecise. The data are for the counties in which the cities were located; data for the incidence of executions in cities are not available.[15]

The comparisons suggest that rates of execution for the cities tended to be lower than the execution rates for the state population outside of the cities. The differences, however, were sometimes small, and in six out of the thirty comparisons the noncity rates were below the city rates. In one case in Boston, during the period 1916–1925, the rates were equal. The city rates also tended to decline from 1880 to 1940. Again, there were exceptions, and the decline was not linear in all cases. However, in eight of the ten cases, the city rates in 1940 were below those of 1880. The decline in the rates for the cities was not consistently greater or smaller than that characteristic of the states in which they were located.

The comparisons, then, do not suggest that execution rates tended to be higher in urban areas. If anything, they suggest once again that, viewed in relation to population, most of those put to death were tried and executed in the smaller cities and towns of the nation for offenses that they were alleged to have committed in smaller cities, towns, villages, and rural areas. Similarly, if rates of execution are taken as an imperfect indicator of rates of violence and capital offenses, then they do not provide evidence that higher levels of violence were associated with greater urbanization.

WHY WERE THEY EXECUTED?

Every execution was a unique event that followed and involved unique circumstances. We do not know all or any significant number of these separate and unique stories. Some generalizations are nonetheless possible. The obvious answer to the question posed above is, of course, because they were convicted of a capital offense. A further assumption is probably also necessary: It is likely that most were guilty of the offense charged or, at least, a similar offense, as manslaughter rather than capital homicide. Some were executed for offenses that would have resulted in a lesser sentence—or no sentence at all—if committed by a member of another racial or ethnic group. We also know that in contemporary years individuals sentenced to death have subsequently been proven innocent, and it is certainly reasonable to believe that an unknown

Table 7.2 Comparison of execution rates in 1880, 1920, and 1940 in the ten largest cities in 1900 with rates excluding the cities in the states where they were located.

City/State	1880 Rate	1920 Rate	1940 Rate
Baltimore	0.05	0.01	0.03
Maryland, excluding Baltimore	0.23	0.27	0.40
Boston	0.03	0.01	0.02
Massachusetts, excluding Boston	0.04	0.01	0.03
Buffalo	0.05	0.22	0.01
New York City	0.07	0.10	0.07
New York State, excluding New York City and Buffalo	0.10	0.09	0.10
Chicago	0.13	0.10	0.06
Illinois, excluding Chicago	0.09	0.04	0.02
Cleveland	0.10	0.11	0.08
Ohio, excluding Cleveland	0.11	0.13	0.07
Philadelphia	0.12	0.09	0.08
Pittsburgh	0.25	0.19	0.04
Pennsylvania excluding Pittsburgh and Philadelphia	0.15	0.20	0.04
St. Louis	0.00	0.00	0.04
Missouri, excluding St. Louis	0.27	0.04	0.07
San Francisco	0.26	0.06	0.11
California, excluding San Francisco	0.59	0.22	0.13

number who were executed in earlier years were actually innocent of the offenses charged.[16] If errors of this sort can occur today, then they were surely more common in earlier years, when the accused had fewer protections and their rights were more limited. A very healthy measure of skepticism is especially warranted where particular categories of offenses are concerned, including African American males executed for the rape of white women, and at least some of the executions for slave rebellion.

It is impossible to assess how often, historically, the death penalty was unjustly applied. A more limited question can be addressed, although it too can only be answered inconclusively. Why did such a disproportionate number of those put to death share the characteristics discussed earlier—if, that is, we have accurately diagnosed those characteristics? Put differently, why did those who were executed include so few of even moderate status and position?

Partial answers to these questions can be summarized in terms of three components, and their interaction, of the process that led, and leads, to executions. One of these is, of course, the individuals accused, convicted, and ultimately executed for capital offenses. A second is the laws, rules, procedures, and offices that make up the institutional framework of the law and criminal justice system. The third, and the most complex, might be called, for want of a better term, the community, referring to the people who animate that framework. These include not only law enforcement personnel, judges, defense and prosecuting attorneys, members of juries, and so on but also the general public, or at least the dominant segment of that public. Here it should be recalled that during most of American history prior to 1945 the large majority of offenders were not only tried and convicted but also were executed in the jurisdictions, usually counties, in which the offense occurred.

Offenders

As we have seen African Americans were heavily overrepresented among those put to death prior to 1945. Although less strong, the available evidence also suggests that other racial and ethnic minority groups also were overrepresented among the executed. The evidence suggests as well that most of those put to death, whatever their race or ethnicity, were of low social and economic status. While the evidence is weaker, it also appears that the executed were disproportionately males in their late teens, twenties, and early thirties.

These are all characteristics that often are seen, individually and collectively, as being associated with high levels of violence. Explanations for this association require little elaboration. In earlier years, the poor and members of racial and ethnic minorities, heavily overlapping groups, had only limited access to education. Schools and education are, of course, primary factors in imposing discipline and inculcating standards and behavior patterns that work to reduce violence and to promote conformity to law and social mores. Family life was frequently truncated, and child-rearing practices often did not impose or teach the same standards of behavior as for established whites. Opportunities for reasonably regular and remunerative employment also were more limited for those of lower socioeconomic status. Opportunities were particularly limited for members of minority groups in areas and time periods characterized by racial and ethnic discrimination, which of course would encompass most of the nation during most of its history. Roger Lane and others have emphasized the disciplining and "civilizing" effects of regular employment, particularly employment that requires interaction with others and routinized behavior.[17] At a minimum, regular employment saps time and energy that might otherwise be available for antisocial activities. All of these factors impacted upon younger males who were still in their formative years.

Members of racial and ethnic minority groups were particularly disadvantaged in these respects. In the eyes of established European Americans, they were of lower status virtually by definition, but they also sometimes held different conceptions of what constituted desirable and acceptable behavior. The point is most clear where Native Americans and whites were concerned. The two groups lacked common values, behavioral norms, and conceptions of law. It is likely as well that immigrant groups that came to the United States from Ireland and southern and eastern Europe in the nineteenth and early twentieth centuries also held views of violence, homicide, and honor that were different from those of the dominant population.[18]

The point is equally obvious in the case of African slaves and whites. It also is relevant but perhaps less obvious in the case of African American immigrants to the North in the late nineteenth and earlier twentieth centuries. In the South violent offenses, including homicide, by African Americans against African Americans were apparently often ignored or went unpunished. In the North such offenses were less likely to be overlooked. It is possible as well that African Americans sometimes adopted and brought with them to the North some of the attitudes of Southern whites toward violence and personal honor. In a detailed study of Omaha, Nebraska, from 1880 to 1920, Clare V. McKanna Jr. argues that the African American community of that city included a "subculture of violence." That subculture involved a profound mistrust of white institutions, an extreme emphasis upon personal honor, and a willingness to resort to violence in response to real or imagined slights.[19]

On the basis of these considerations it might be expected that, historically, African Americans, and probably at least some other racial and ethnic minority groups, had higher homicide rates than the general population or than established white Americans. Higher homicide rates would provide at least a partial explanation for disparities in rates of execution. Unfortunately, only limited evidence is available to test this expectation for the years prior to 1945.[20] Studies of Chicago, New York City, Omaha, and Philadelphia provide evidence that in the late nineteenth and earlier twentieth centuries African American homicide rates were higher than rates for the general population of these cities or for whites. In New York and Philadelphia, it appears that during the early years of their migration to the United States Irish and Italian homicide rates also were higher than those of other whites and were comparable to those of African Americans.[21] The degree to which these findings would hold for other parts of the nation is unclear.

The Criminal Justice System

It is reasonable to believe, in short, that at least in some places and at some times differences in homicide rates between racial and ethnic groups help explain disparities in execution rates. That view, however, is based upon limited historical data and research and also rests heavily upon present-day experience. On the other hand, there is abundant evidence that during most of the years prior to 1945 the institutions and practices that made up the historical law and criminal justice system were biased against the poor, members of minority groups, and those of lower status more generally. These biases also played a role in explaining disparities in execution rates, although with many variations over time and space. Here again, the relative weight of these factors in explaining disparities cannot be assessed.

Bias was most clear in the case of African Americans. As noted earlier, in the antebellum slave states a variety of offenses were subject to the death penalty when committed by African Americans but not if committed by whites, and in some cases, not punishable at all when whites were the perpetrators. African Americans could not serve on juries or testify on their own behalf. Many of these liabilities also were present in the Northern states. In these states African Americans also were precluded from serving on juries or testifying on their own behalf, and of course, the criminal justice system was exclusively white and male.[22] Technically, many of these liabilities ended with the Civil War. In the former slave states they were perpetuated in a variety of formal and informal ways after Reconstruction. In the North as well, formal and informal ways could be found to perpetuate the lily-white character of the criminal justice system.

It is difficult to know the degree to which these and similar legal liabilities extended to other racial and ethnic groups. It is likely, however, that many of these groups also suffered from disadvantages before the law. In some cases members of ethnic and racial minority groups were not citizens—or at least not regarded as citizens. As a consequence, their eligibility for the legal protections of other Americans could be challenged and denied.

As noted elsewhere, the historical criminal justice system placed the poor at a disadvantage whatever their racial or ethnic characteristics. The right to counsel is an example. Since 1932 those accused of capital offenses have had the right to counsel, although not necessarily the right to effective counsel or to the resources required to mount a fully meaningful defense. In earlier days not even these limited rights were routinely available. In many jurisdictions during much of the past defendants had a right only to the counsel they could afford. For the poor, that often meant no counsel. Whether represented or not, during most of American history the accused faced juries and a judiciary that were exclusively white, male, and middle or upper class.[23]

It appears that the large majority of those put to death during most of American history did not appeal the convictions and sentences handed down by local courts. In the nineteenth century and earlier appeals to higher state courts seem to have been rare, and appeals beyond state courts even rarer still. Even if an appeal was possible, the process was costly and, it is likely, beyond the reach of most of those convicted of capital crimes. Appeals became more common after the centralization of the conduct of executions to the state level. Even after centralization, however, many of the executed did not appeal their convictions. Prior to 1900, when eleven states and the District of Columbia had centralized executions, only about 45% of the condemned appealed their convictions. In the first decade of the twentieth century, when twenty-two states, including the District of Columbia had centralized executions, the percentage that appealed remained at roughly 45%.[24] After centralization, appeals followed a predictable racial and regional pattern. During most of the years prior to 1945, appeals were less common in the South than in the North and West, and nonwhites were somewhat less likely to appeal than whites.[25]

Communities

The third component of the process that led to execution, as we have treated that process, is the most complicated. Not only was it a major element of the underpinning of the other two, but it also poses the difficult, perhaps impossible, task of diagnosing historical popular attitudes. It appears that during most of the years prior to 1945 the verdicts and sentences of local courts tended to be final, including death sentences. Pardons and commutations did occur (how many is unknown), but appeals were rare. Historically, the administration of criminal justice has been highly decentralized, seen as primarily the prerogative of state and local authorities with enforcement largely left to local authorities. In accordance with traditional political values, deference was paid to local values and to popular attitudes and preferences, even when these conflicted with more universal norms and principles. This meant, of course, the attitudes and values of the white male majority, or at least the respectable, established, and substantial segments of that majority. The gradual extension to the state and local levels of the restraints and protections of the accused embodied in the federal constitution came only toward the very end of the period considered here.[26]

In these terms, local values and attitudes played a major role in determining who would be executed and who would not. With immense variation over time and place, the many decisions involved in the process that led from accusation to execution could be influenced by the ethnic, class, and religious animosities, prejudices, stereotypes, and misunderstandings that characterized the dominant majority. It has been noted that juries—and, indeed, judges, members of the bar, and law enforcement personnel—were all drawn from the same pool as the members of lynch mobs and vigilante groups. Thus the same attitudes that animated lynch mobs and vigilantes also could find their way into the jury box, the police force, and the bench and the bar.

It also is fair to say that if the criminal justice system was biased against the poor, ethnic and other minority groups, and those of lower status more generally, then it was because the dominant majority agreed with or at least accepted that bias. By the same token, if these groups were denied opportunities and that denial contributed to their violent proclivities, then it was with the agreement or acceptance of the dominant segment of the white majority. All of this may paint an excessively dark picture. There were eminently fair trials. Probably most were fair, at least in terms of the standards of the time, recalling that in earlier periods the law differed from one racial or ethnic group to another.

From the standpoint of the twenty-first century, the process that led to execution as it was carried out in the communities of the past might be seen as heartless and unfair, even grotesquely unfair. That was not the opinion of the dominant members of those communities. If we cast the picture in larger terms, it is likely that during most of American history the majority of the national population saw the death penalty as an appropriate, even a necessary response, to a gradually narrowing range of offenses. Diagnosing popular attitudes in the historical past is a very difficult, if not an impossible, task. There were no surveys of public opinion before the mid-1930s, and even those of the 1930s and earlier 1940s were few and relatively unsophisticated by present-day standards. Other sources bear only indirectly on popular attitudes in the more distant past and are at best marked by major limitations. Even so, plausible inferences are possible, although they inevitably involve a large element of conjecture.

It is at least reasonable to believe that, historically, capital punishment enjoyed widespread but perhaps fluctuating popular support. Essentially, anecdotal evidence is available, however, that might be taken as suggesting popular opposition to the death penalty. There were numerous efforts to abolish the institution. The early-nineteenth-century committees and societies that formed to seek abolition were most active in the Northeast, particularly in New England, and they were apparently at least led by groups perhaps primarily composed of professionals, prominent citizens, and other members of the upper middle class.[27] It also is true that a number of popularly elected state legislatures, a territorial legislature in the case of Michigan, voted to abolish capital punishment. It is true as well that several also voted to reinstate the institution. In 1914, Oregon abolished capital punishment by popular initiative. The initiative was carried by a margin of 157 votes out of a total vote that probably was in the neighborhood of 200,000. In 1920, apparently out of fear of a "wave of crime," Oregon restored capital punishment also by popular vote, in this case with a 17,000 majority vote. Arizona also abolished the death penalty by popular referenda but restored it the following year.[28] Most states, of course, did not abolish capital punishment, even temporarily. Evidence of this sort is, in short, conflicting and far from completely convincing that there was strong and widespread popular opposition to capital punishment in the earlier years.

It is, of course, highly risky to infer past attitudes from evidence bearing on more recent years. It may be possible, however, to gain a few plausible insights into past popular attitudes toward the death penalty by briefly examining evidence provided by more recent public opinion surveys. From 1972 through 2002, approximately 43,600 individuals were interviewed in twenty-four separate surveys for the General Social Survey and asked, "Do you favor or oppose the death penalty for persons convicted of murder?" Of the total interviewed, seven out of ten responded that they favored the death penalty. In the individual surveys the favorable response fluctuated between 64% (in 1975) and over 79% (in 1985) of the total. Groups differed in their support for the death penalty. African Americans were less favorable to the death penalty. Of all African Americans interviewed slightly less than 50% said they supported the death penalty compared to 79% of whites. The results of the 2002 survey taken alone indicate that 69% of those interviewed supported the death penalty, and 31% opposed it.[29]

Surveys conducted from 1953 through 1972, using a somewhat different question, show a lower level of support for capital punishment. According to these surveys support ranged from 64% in 1953 to a low of 42% in 1966, rising to 57% in 1972 and to still higher levels in later years, as indicated earlier. The rise in support appears to have coincided with an increase in the murder rate. To look farther back in time, three surveys conducted in 1936 and 1937 place support for capital punishment between approximately 60% and 66%.[30] Clearly, support for capital punishment has fluctuated from the comparatively low levels of the reform-minded 1960s to higher levels in subsequent and earlier years.

Numerous reservations and qualifications can be held concerning the meaning of data such as these. Would people who say they support the death penalty, for example, actually vote for conviction in a jury trial when conviction meant execution? In some surveys the number of respondents is too small to allow for an adequate examination of the many socioeconomic, educational, ethnic, and other factors that may be relevant to opinions concerning the death penalty. But the most serious reservation has to do with the anachronistic nature of the argument. It is risky, indeed, to draw inferences about the more distant past on the basis of evidence bearing on more recent years. On the other hand, it would be difficult to make the case that the institution of capital punishment and the way it was used historically were somehow undemocratically imposed on the nation. With evidence of this sort, the case is even more difficult to make.

Chapter 8

The Death Penalty after 1945

Use of the death penalty in American history was marked by clear patterns. "Stark" might be the better word. It is possible that more perfect data would work to muddy the clarity of these patterns. In our view, however, it is at least equally likely that they would appear even more stark. Use of the death penalty did not end in 1945. During the years that immediately followed, however, the rate of executions in relation to population dropped sharply, and in these years, unlike earlier years, the number executed also declined. From 1936 through 1945, almost 1,500 executions were carried out. During the following ten-year period, the number dropped to slightly more than 1,000 and slightly over 400 from 1956 through 1965. In 1967, only two executions took place. In 1972, the Supreme Court ruled the death penalty unconstitutional, but the decision left open the possibility that capital punishment statutes could be crafted that would be constitutional. Beginning in 1976, capital punishment was progressively reinstated, and the first execution was carried out in Utah in 1977.

This chapter compares the use of the death penalty after 1977 with the use prior to 1945. In examining the contemporary use of the death penalty, we address three of the four questions posed for the years prior to 1945: How frequently has the death penalty been used, and how has this use changed? Where was the death penalty used most frequently? What were the characteristics of the executed? Contemporary use of the death penalty at the state level has been limited primarily to offenses involving the death of a victim. In the final chapter of this book we attempt to cast change in the use of capital punishment in terms of a larger conceptual framework. Before turning to these issues, it may be useful to summarize briefly the historical patterns in the use of the death penalty.

Historically, most of those put to death were members of minority groups. It is reasonable to expect that if more complete data were available for the early years, then members of minority groups would constitute an even larger proportion of those executed. This speaks only of the legal use of the death penalty. If more comprehensive records of lynching and other forms of mob violence were available, then the balance would tip even more disproportionately toward minority groups. Although the evidence is less satisfactory, it is reasonable to conclude that those put to death were disproportionately younger, lower-class males of whatever race or ethnicity. During the course of American history the death penalty has impacted most heavily upon those at the bottom of the social order.

African Americans made up a near majority of those put to death; whites were in the minority. During most time periods from the mid-eighteenth century onward, more African Americans than whites were executed, and of course, African Americans were executed at higher rates in relation to population, usually many times higher, than whites. Other differences also existed between these two groups in the use of the death penalty. It appears that more extreme and brutal methods of execution continued to be used for African Americans after these methods had largely been discontinued for whites. Similarly, African Americans continued to be executed for crimes other than homicide, primarily rape, while the death penalty for whites was increasingly confined to homicide.

Continuities in the geographical distribution of capital punishment also are apparent. After the late eighteenth century, most executions took place in the South. Most lynchings also took place in that region. Rates of execution also tended to be higher in the Southern and Border regions, in other words, in the states where slavery remained a legal institution for the longest period. Execution rates tended to be lowest in New England. There were exceptions, however. Even in New England a small number of executions of African Americans combined with a small African American population sometimes resulted in higher execution rates than in the South or the Border region. During much of the history of the Pacific Coast and Mountain West regions, execution rates often were higher or comparable to those of the South and the Border regions.

The most striking historical change is the relative decline in the use of capital punishment. From the seventeenth to the mid-twentieth century, the number executed increased with relative consistency as the population increased, and the death penalty continued as a prominent fact of national life. Viewed in relation to population, however, the use of the death penalty declined also with relative consistency. In the 1930s and 1940s rates of execution per 100,000 population were at the lowest level in the history of the nation up until that time.

Several factors were undoubtedly involved in this long decline. The link between crime and capital punishment is tenuous. However, long-term decline in execution rates may have been related to long-term decline in violent crime rates from the seventeenth or eighteenth centuries through the early twentieth, although the evidence supporting the latter trend is limited.[1] Patterns of settlement also may help account for decline in both the use of capital punishment and the decline in crime rates, if the latter trend actually occurred. During the early years of settlement, all regions appear to have been marked by high rates of execution. As settlement progressed and the regions became more socially and economically complex, execution rates tended to decline.

Institutional change in the legal and criminal justice systems, discussed earlier, also helps explain the long-term decline in execution rates. Making the death sentence discretionary rather than mandatory was one change, as was the progressive redefinition of capital crime to include primarily offenses that involved the death of a victim. Gradual extension of the guarantees provided by the U.S. Constitution to criminal proceedings at the state and local levels undoubtedly also worked to reduce the incidence of capital punishment. That extension meant as well at least a measure of greater uniformity in criminal justice and was a small step toward a national criminal justice system and away from the welter of often conflicting state and local systems. It is likely that the centralization of the conduct of executions from the local to the state level also reduced the incidence of capital punishment by making appeals and commutations more likely.

These considerations, of course, only push the question back a step. If these institutional changes worked to reduce the use of the death penalty viewed in relation to population, then why were they made? To answer this question would require a substantially different study than that carried out here. It would be tempting to believe that the decline in execution rates reflected decline in popular support for capital punishment. It is certainly possible that such a change did occur, but little in the way of direct evidence is available to support that possibility. Moreover, the continuing high level of support for the death penalty in contemporary years raises questions about the magnitude of any such change that may have occurred. Indeed, it also is possible to suspect that the decline in the use of the death penalty had little to do with democratic demand.

THE LATE TWENTIETH CENTURY

Beginning in 1977 capital punishment was progressively reintroduced, and by the end of June 2003, the death penalty was in force in thirty-eight states and the U.S. government and military. Ethnic, regional, and socioeconomic patterns characteristic of the use of capital punishment prior to 1945 reappeared after 1976, but with major differences. While the number put to death gradually increased across the period, fewer executions were carried out during the twenty-nine years from 1977 through 2005 than in any other equivalent period since the late eighteenth century. According to information available from the Death Penalty Information Center, as of the end of 2005, only 1,004 executions (1,001 by the states and three by the federal government) had been carried out during these years compared to slightly more than 4,200 during the thirty years from 1916 through 1945.[2]

Differences between the states and regions in the use of capital punishment reappeared after 1977 in more extreme form. The number of states without the death penalty doubled. In 1945, six states—Michigan, Rhode Island, Wisconsin, Maine, Minnesota, and North Dakota—were without the death penalty. Alaska and Hawaii entered the Union without capital punishment. As of early 2001, four additional states—Iowa, Massachusetts, Vermont, and West Virginia—and the District of Columbia had not reinstituted the death penalty. Of the states with the death penalty, however, Kansas, New Hampshire, New Jersey, New York, and South Dakota carried out no executions, and none were carried out by the U.S. military. In June 2001, the federal government carried out its first executions since 1963.

As in earlier years, the ten states of the Old South led the nation in the use of the death penalty but, again with differences. All of the Southern states reinstated capital punishment, and all carried out executions. The Southern states were among the first to resume executions after 1976. By 1985, all Southern states, except Arkansas, had conducted executions. Arkansas carried out its first execution in 1990. Outside of the South, only Utah, Nevada, and Indiana had carried out an execution by 1985. In addition to the states that carried out no executions, by the end of 2005, fifteen states had conducted seven executions or fewer. Mississippi, with seven executions, was the only Southern state in this group. Among the remaining Southern states Arkansas had the next smallest number, twenty-seven. After 1977, the South dominated the regional distribution of the use of the death penalty to an even greater degree than in earlier years (Table 8.1). During the period 1926–1945, approximately 46% of all executions were in the South. The region accounted for almost 72% of the executions after 1977. The South, however, was much less uniform in its use of the death penalty than in earlier years. Slightly over 73% of all executions in the South from 1977 through 2005 were carried out in three states—Texas with 355, Virginia with ninety-four, and Florida with sixty. Taken in total, the three states accounted for approximately 51% of all executions in the nation.

The other regions were marked by some of the same diversity in the use of the death penalty as the South. Only one person was executed in New England, in keeping with a trend that had appeared much earlier. Only three executions were carried out in the Middle Atlantic states—all in Pennsylvania. Two of the Border states—Missouri, with sixty-six and Delaware, with fourteen—accounted for most of the executions in that region. Of the executions in the East North Central states, nineteen took place in Ohio, twelve in Illinois, and sixteen in Indiana. The West North Central region was marked by an even more extreme imbalance; of the eighty-two executions in the region, three were in Nebraska and seventy-nine in Oklahoma. Twenty-two of the forty-five executions in the Mountain states took place in Arizona, another eleven in Nevada, and six in Utah. California carried out twelve executions, Washington four, and Oregon two. All told, thirty-five states carried out executions after 1976. Texas, Virginia, Florida, and Missouri, however, accounted for over 65% of the total. Both the regions and the states within the regions were more diverse in their use of the death penalty than in earlier years.

Racial and ethnic disparities in the use of the death penalty reappeared after 1977, but also with differences. Of those executed during the twenty years ending in 1945, whose ethnicity is known, slightly less than 50% were African American, and almost 45% were white. After 1977, a majority (approximately 58%) of the executed were white, and a little over one third (34%) were African American (Table 8.1). The several regions were marked by a generally similar distribution. Most of the African Americans put to death (approximately 77%) were executed in the South. In all regions, however, the majority of those put to death were white. In the Mountain and Pacific regions, over 70% of the executed were white. Small numbers of members of other ethnic groups also were executed, with Hispanics making up the largest number. Most Hispanics were executed in the South, primarily in Texas.

After 1977, the death sentence was imposed much more frequently than it was carried out. As of July 1, 2005, over 3,400 inmates were in state and federal prisons awaiting execution. It is, of course, impossible to know how many of these prisoners will ultimately be put to death. On the other hand, it is virtually certain that most will never be released. The regional racial and ethnic distributions of these prisoners resemble that of the executed, but with differences (Table 8.2). Whites were slightly in the minority (46%) in this group. African Americans made up 42%, Hispanics over 10%, and Native Americans and Asians a little over 1% each. In the East North Central states and in federal prisons, African Americans were in the majority.[3]

As perhaps would be expected, states that carried out only small numbers of executions often had large numbers of prisoners under the death sentence, although there were noteworthy exceptions. California carried out only twelve executions during the period but had the largest number (648) of prisoners on death row. Pennsylvania, with three

Table 8.1 Number executed by region, race, and ethnicity, January 17, 1977–December 31, 2005

	African American	White	Hispanic*	Native American	Asian	Other	Total**
New England	0	1					1
Mid-Atlantic		3					3
East North Central	16	32					48
South	260	394	57	3	3	2	719
Border	35	51	0	2			88
West North Central	23	47	0	6	2	1	79
Mountain	2	36	5	1	1	0	45
Pacific	2	14	0	1	1	0	18
Total	338	578	62	13	7	3	1,001

Note: *Corresponds to Death Penalty Information Center category "Latina/o"
Note: **Does not include one African American, one white, and one Hispanic executed by the U.S. government

executions, had 233 prisoners under sentence of death and Ohio, with nineteen executions, had 196. On the other hand, as the table indicates, the South had the largest death row population, approximately 47% of the national total, and also had the largest number of executions. Of the Southern states, Texas and Florida had the largest death row populations, 414 and 388, respectively, and as indicated earlier, the two states also ranked first and third in the nation in the number of executions carried out.[4]

In states with the death penalty, approximately .97 of every 100,000 population was on death row. In eighteen states the numbers per 100,000 on death row were above the national level. These included eleven Southern and Border states and Arizona, California, Idaho, Ohio, Oklahoma, Nevada, and Pennsylvania. In seven states the death row population exceeded two per 100,000. Alabama led the nation, with approximately 4.29 per 100,000 on death row. Oklahoma was second, with 2.81, and Arizona was third, with 2.49. The remaining states in the group were Mississippi (2.46), Delaware (2.42), Florida (2.43), and North Carolina (2.39). Four Southern and Border states were among the eighteen states with rates below the national level.[5]

While African Americans were a minority of those executed and a narrower minority of those sentenced to death, they were overrepresented in relation to the population as in earlier years. In 2000 they made up only 12.3% of the national population. Table 8.3 provides an indication of the overrepresentation and underrepresentation of the several ethnic and racial groups among those executed and on death row. The table gives the ratio of the percentage of each group among the executed and of the death row population to the percentage that each group constituted the regional populations in 2000. As can be seen, African Americans were the only group consistently overrepresented in all regions, both among those sentenced to death and those executed, although the margin among the executed was very small in the Pacific region. Native Americans also were frequently overrepresented among the executed and the death row population, although not as consistently as those of African descent.[6]

Systematic information bearing upon the socioeconomic characteristics of those put to death is not available. However, the Bureau of Justice Statistics has published limited information concerning the characteristics of the death row population as of the end of 2002.[7] There is no reason to believe that those put to death differed significantly from those under sentence of death. The latter population was overwhelmingly male; only slightly over 1% were women. At the time of their arrest, almost 80% were thirty-four years of age or younger. According to the 2002 Census estimate, approximately 27.9% of the national population was in the age range of fifteen to thirty-four.[8] Among those

Table 8.2 Number on death row, July 1, 2005, by region, race, and ethnicity*

	African American	White	Hispanic**	Native American	Asian	Total
New England	3	3	2	—	—	8
Mid-Atlantic	151	78	18	—	2	249
East N. Central	119	109	4	2	2	236
South	724	694	155	11	10	1,594
Border	86	146	8	0	0	240
West N. Central	41	66	5	6	0	118
Mountain	50	166	31	4	2	253
Pacific	239	285	130	15	20	689
U.S. Government	12	23	—	1	—	36
Military	6	1	—	—	1	8
Total	1,431	1,571	353	39	37	3,431

Note: *When added, state and regional totals are higher than the actual count, because some inmates were sentenced to death in more than one state.

**Corresponds to Death Penalty Information Center Category "Latino/a"

Table 8.3 Ratio of the percentage of racial and ethnic groups among those executed between 1996 and 2005 and the death row population that each group represented in the regional populations in 2000.

	African American	White	Hispanic	Native American	Asian
New England					
Executed	—	1.22	—	—	—
Death row	6.54	0.52	1.95	—	—
Mid-Atlantic					
Executed	—	1.44	—	—	—
Death row	4.72	0.45	0.65	—	0.18
East North Central					
Executed	2.72	0.86	—	—	—
Death row	3.88	0.65	0.12	4.38	0.38
South					
Executed	1.69	0.90	0.61	2.54	0.11
Death row	2.34	0.69	0.69	1.43	0.37
Border					
Executed	2.10	0.81	—	6.45	—
Death row	2.33	0.74	0.58	2.88	0.45
West North Central					
Executed	6.04	0.70	—	1.34	1.98
Death row	5.86	0.71	0.71	1.30	0.55
Mountain					
Executed	—	1.07	0.88	1.13	1.65
Death row	7.50	0.91	0.62	0.50	0.55
Pacific					
Executed	2.55	1.32	0.00	10.13	0.73
Death row	6.04	0.78	0.69	3.18	0.29

on death row, some 64% had prior felony convictions. Approximately 22% were married, 21% were divorced or separated, 3% were widowed, and approximately 54% had never married. The education of the death row population is a particularly telling indication of socioeconomic status. A little over 50% were not high school graduates, compared to 15.5% of the general adult population (twenty-five years of age or older) that in 2000 had attended twelve years of school or less without earning a diploma. Less than 10% had attended some college, in contrast to 50% of the national population ages twenty-five or older.[9] As was characteristic of the past, the lower end of the social order received the death sentence most frequently.

As the number of executions suggests, after 1977 rates of execution in relation to population were well below those of earlier years. Whether the long-term declining trend in the use of capital punishment continued after 1977 is a different matter. Table 8.4 gives average execution rates for African Americans and whites for four time periods, 1926–1935, 1936–1945, 1986–1995, and 1996–2005. (Only states with capital punishment are included in the population base for calculating execution rates.) As can be seen, in all regions and during both of the later time periods, average execution rates were below those of the pre-1945 years, usually by considerable margins.[10] The declining trend in execution rates did continue in the Middle Atlantic and South. In the other regions where a comparison was possible, most execution rates increased and were somewhat higher during the period 1996–2005 than in the preceding ten-year period.

The differences, however, are small and are as would be expected. The states did not reintroduce capital punishment simultaneously but did so in piecemeal fashion. In all states there were usually prolonged periods between the reintroduction of capital punishment and the conduct of an execution. Thus it could be expected that the number executed would tend to increase with the passage of time. The regional rates also are often a product of the execution rates of particular states, as suggested earlier. During the period 1996–2005, five states had the highest average execution rates. Oklahoma led, with an average rate of .212 per 100,000 population, followed by Texas (.120), Delaware (.115), Virginia (.092), and Missouri (.088). A significant gap was evident between these states and those with the next highest rates, South Carolina (.082) and Arkansas (.069). Obviously the states and the regions, including the South, were diverse in their use of capital punishment. Indeed, it would be possible to describe the states as polarized in these terms, with most states making no or little use of the death penalty in contrast to a few that made comparatively heavy use of it.

Execution rates in the latter two time periods also differed from those of the earlier periods in another respect. As indicated in Table 8.3, African Americans were overrepresented, both among those put to death and among death row inmates. However, the discrepancies between execution rates for the two groups during the period 1996–2005 were sharply below those of the years prior to 1945 as the ratios of African American to white rates, given in Table 8.4, indicate. On the other hand, it appears that in three of the four regions where a comparison could be made, the average discrepancy increased in the period after 1996.[11]

Table 8.4 Rates of executions of African Americans and whites by region and by selected ten-year periods

	1926–35	1936–45	1986–95	1996–2005
New England				
African American	0.120	0.110	—	—
White	0.040	0.030	—	0.003
Mid-Atlantic				
African American	0.610	0.400	—	—
White	0.080	0.050	0.001	0.0003
East North Central				
African American	0.690	0.340	0.009	0.03
White	0.070	0.040	0.002	0.01
South				
African American	0.610	0.640	0.068	0.10
White	0.090	0.090	0.024	0.05
Border				
African American	0.650	0.720	0.030	0.16
White	0.050	0.060	0.007	0.02
West North Central				
African American	0.540	0.190	0.046	0.49
White	0.050	0.060	0.007	0.06
Mountain				
African American	1.290	2.430	0.054	—
White	0.130	0.100	0.009	0.14
Pacific				
African American	1.320	1.340	—	0.02
White	0.120	0.090	0.001	0.004

DISCRIMINATION AND THE DEATH PENALTY

One of the most consistent characteristics of the use of the death penalty in American history is the disparity between African Americans and whites among those sentenced to death. That disparity appeared in the eighteenth century, continued until the use of the death penalty was suspended, and reappeared in somewhat diminished form in the 1970s. Overrepresentation of African Americans, of course, is not limited to those executed or on death row but extends to the prison population more generally. Given the long history of discrimination against minority groups by white America, or at least the dominant segments of white America, it would be easy to assume that these disparities are evidence of continuing discrimination.[12]

As is often pointed out, however, overrepresentation does not in itself demonstrate discrimination or anything else. Reflecting that consideration, a large literature has appeared that attempts to assess the degree to which discrimination does, or does not, influence the criminal justice process and to explore alternative explanations for these disparities. A detailed discussion of this literature is beyond the purposes of this study, however, a few salient points can be touched upon.

It appears that by the 1990s the balance of opinion among researchers was that differences in crime rates account for a significant proportion of the overrepresentation of African Americans compared to whites in the prison population. In an influential article published in 1982, Alfred Blumstein was able to show that 80% of the disparity between African Americans and whites in the national prison population could be statistically explained by "differential involvement in crime" as measured by arrest rates.[13] In a subsequent article, Blumstein refined and extended his research using data for a later period, and he found in this case that 76% of the racial disparity in the prison population was related to arrest rates.[14]

On the basis of Blumstein's work and that of others following this same general line of inquiry, it was widely accepted that discrimination had been substantially reduced, if not eliminated, from the law and criminal justice system. It is worth noting that few if any argued that discrimination did not occur. It was, rather, that discrimination was seen as an essentially random factor. Individual jurors, prosecutors, judges, or particular jurisdictions might act in a discriminatory fashion, but discrimination was neither pervasive nor a systemic factor in the criminal justice process.[15]

There were also challenges and qualifications on methodological grounds. It was pointed out, for example, that arrest rates were sometimes biased by discrimination, lessening their validity as a measure of criminal activity. The use of data aggregated to the national level also was questioned. Further research showed that the states varied widely in the degree to which arrest rates could account for differences in incarceration rates.[16] Similarly, a finer-grade treatment of offenses showed a larger variation in the degree to which arrest rates could statistically explain prison commitment rates than when offenses were aggregated to more general categories. In general, this research showed that arrest rates left more variance in incarceration rates unexplained than earlier studies had shown. Hence, the possibility of discrimination also was greater than studies such as Blumstein's had suggested.[17]

Qualifications such as these to the side, even some of those who stress the continued importance of discrimination also indicate that it is not the most important factor explaining the racial imbalance in the prison population.

While the literature just touched upon is not primarily concerned with capital punishment, it raises questions concerning any tendency to see the racial imbalance among those executed or sentenced to death as no more than evidence of racial discrimination. However, a large number of studies of the process leading to the death penalty have been carried out, and most provide evidence of at least limited racial discrimination. In a methodologically sophisticated study of capital punishment in Georgia, James Baldus, Charles Pulaski, and George Woodworth controlled statistically on over 200 variables that enter into "death-eligible" cases at all stages from the prosecutorial decision to charge with a capital offense through sentencing. They found that the race of the victim affected the likelihood that a defendant would receive a death sentence. Regardless of their race, defendants charged with the murder of a white victim were more likely to be sentenced to death than defendants—again, regardless of race—charged with the murder of an African American victim. They also found that in rural areas of Georgia, African American defendants were more likely to receive a death sentence than whites, but in urban areas the opposite was the case.[18]

A report released in 1990 by the U.S. General Accounting Office (now the Government Accountability Office) had similar findings. Twenty-eight studies, published from 1976 through 1990, were analyzed for the report. It was found that 82% of these studies showed that the race of a victim affected the likelihood that a defendant would be charged or sentenced to death. The report described the finding as "remarkably consistent across data sets, states, data collection methods, and analytic technique." On the other hand, the report described the effect of the race of the defendant as "equivocal."[19]

In a study of Philadelphia that was, if anything, methodologically more advanced than the Georgia study, Baldus and collaborators again found that the race of the victim influenced the likelihood of a death sentence, but they found that the race of the defendant had an effect as well.[20] In reporting the results of their Philadelphia study, Baldus and colleagues summarized the results of work in other states. A New Jersey study sponsored by the Supreme Court of that state found that both the race of the victim and the race of the defendant influenced the likelihood of a death sentence.[21] They also summarized data—sometimes apparently quite limited—bearing upon the twenty-nine death penalty states that had carried out an execution since 1973. In twenty-six of these states they found "some evidence" of a race of victim effect and in sixteen "some evidence" of a race of defendant effect. The race of defendant effect, however, was not always to the disadvantage of an African American defendant.[22]

There is, then, convincing research that shows racial discrimination in the administration of the death penalty, although in diminished degree compared to earlier studies. Whether this research demonstrates that discrimination is a systemic factor in the criminal justice process rather than the effectively random actions of individuals is probably debatable. It is worth noting that the distinction between the criminal justice system, on the one hand, and the sometimes prejudiced people who animate that system, on the other, is an analytic one that, from some points of view, makes little practical difference. Moreover, if people who make discriminatory decisions can affect the operation of the criminal justice system, then it is a systemic, not a purely random, problem.

While the research is convincing, it is clear that discrimination in the criminal justice process is not the only factor the accounts for the overrepresentations of African Americans among those executed or on death row. An equally and probably more important factor is the difference in estimated homicide rates. As examples, in 2002, African American homicide and non-negligent manslaughter rates per 100,000 were estimated at approximately 6.9 times those of whites. For African American males ages eighteen to twenty-four, homicide rates were 7.7 times those of whites, and for African American males ages twenty-five and older approximately 7.4 times those of whites.[23] The estimating procedures can be debated, but the discrepancies between African American and white homicide rates, and rates for other violent crimes, are unavoidable. This, of course, raises a further question: How are these discrepancies to be explained?

Here again, there is a very large literature composed, unfortunately, of both careful empirical research and ideological polemics. At the risk of egregious oversimplification, as we read it, this literature seems to have two extreme poles. On one side are those who argue that discrimination has been largely purged from American society and its institutions, including the law and criminal justice system. The pathologies that remain within the African American community, including high crime rates, can be ameliorated and eventually eliminated if the market economy is allowed to work, and if policies that undermine accountability, initiative, and a sense of accomplishment are avoided. Personal responsibility is stressed, and in this view the appropriate admonishment is "just say no."[24]

The opposing point of view contends that discrimination remains an obstacle to African American progress but has become more subtle and less overt, more a matter of unconscious stereotypes than of conscious, overt behavior. The disrupted families, the underemployment and unemployment, the crime rates, and the other social ills suffered by the African American community are the cumulative products of hundreds of years of slavery, discrimination, segregation, and economic, political, and educational disadvantage. That poor life decisions are made is not denied, but the social and historical context is stressed as conditioning such decisions. In this view, the problems characteristic of the African American community will not disappear by themselves. To eradicate them will require conscious and deliberate national action.[25]

By the closing years of the twentieth century, the use of capital punishment had undergone significant change. Fewer executions were carried out than during comparable periods prior to World War II, and rates of execution in relation to population continued their long decline. The disparity between white rates of execution and those of other ethnic and racial groups remained but was now substantially smaller. Convincing research showed that discrimination in the administration of the death penalty persisted but had also been significantly reduced. Regional patterns in the geographic distribution of the death penalty also persisted, but in sharply weaker forms.

Chapter 9

The Death Penalty
in American History

The use of capital punishment in American history has been marked by elements of seeming paradox. On the one hand, the frequency of executions and the way in which they are conducted have changed radically; on the other, regional, racial, and economic patterns of use from the distant past have persisted into the twenty-first century. It is probably fair that the most significant change has been the long-term decline in the incidence of capital punishment when viewed in relation to population.

However, for an observer from the colonial period or the early nineteenth century, if that could be imagined, other changes might seem even more striking. In those early years executions were public events, often accompanied by a measure of ceremony and fanfare. In contrast, executions are now carried out in the utmost privacy, and the only fanfare is an occasional protest in front of a governor's office or outside the walls of a prison. That hypothetical observer from the past might be surprised to find that the population of the nation's death rows in 2005 was well over three times greater than the total number executed since 1976, without counting those who died on death row of other causes or who were exonerated or otherwise reprieved. The discovery that a single offense, homicide, and not all forms of homicide at that, accounts for virtually all of those executed and on death row also might come as a surprise.

On the other hand, other characteristics of contemporary capital punishment might be less surprising. The same regions that made the heaviest use of capital punishment in the past continue to do so in the present. Differences exist in the incidence of executions and in the degree of uniformity of use within the regions, but the similarities are clear. The same racial and economic groups that were overrepresented among those sentenced to death in the past continue to be overrepresented in the present. The magnitude of differences may be smaller, but overrepresentation continues.

The empirical data document these elements of change and continuity, but they do not explain them. Rather, they leave us with several basic questions. What accounts for the long-term decline in the use of the death penalty, and for the change in the way the death penalty is used? What explains the continued presence of racial, ethnic, economic, and regional disparities in the incidence of capital punishment? How can the imbalance between the number sentenced to death and the number actually executed be explained? At best, only partial answers are available to these questions, and even the partial answers are debatable and sometimes hotly controversial.

It remains to be asked whether historical characteristics of the use of the death penalty and patterns of persistence and change in use can be usefully fit, if only for heuristic purposes, into a larger and more general conceptual framework. The work of Norbert Elias, particularly as interpreted and applied to punishment practices by David Garland, suggests such a conceptual framework.[1] To attempt in a short space to apply a complex body of ideas to patterns characteristic of empirical data risks distorting both ideas and data. Even so, Elias provides a suggestive starting point for explaining the long-term decline in the use of capital punishment and for change in the character of the death penalty.

As we understand him, Elias argues that the histories of Western societies have been marked by increasing "differentiation" of social functions. As he puts it:

> The more differentiated [social functions] become, the larger grows the number of functions and thus of people on whom the individual constantly depends in all his actions, from the simplest and most commonplace to the more complex and uncommon. As more and more people must attune their conduct to that of others, the web of actions must be organized more and more strictly and accurately, if each individual action is to fulfill its social function.[2]

To maintain social integration and organization, "the more animalic human activities," including violence, "were progressively thrust behind the scenes of people's communal social life." Suppression initially depended upon external restraints imposed by others; over time, however, external constraints were supplemented or replaced by "self-restraints" through which particular forms of behavior were inhibited and "invested with feelings of shame." In Elias's view, in short, the civilizing process has involved a continuing restructuring of human behavior and psychology. One element of that restructuring has been the rejection and suppression of violence.[3]

For the development of "self-restraints" and for restructuring to occur, other changes also are necessary. Particularly, the development of stable central authorities exercising a monopoly over the use of force is required. Again, as Elias puts it:

> Only with the formation of this kind of relatively stable monopoly [over physical force] . . . do societies acquire those characteristics as a result of which the individuals forming them get attuned, from infancy, to a highly regulated differentiated pattern of self-restraint; only in conjunction with these monopolies does this kind of self-restraint require a higher degree of automaticity, does it become, as it were, "second nature."[4]

These two patterns of change tend to go hand in hand and are, in some senses of the word, dependent upon one another. Societies without stable monopolies over the use of force are "societies in which the division of functions is relatively slight and the chains of action binding individuals together are comparatively short." On the other hand, societies with a greater monopoly over the use of force are characterized by a "more or less advanced" division of functions, "in which the chains of action binding individuals together are longer, and the functional dependencies between people greater."[5]

The history of capital punishment in America is in a number of respects congruent with these formulations. We know that over time the United States has become socially and economically more complex, that a more urban society has replaced a predominately rural one, and that interaction and interdependencies between individuals have increased. The growth of industry required a predicable and, in some respects, a regimented workforce composed of individuals working in cooperation with each other in performing the tasks of production.[6] We know as well that governments have tended to become stronger, and that their functions have grown.

Whether change in the incidence of homicide, the primary occasion for capital punishment, coincided with these broad patterns of social, economic, and political change is imperfectly documented over the course of American history, but it is probable that viewed in relation to population, its incidence has declined. We do know, however, that the use of violence for punishment and discipline has become less common in American life, as Elias might have predicted. In the not-too-distant past, violence was a routine element of life in the home, the workplace—farm and factory—schools, prisons, in the military, and on shipboard. Wives, children, servants, slaves, apprentices, prisoners, soldiers, sailors, and animals were routinely beaten and subjected to other forms of corporal punishment.

The incidence of these forms of violence has declined, and actions of this sort, whether carried out by governmental agencies or private individuals, were increasingly viewed if not as crimes then certainly as shameful, unacceptable aberrations. At the same time the evidence suggests that the willingness to use death as punishment also declined. The number of capital offenses has been steadily reduced and capital punishment hedged around with restrictions. In the United States, as in other Western nations, the use of the death penalty has declined. As we have seen, in American history the number put to death increased from the seventeenth through the first half of the twentieth century, but not as rapidly as the population. Thus viewed in relation to population, the use of the death penalty has declined.

The way in which the death penalty was administered also changed over the history of the nation. Executions are no longer public spectacles as they once were but are carried out in circumstances approaching absolute privacy. And that understates the point. From the latter eighteenth century to the present, executions have been progressively sanitized and hidden from the public eye. New modes of execution have been employed, each said to be more instantaneous and less painful than its predecessor. Efforts have been made to shield executioners from any sense of personal responsibility for death. They are now often physically separated from the condemned, and only a minimal number of witnesses is allowed. Drawing upon Elias, David Garland argues that these changes reflect the change in "sensibilities" particularly, although by no means uniformly, among elite groups. Deliberate infliction of death upon another human being has progressively come to be seen as shameful, embarrassing, and demeaning to observers and participants— hence something that should be carried out, if carried out at all, "behind the scenes."[7]

These same sensibilities also may suggest at least a partial explanation for the fact that the death sentence is handed down much more frequently than it is carried out with the consequence of a steadily growing death row population. We cannot know the ultimate fate of that population, but at this point its existence might seem oddly reminiscent of the symbolic executions of the colonial years. In those years, some offenders, perhaps particularly those charged with such offenses as blasphemy and adultery, were sentenced to death but subjected to only symbolic execution in order, it may be, to provide deterrence while avoiding the onus of deliberately inflicting death.[8] It might be conjectured that present-day practices serve a similar function—maintaining the appearance of conforming to the law and providing deterrence but avoiding the shame and embarrassment of actually inflicting death. Elias's formulations provide, in short, at least a suggestive indication of why contemporary use of capital punishment has taken on the form that it has.

Change in the incidence and administration of capital punishment did not occur uniformly in American history. Rather, in both respects, the nation was marked by considerable variation between regions and states and between social groups. Here again the history of capital punishment in the United States and its colonial beginnings suggests congruencies with Elias's formulations. Three sections stand out as marked by the highest rates of use of the death penalty in relation to population and by the persistence of public executions as compared to other regions at the time: the South and, to a lesser degree, the Border states during most of their history, and the farther West during the last half of the nineteenth century and into the twentieth. These regions also were comparatively the least complex in social and economic terms, less differentiated, and, as Elias might put it, marked by only relatively short "chains of mutual interdependence."

In these regions monopoly over the use of force by central authorities was comparatively imperfect as witnessed by the frequent lynchings and vigilante actions. In these regions an emphasis upon the right to self-defense, upon personal honor, and upon the right and obligation to take personal action to redress grievances was virtually legendary. Such attitudes, of course, reflect an unwillingness to accord to government a monopoly over the use of force. Although Elias does not generally address regional differences within nations, his views are noteworthy, as they apply to such differences in the United States. In the United States, of course, the use of force for punishment and public order is decentralized and largely under the control of individual states or, in earlier years, lesser jurisdictions. We know that the states and jurisdictions varied widely in the degree to which they attempted to exercise a monopoly over the use of force. In the three sections in question, however, the monopoly of the use of force by central authorities was more limited than in the rest of the nation.

Drawing upon Elias, Garland adds to our understanding of the history of capital punishment in America by suggesting that an element of the psychological change involved in the civilizing process is the gradual recognition of the humanity of others.[9] That recognition does not come about instantaneously, and it is only gradually that respect is extended to others by elite groups. In the United States, as in other countries, people of lower status and particular ethnic, racial, religious, and even linguistic minority groups have been regarded as less than human or, at least, as clearly inferior and not entitled to the same rights and protections as other groups. In the United States, that assessment of various minority groups has been manifested in higher rates of execution and lynching as well as in other forms of violence, discrimination, and persecution.

A further point also is relevant. Through discrimination and persecution members of these groups were denied civilizing experiences. They were denied access to education and to regular and adequately remunerative employment. They did not receive the same protection under the law and by government authorities as was accorded to the dominant white community. As a consequence, the development of "self-restraints" against violence and other anti-social behavior was slowed. Similarly, respect for the law and established authority and its institutions was hindered. Among the members of these groups reliance was placed instead upon self-defense, realized both through violent reactions to real and imagined injuries and by insistence upon respect for personal honor. In either case, monopolization by force by government authorities was frustrated. The references here apply most obviously to African Americans during and after slavery. They also apply, although the application is less well documented, to Native Americans, Hispanics, and, particularly during earlier years, Asians.[10]

From Elias's perspective, the civilizing process is never complete. Neither the capability nor the proclivity for violence is eliminated, but only "thrust behind the scenes." The legitimate exercise of violence is increasingly confined to specialized groups—the military, the police, prison guards, and the like. The proclivity of individuals for violence is legally suppressed; of greater importance, it is psychologically repressed. The capability and proclivity for violence, however, are always present. This may help us understand that under particular circumstances even the most advanced—the most "civilized"—societies can erupt in outbursts of ethnic cleansing, genocide, lynching, and warfare.[11] Similarly, under particular circumstances, the most civilized nations can resort to and justify torture and war crimes. We also can understand that lower-status groups, ethnic minorities and other groups that have not yet been accorded full humanity, are likely targets of such outbursts. Here it is worth recalling that the lynch mobs of the South, the Border states, and the West were not made up of only the community riffraff or of a few homicidal fanatics and their followers. They also included, usually in the majority, individuals best described as ordinary Americans, and they were led, or at least supported and justified, by prominent figures at the local, state, regional, and even national levels.

It also can be recognized that the civilizing process can be incomplete in another respect. Members of particular groups can be, in some sense of the term, "left out." The example of African and Native Americans as well as other racial and ethnic groups is noted earlier. The populations of the contemporary central cities can be seen as further cases in point. These populations have as part of their legacy generations of exclusion and disadvantage that stretch far into the past. Chronic underemployment and unemployment, inadequate education, and disrupted families and communities mean that in the central cities chains of interdependency are relatively short. As a consequence, for segments of these populations, the internalized restraints against violence and other forms of anti-social behavior are underdeveloped.

In the central cities the monopoly over the use of force by central authorities is imperfect. And it is not just the seemingly uncontrollable street gangs that demonstrate imperfection. On the basis of history, their own experience and that of their elders, other segments of these populations, particularly the young, see little reason to look to the law, the police, or other institutions of central authority for protection and justice. For protection they rely instead upon their own resources, which often means their capacity for violence, while their definition of justice involves an exaggerated sense of personal honor. For these segments of inner-city populations, the legacy of exclusion and disadvantage includes high rates of homicide and overrepresentation, both in the prison population and among those sentenced to death.

Capital punishment in America has undergone radical change. Over the long sweep of American history, its use has declined. In a few states, it is no longer a sentencing option; in others, it is rarely, if ever, used. The manner of its use, when it is used at all, also has changed, and in these terms it is a strikingly different institution than it once was. But despite change, regional, racial, ethnic, and economic imbalances out of the distant past continue into the present, albeit in a somewhat attenuated form. Differences and continuities of this sort, and what they tell us about the larger society, remain to be explained. Elias suggests some beginning points, but at best only beginning points.

Appendix

DATA SOURCES

The characteristics and limitations of the several data collections employed in this study are discussed at various points in the text. The limitations of data from historical censuses and the available estimates of historical populations are well known. Some of these are touched upon in the text as they bear upon our findings. The M. Watt Espy Jr. collection is less well known and is of central importance to this study. That collection requires, therefore, a more extended discussion. Data on lynching present some of the same issues as the Espy collection and also require consideration.

Before turning to these issues, it is first necessary to describe the version of the Espy collection that we have used. Our examination of executions prior to 1945 draws upon computer-readable data supplied by Espy to the Inter-university Consortium for Political and Social Research (ICPSR), first released for general scholarly use in 1987. A second version of the collection, incorporating corrections supplied by Espy, was released in 1992. We have used this second and revised version of the collection. The codebook for the collection provides detailed information concerning the methods employed by Espy in collecting the original data.[1]

The data we have used from this version of the collection bear upon 12,991 executions carried out from 1608 through 1945. The variables included in the collection are the race (ethnicity) of offenders (categorized as White, Black, Native American, Asian or Pacific Islander, Hispanic, and Other); the age at execution; the name of offender; the place of execution (city, county, state, or other); the jurisdiction of execution (local, state, federal, territorial, Indian tribunal, and other, defined as military courts and courts of admiralty); the offense charged; the method of execution; the date of execution (day, month and year); the colony, territory, state, or district of execution;

191

the county of conviction; the gender of offenders; whether compensation was paid (to owners in the case of slaves); and the occupation and status of the offenders.

Espy also provided us with summary data bearing upon executions identified from 1986 through early 1996. For this study we have used summary data concerning 4,139 executions conducted from the early seventeenth century through 1945. These data include three variables: the ethnicity of the executed (as defined earlier); the state, territory, district, or colony of execution; and the decade of execution, as defined in chapter 1 of this text. We combined these two bodies of data, amounting to 17,130 executions, to provide the basis for this study.[2] It will become apparent that our generalizations concerning the temporal, geographical, and ethnic distribution of the use of the death penalty, the central issues addressed by the study, are most strongly grounded. Findings concerning such issues as redefinition of capital offenses, age, and other characteristics of offenders are less strongly grounded. However, we have stated our findings in a way that, we think, understates rather than overstates.

Most of the executions identified between 1986 and 1995 for which we have used summary data occurred disproportionately in the South, approximately 64%, and the Border region, slightly less than 19%. About 9% took place in the Middle Atlantic region. The small remainder of executions with only summary data is scattered across the other regions, with New England accounting for the largest percentage. Table A.1 gives the temporal and regional distribution of the summary data provided by Espy in greater detail in order to provide an indication of the biases and other limitations characteristic of the combined data collection and as a means to better assess support for findings reported earlier. The concentration of these executions in the Southern and Border regions is readily apparent. The temporal distribution differs from region to region but tends, in very general terms, to coincide with the earlier years of settlement and development. In New England and the Middle Atlantic region, most of the executions for which only summary data were used took place in the seventeenth and eighteenth centuries.

In the South and Border regions, executions with only summary data took place disproportionately in the colonial years and in the early nineteenth century. Here it should be recalled that for much of these regions settlement and the early stages of development took place throughout the nineteenth century. In the Border region, executions with only summary data tended to concentrate in the eighteenth century, largely due to the large number of executions in Maryland.

Approximately 54% of the executions with summary data were of African Americans, 37% were of whites, and a little over 3% were of Native Americans. Approximately 80% of these African Americans were

Table A.1 The Summary file as a percentage of total known executions by region, 1606–1945*

	1606–1695	1696–1785	1786–1865	1866–1905	1906–1945	1608–1945
New England						
Number of cases, Summary data	58	55	17	3	0	133
Total number of cases	171	201	144	79	116	711
% Summary data	33.9	27.4	11.8	3.8	0.0	18.7
Mid-Atlantic						
Number of cases, Summary data	9	254	107	14	2	386
Total number of cases	22	604	505	552	1,053	2,736
% Summary data	40.9	42.1	21.2	2.5	0.2	14.1
East North Central						
Number of cases, Summary data	0	1	47	18	4	70
Total number of cases	2	7	181	262	459	911
% Summary data	0.0	14.3	26.0	6.9	0.9	7.7
South						
Number of cases, Summary data	28	464	1,226	633	300	2,651
Total number of cases	38	962	2,801	2,388	2,643	8,832
% Summary data	73.7	48.2	43.8	26.5	11.4	30.0
Border						
Number of cases, Summary data	20	348	302	87	23	780
Total number of cases	37	399	638	621	601	2,296
% Summary data	54.1	87.2	47.3	14.0	3.8	34.0

continued on next page

Table A.1 (continued)

	1606–1695	1696–1785	1786–1865	1866–1905	1906–1945	1608–1945
West North Central						
Number of cases, Summary data	—	—	18	28	15	61
Total number of cases	—	—	79	138	150	367
% Summary data	—	—	22.8	20.3	10.0	16.6
Mountain						
Number of cases, Summary data	—	—	8	14	4	26
Total number of cases	—	—	36	211	223	470
% Summary data	—	—	22.2	6.6	1.8	5.5
Pacific						
Number of cases, Summary data	—	0	12	20	0	32
Total number of cases	—	4	148	259	396	807
% Summary data	—	0.0	8.1	7.7	0.0	4.0
Number of cases, Summary data	115	1,122	1,737	817	348	4,139
Total number of cases	270	2,177	4,532	4,510	5,641	17,130
% Summary data of total	42.6	51.5	38.3	18.1	6.2	24.2

Note: *Excludes eight Hispanics executed in Spanish Southwest in 1640s.

put to death in the South, over two thirds of them during the period 1786–1905. Another 15% of African Americans were executed in the Border region, most of them during the eighteenth and early nineteenth centuries. Most whites included in the summary file also were executed in these same two regions during the same time periods. The disparity between the South and the Border regions, on the one hand, and the other regions, on the other, is much smaller in the case of whites than of African Americans.

In these terms, support for findings, reported earlier, that go beyond the temporal, geographical, and ethnic distribution of the use of capital punishment is weaker for the South and, to a lesser degree, for the Border regions than for the other regions. Support also is less strong for African Americans in the South than for other ethnic groups in that region. Support for these findings also tends to be least strong for the earlier years of settlement than for later years. On the whole, however, the reported differences and contrasts are sufficiently sharp, even for the South, thus it appears unlikely that they would be eradicated by more complete data.

Beyond these issues, basic questions concerning the Espy data involve the degree to which the collection includes all executions that occurred during the years of interest here and only and without duplication executions that actually occurred. As we have noted at various points, the Espy collection is a continuing effort, and it is virtually certain that additional executions have been identified since 1995, and that more will be discovered in the future. It also is likely that given the nature of historical records and record keeping, or the lack thereof, an unknown number of executions that actually occurred will never be identified.

For these same reasons, it is plausible to assume that executions that are not reflected in the combined data collection we have used, including those yet to be identified, probably occurred disproportionately in the earlier years of development of the various regions. The isolation and remoteness of early settlements, the primitive nature of communication mechanisms, and the greater attrition of source material that would be likely in frontier, rural, and small-town circumstances suggest as much. It also is plausible to think that these executions were disproportionately of members of minority groups. We have found limited evidence that suggests, for example, that executions of Native Americans during the early history of the several regions may have been undercounted. If these surmises are correct, then the identification of executions not included in the data collection we have used would work to accentuate rather than attenuate many of the findings discussed here. These conjectures to the side, the temporal, regional, and ethnic differences that we have found are large. A substantial number of executions would be necessary to eradicate or reverse these differences.

Another set of problems is the obverse of executions not identified. These, of course, concern whether, or the degree to which, the collection includes executions that actually did not occur, or reports that the same execution occurred more than once. It is easy to see how the inclusion of spurious or duplicate executions might occur. It is possible that some executions actually did not take place because of last-minute pardons or commutations or even escapes but were reported in newspapers or other sources as if they had occurred. Variant spellings of names in newspaper reports or the use of aliases for the same person also might result in duplication. Similarly, the same execution may have sometimes been reported in newspapers and other sources as occurring in two different towns, counties, or even states or territories, resulting in duplication. As noted later, a further problem involves questions concerning the definition of legal executions, which can lead to inappropriate inclusion or exclusion of executions.

With these issues in mind, we have taken several steps to assess the Espy collection. These include a comparison to two older and more limited collections. Prior to Espy's work, the most extended list of historical executions was that compiled by Negley K. Teeters and Charles J. Zibulka. William J. Bowers published the first complete version of this compilation.[3] The original version was intended as a comprehensive inventory of executions carried out under state authority and included approximately 5,700 executions, beginning with Vermont in 1864, and the District of Columbia in 1853, and ending in 1967. Approximately 4,300 executions were listed as carried out in 1945 or earlier. Espy reconfirmed all of the executions included in the original Teeters-Zibulka inventory. A second version of the inventory was then published by Bowers with Glenn L. Pierce and John F. McDevitt. Based on information provided by Espy, this version includes some 2,900 corrections to the original inventory and adds forty executions.[4] These executions and corrections are, of course, included in the Espy collection.

It appears, in short, that the Espy collection provides a virtually complete list of executions carried out under the jurisdiction of the various states and the District of Columbia. Executions under state jurisdiction, however, account for only about one quarter of all executions carried out in 1945 and earlier. Many more were conducted under local jurisdiction. These executions pose greater difficulties of identification and verification and require a more extended discussion.

In addition to his work with executions carried out under state authority, Negley K. Teeters also compiled an extended list of executions in Pennsylvania from 1682 through 1962.[5] The bibliography provided in the codebook for the Espy file indicates that the Teeters compilation was drawn upon in preparing the Espy collection. Differences between the two compilations suggest that in preparing the latter collection considerable independent work was directed to identifying additional executions and to verifying and correcting entries in the Teeters compilation. The Teeters compilation lists 1,035 executions carried out from 1682 through 1962, 685 of them prior to 1915, when the conduct of executions was shifted from local to state jurisdiction. The Espy collection includes 675 executions between 1693 and 1915. The first execution identified in the Teeters compilation took place in 1688; the first in the Espy collection was in 1693. To the degree that names can be compared, eight executions appear in the Teeters compilation that are not in the Espy collection; six appear in the latter collection but not in the former. Thirty-seven more are included in the summary information provided by Espy, referred to earlier. In addition to differences in the number of executions included in the two collections, there are also differences in the spelling of names, in the offenses charged, in the dates of execution, and in the ages given for the executed.[6]

Two more recent volumes by Daniel Allen Hearn provide further opportunities to assess the Espy collection.[7] Hearn's volumes provide more or less extensive information, sometimes running to several pages, bearing upon the offenses charged, characteristics of the victims and executed, the circumstances surrounding both offenses and executions, and other information for executions carried out in New York and New England from 1639 through 1963. Thus the Hearn volumes include substantially more information than does the computer-readable version of the Espy collection. Both lists are intended, as far as source material permits, to include all executions that occurred in the two areas during the years indicated. Hearn expresses high regard for Espy and his work but also indicates that the volumes are based upon his own research and, in the case of the New England volume, that he did not ask Espy to supply information.[8] In these terms Hearn's studies appear to provide an independent basis for comparison with the Espy collection.

The executions included in the Hearn volumes are marked by relatively close correspondence with those included in the Espy collection, but there are differences most notably for the earlier years. Hearn lists a somewhat smaller number of executions than does Espy. For New York, Hearn lists approximately 1,250 executions during the period 1639–1945; Espy lists 1,269. Espy lists 711 executions in New England from 1623 through 1945, while Hearn lists about 660. For both areas, however, Hearn lists a greater number of whites put to death than does Espy (in New York, about 950 compared to 890 and about 500 compared to 460 for New England, both during the periods just indicated).

These differences are explicable, in part by the relatively large number of individuals listed in the Espy collection as being of unknown ethnicity, ninety-six in New York and seventy-nine for New England. Hearn, in contrast, lists none as being of unknown ethnicity. For a number of those listed by name in the Espy collection as being of unknown ethnicity, the Hearn collection assigns ethnicity, usually white, and sometimes on the basis of what appear to be reasonable assumptions. Even if Hearn's assignment of ethnicity in these cases is accepted, a number of cases in the Espy file remain of unknown ethnicity, and these account for a large proportion of the differences in the total number of executions given by Espy and Hearn. One consequence of these differences is that the rates of execution for whites in relation to population based upon the Hearn collection are marginally higher than those based upon the Espy collection. Even so, the differences in rates and in numbers put to death, including those for the specific ethnic groups, are comparatively small.

As a limited step toward verification of executions under local jurisdiction, we have also examined executions listed in the collection for two states. The Espy collection lists 248 executions carried out in Illinois during the period 1779–1928, when the conduct of executions was centralized at the state level. With a single exception, all executions in a one in ten sample were verified using newspapers and local histories. All of the thirty-two executions carried out in Washington Territory and State between 1849 and 1904, the date of centralization at the state level, also were verified using similar sources.

It will be recognized that this process involves only a sort of "one-way" verification. That is, it provides evidence that the executions listed in the collection actually occurred, but it does not test whether only these executions took place. As was noted in chapter 6, we found an indication of executions of Native Americans by military forces in the field during the Indian Wars of mid-nineteenth Washington Territory not included in the collection. As we have indicated, this discrepancy may suggest that executions of Native Americans were more or less consistently underreported. On the other hand, it also suggests a definitional problem confronted in attempting to create definitive lists of historical executions. It is not always clear that tribunals that imposed death sentences actually had jurisdiction or followed appropriate processes. This issue is briefly touched upon in more concrete terms later.

The secondary literature bearing upon the historical criminal justice system is voluminous. While we do not claim to have examined all of that literature, it appears that most of it does not have capital punishment as a primary or even as an important secondary focus. As a consequence, we have found few systematic lists of executions or references to numbers of executions carried out that could be used to assess the Espy collection.

There are, however, important exceptions. George C. Wright provides a list of executions carried out in Kentucky from 1872 to 1939.[9] Wright lists 229 executions conducted during these years with the names and race of the executed, the counties in which trials were held, the dates, and the offenses charged. The Espy collection includes 251 executions during these years, fifteen reflected in the summary file alluded to earlier. To the degree that names can be matched, Wright includes fifteen executions that are not in the Espy collection. (It is possible, of course, that these fifteen executions are included in the summary file.) The Espy collection includes twenty-four executions that are not included in the Wright tabulation. Most of the discrepancies between the files occur in the nineteenth century, as might be expected.

John D. Bessler's study of capital punishment in Minnesota provides information bearing upon sixty-eight executions carried out between 1854 and 1911, when the death penalty was abolished in that state.[10] The Espy collection, however, lists only sixty-six executions during the same period. Here again, the discrepancies are somewhat larger than the totals suggest. Bessler, as other sources, indicates the mass execution of thirty-eight Native Americans in 1862 after conviction by a military tribunal. The Espy collection records the number at thirty-nine. Bessler also lists two Native Americans and one white as having been executed, but they do not appear in the Espy collection. Once again, the match between the two sources is imperfect but reasonably close.

Colorado provides a further opportunity for comparison with the Espy file and also illustrates definitional differences. In his study of lynching in the territory and state, Stephen J. Leonard indicates that twenty legal executions took place under local jurisdiction from 1863 to 1890, when the conduct of executions was shifted to the state level.[11] The Espy file lists twenty-seven. Five hangings after trial by a "people's court" in Denver in 1859 and 1860 account for most of the difference. Although the trials were open, with juries and defense counsels, Leonard treats these technically as lynchings, since the "court" did not have legal jurisdiction.[12] Espy treats these as legal executions.

In his study of New York City, Eric H. Monkkonen reported that nine individuals executed there between 1727 and 1852 are not included in the 1992 version of the Espy collection. However, the summary data provided by Espy, described earlier, include 197 individuals executed in New York Colony and State between 1726 and 1855. While we cannot be certain, it is at least possible, and perhaps likely, that the executions indicated by Monkkonen are included in the summary data provided by Espy.[13]

The colonial period and, particularly for the South and the Border region, the earlier nineteenth century present the most serious difficulties for the development of a complete inventory of historical executions. In chapter 2 we noted the correspondence, or near correspondence, between the Espy collection and several secondary studies (see chapter 2, notes 5, 6, 10, 11, and 12). These refer, however, to events that have been more or less widely studied, including the Salem witch trials and executions and the two slave uprisings in eighteenth-century New York City. The correspondence is, therefore, perhaps not surprising.

Although there were few executions in the history of Vermont, Randolph Roth's study of capital punishment in the colony and the state also has some correspondence to the Espy collection. Roth puts the total number of executions in Vermont at twenty-seven between 1777 and 1954, when the last execution in the state took place.[14] The Espy collection includes twenty-nine. Roth indicates that twenty were executed after centralization at the state level in 1864; both the original and revised versions of the Teeters-Zibulka compilation list twenty-one, as of course does the Espy collection. For the years prior to 1864, Roth lists seven individuals as having been executed. The Espy collection places the number at eight. Two executions during these years listed by Roth are not included in the Espy collection. One of these is a further illustration of a definitional problem confronted in attempting to identify executions in the more distant past.

The execution in question was of a Native American, Toomalek, who was sentenced to death by an Abenaki tribal council. The execution took place in 1779 or 1780 in a Vermont county court house with the approval of local white authorities. The execution was carried out by the father of the victim in accordance with Abenaki law. Rowe lists this execution with reservations; it is not included in the Espy collection. The execution of David Redding in 1778 is included in the Espy collection and also in the Rowe collection, but again with reservations. Redding was executed in Vermont for treason against the United States, although the treasonous acts did not occur in Vermont. Vermont at the time was not a part of the United States and had no authority to act on behalf of the United States. Both cases raise questions as to how "legal" executions ought to be defined and suggest that different investigators may sometimes use different definitions and arrive at different judgments.

Four additional studies bear on the earlier nineteenth century and the colonial period and suggest ambiguities confronted in identifying executions in the Southern and Border regions. Michael Hindus's comparative study of Massachusetts and South Carolina is marked by the largest divergences from the Espy collection. Hindus indicates that there were sixty-one executions in Massachusetts during the period 1780–1845. The Espy collection indicates eighty-six, and although the decade-by-decade distribution of executions shows some similarities to the Espy collection, the differences are large. Hindus cites as his source an 1851 issue of the *Prisoners' Friend*. While the *Prisoners' Friend* is a well-known and frequently cited anti-capital punishment journal, it is plausible to believe that subsequent investigations may have resulted in the identification of a larger number of executions.[15] The divergences in South Carolina are much larger. Hindus indicates that "at least" 296 slaves were executed in the state from 1800 to 1855, an average of over five each year. The Espy collection, in contrast, includes only 201, and a comparison by five-year time periods reveals few similarities.[16] As we discuss at a later point, Hindus also implicitly suggests ambiguities concerning at least some of these executions.

In his study of slavery and criminal law in Virginia, Philip J. Schwarz gives numbers of executions that are both similar to and divergent from the Espy collection.[17] As an example, he finds that from 1706 to 1784, at least 555 slaves were sentenced to be hanged, and that from 1785 to 1865, at least 628 were hanged. These numbers are of the same general magnitude as provided by Espy. A death sentence, as Schwarz makes clear, was not tantamount to execution, and the Espy collection indicates that approximately 450 slaves were actually executed from 1706 to 1784. For the period 1785–1865, the Espy collection places the number of slaves hanged at approximately 682. There are other examples of similarities. Schwarz indicates that 165 slaves were executed for murder between 1785 and 1829. To the degree that offenses are given, the Espy collection lists 161 slaves as having been executed for murder, and the five-year distribution of these executions shown in the Espy collection is generally similar to that given by Schwarz.[18] However, the offenses charged are not given for a significant portion of the executions reflected in the Espy collection, and it is likely that the actual number of executions for murder as well as other offenses was greater than that given by Schwarz.

Donna J. Spindell also provides information in her study of colonial North Carolina that is useful in assessing the Espy collection and also confirms the discrepancy between the number of African Americans and whites put to death. She indicates that between 1663 and 1776, only sixty-seven whites were sentenced to death. The sentences of twenty-four were remitted, either through benefit of clergy or pardon, and one was deported. For many of the remaining forty-three, Spindell suggests, the death sentence may not have been carried out.[19] The Espy collection indicates that twenty-one whites were executed between the early 1720s and 1776; and in a general sense, this might be taken as corresponding to Spindell's assessment. In their study of North Carolina in the latter eighteenth century, Marvin L. Michael Kay and Lorin L. Cary indicate that between 1748 and 1772 at least 100 slaves were executed.[20] Espy puts the number of slaves executed at eighty-two during the same period, a substantial discrepancy. In either case, however, African Americans significantly outnumbered whites among those put to death, and the discrepancy is particularly impressive when it is noted that the white population far exceeded the African American population of the colony.

A comparison of the Espy file with various secondary studies suggests both similarities and differences in the count of executions. A comparison of four secondary studies bearing upon three states and colonies suggests that the Espy file may in balance underestimate the number of slaves put to death in these areas.[21] It cannot be assumed that these areas were representative of the entire South and the Border region. However, these regions were marked by similar institutions, by the same labor system, and by similar needs to control a subject and a potentially dangerous segment of their population. It is, therefore, at least reasonable to suspect that the collection also underestimates the number of executions in other parts of the two regions.

These studies also suggest ambiguities confronted in identifying executions. One set of ambiguities might be summarized by the question, what counts as a legal execution? Both law and practices concerning slaves thought to be guilty of serious offenses varied from one colony and state to the other and also changed with the passage of time. In North and South Carolina, and probably in other states and colonies, several procedures could result in a sentence of death for accused slaves. What the practice of "plantation justice" actually involved is unclear. Through this practice, which probably was most common in the early colonial days, a plantation owner could judge and impose punishment on his slaves, perhaps with the assistance of a "court" composed of members of his family and white employees.[22] Whether a slave was ever executed through this practice is unknown.

Whatever the nature of plantation justice, in the Carolinas, and undoubtedly in other jurisdictions, there were other ways that slaves could be legally killed, including, of course, during the pursuit of or apprehension for an alleged offense. In North Carolina, an outlawed slave could be legally killed by any white.[23] Similarly, in South Carolina, any white could legally kill slaves who were found away from their home plantation if they resisted interrogation.[24] Local courts that tried cases involving slaves also could impose the death penalty. For these courts local magistrates convened juries composed of freeholders, as need arose. Grand jury indictment was not required, juries were not randomly selected, and a unanimous vote was not required for conviction. In South Carolina, written records of proceedings were apparently not mandatory until 1833.[25] These courts, it appears, were sometimes marked by a variety of irregularities. As Hindus puts it, "Although the criteria for assembling a magistrate's and freeholder's court were not rigorous, they were not always followed." Or, as he notes at another point, in some instances "the line between formal justice and vigilantism became fine indeed."[26]

The point is, of course, that in compiling lists of executions the distinction between legal executions and extralegal killings often is difficult or impossible to make.[27] Petitions by slaveholders seeking compensation for executed slaves, the source of Hindus's count of slaves executed in South Carolina, are evidence of the death of slaves. Such petitions do not indicate whether the slaves were summarily killed, as whites could do under certain circumstances, or whether the procedures followed in trials or in constituting courts were in keeping with the legal requirements of the time.[28]

A second set of ambiguities concerns evidence of the occurrence of executions. Secondary studies of the earlier South and Border region as well as the frontier West are virtually uniform in their comments on the gaps in records series, missing series, and other shortcomings of the available historical records. It also is clear that court records, to the degree they exist, may be reliable evidence of death sentences rendered but not of executions actually carried out. Death sentences often do not result in executions. Given the frailties of record keeping and preservation, executions may have left no evidence of their occurrence, particularly in rural and remote areas, where newspapers were rare and travel and communications slow. In these circumstances, lists of historical executions may omit an unknown number of executions that actually occurred or, conversely, executions that did not occur.

This is only to say that completely definitive lists of historical executions will never be compiled. The best that can be hoped for is reasonable approximations. The degree of approximation will be greatest for earlier years and for remote and rural areas and smaller as the present is approached. In our assessment, the Espy collection is a reasonable approximation of the incidence and distribution of capital punishment and the characteristics of those executed across the long sweep of American history. The collection will improve as Espy's work, and others' work as well, continues, but it will remain an approximation. We doubt that improvements in the collection as they occur will seriously affect the findings reported here.

Lynching presents the same problem as executions, but with added complexities. One of these concerns definitions. How often did posses turn into lynch mobs? How big a group is necessary to constitute a lynch mob? Should some of those killed in riots be counted as lynched?[29] A larger problem is that lynching was a criminal act. In the South and in the Border states and the West, an effort was sometimes made to publicize lynchings in order to terrorize and intimidate targeted groups. On the other hand, lynchings were also carried out in secret out of fear of recriminations. And lynchings in remote areas could escape the attention of all but a purely local and limited population. As a criminal act, lynching did not leave a trail of records aside, perhaps, for an occasional coroner's report, or in the rare event that an attempt was made to apprehend and prosecute perpetrators. The evidence suggests that lynching was a much more ubiquitous fact of American history than is usually recognized, but as Leonard indicates, the number actually lynched will never be known.[30] Here again, the best that can be hoped for is an approximation.

The present study is, in short, based on imperfect data. Imperfect data are, however, the lot of historians. In our view it is unlikely that a completely definitive list of executions, or of lynchings, if such lists could be created, would lead to findings significantly different from those reported here. The observed racial and ethnic and regional and temporal differences are pronounced and highly consistent. They also are consistent with other knowledge of American history. Better data would result in some modification of these differences but not, we think, in refutation. The case is less strong where generalizations, bearing upon such issues as change in the definition of capital offenses or the characteristics of the executed, are concerned. Here as well, however, the differences are sharp and consistent.

Notes

INTRODUCTION

1. George C. Wright, *Racial Violence in Kentucky, 1865–1940: Lynchings, Mob Rule, and "Legal Lynchings"* (Baton Rouge: Louisiana State University Press, 1990), 12–13, 251–305.

2. Lawrence M. Friedman, *Crime and Punishment in American History* (New York: Basic Books, 1993), 461.

3. Norbert Elias, *The Civilizing Process: Sociogenetic and Psychogenetic Investigations*, rev. ed., ed. Eric Dunning, Johan Goudsblom, and Stephen Mennel (Oxford: Blackwell, 1994).

4. David Garland, *Punishment and Modern Society: A Study in Social Theory* (Chicago: University of Chicago Press, 1990), esp. chap. 10.

5. Descriptions of the Espy project can be found in William J. Bowers, with Glenn L. Pierce and John G. McDevitt, *Legal Homicide: Death as Punishment in America, 1864–1982* (Boston: Northeastern University Press, 1984), 43–45, 395–97; M. Watt Espy Jr., "Capital Punishment and Deterrence: What the Statistics Cannot Show," *Crime and Delinquency* (October 1980): 537–44; Ronald Smothers, "Headland Journal: Historian's Death Penalty Obsession," *New York Times*, October 21, 1987; Michael A. Radelet, "Execution of Whites for Crimes against Blacks: Exceptions to the Rule?" *The Sociological Quarterly* (1989): 30:4: 529–44. The computer-readable version of the collection and the project are described in M. Watt Espy and John Ortiz Smykla, "Executions in the United States, 1608–1991: The Espy File" (computer file). 2d ICPSR ed., comp. John Ortiz Smykla, University of Alabama (Ann Arbor, MI: Interuniversity Consortium for Political and Social Research [producer and distributor], 1992).

Studies that make use of the Espy collection include Stuart Banner, *The Death Penalty: An American History* (Cambridge, MA: Harvard University Press, 2002), Keith Harries and Derral Cheatwood, *The Geography of Execution: The Capital Punishment Quagmire in America* (Lanham, MD: Rowman and Littlefield, 1997), xiii passim; Stewart E. Tolnay and E. M. Beck, *A Festival of Violence: An Analysis of Southern Lynchings, 1882–1930* (Urbana: University of Illinois Press, 1995), 108–11; Victoria Schneider and John Ortiz Smykla, "A Summary Analysis of Executions in the United States, 1608–1987: The Espy

File," in *The Death Penalty in America: Current Research*, ed. Robert M. Bohm, 1–19 (Cincinnati: Anderson Publishing and Academy of Criminal Justice, 1991); Ted Robert Gurr, "Historical Trends in Violent Crime: Europe and the United States" in *Violence in America: The History of Crime*, ed. Ted Robert Gurr, 1: 35–36 (Newbury Park, London, and New Delhi: Sage Publications, 1989).

6. The original data collector, ICPSR, nor the National Science Foundation does not bear any responsibility for our use of the data or for our interpretations and inferences.

7. The Death Penalty Information Center Web site is http://www.deathpenaltyinfo.org.

8. Stewart E. Tolnay and E. M. Beck, *A Festival of Violence: An Analysis of Southern Lynchings, 1882–1930* (Urbana: University of Illinois Press, 1995).

9. George C. Wright, *Racial Violence in Kentucky, 1865–1940: Lynchings, Mob Rule, and "Legal Lynchings"* (Baton Rouge: Louisiana State University Press, 1990), Appendix A, 307–23; W. Fitzhugh Brundage, *Lynching in the New South: Georgia and Virginia, 1880–1930* (Urbana: University of Illinois Press, 1993) 268–83.

10. Jessie P. Guzman, Lewis W. Jones, and Woodrow Hall, *Thirty Years of Lynching in the United States, 1880–1930* (New York: National Association for the Advancement of Colored People, 1919; reprinted New York: Negro Universities Press, 1969), 27–279.

11. Richard Maxwell Brown, *Strain of Violence: Historical Studies of American Violence and Vigilantism* (New York: Oxford University Press, 1975), Appendix 3, 305–19.

12. Inter-university Consortium for Political and Social Research, "Historical, Demographic, Economic and Social Data: The United States, 1790–1970" (ICPSR 0003) (Ann Arbor, Michigan).

13. U.S. Bureau of the Census, *Historical Statistics of the United States, Colonial Times to 1970, Bicentennial Edition* (Washington, DC: U.S. Government Printing Office, 1975), part 1, 24–35; part 2, 1168.

CHAPTER 1

1. The first person executed in English America was George Kendall, who was found guilty of mutiny and shot. See H. L. Osgood, *The American Colonies in the Seventeenth Century* (New York: Columbia University Press, 1904; reprinted Gloucester, MA, 1957) 1, 48.

2. Unless otherwise indicated, the rates of execution in this study are based on the annual average number of executions in each ten-year period.

3. Other types of errors are also likely to be found in this collection. These include errors made in data preparation and entry, the misspelling of names in original sources, the misidentification of the locations and dates of execution, and the ages of the executed. Errors of this sort tend to be random in nature and are more likely to mask patterns and relationships that actually exist. As a consequence, they prevent findings rather than lead to erroneous

findings. Systematic errors, such as the failure to discover executions or undercounts of populations, are more likely to lead to erroneous conclusions.

4. The ethnic categories used in Table 1.1 and hereafter are those used in the Espy collection. These are not to be taken as biological categories in any sense of the word. As in the case of categories used in the United States Census, they reflect "common usage." See U.S. Bureau of the Census, *Historical Statistics of the United States, Colonial Times to 1970, Bicentennial Edition* (Washington, DC: U.S. Government Printing Office, 1975), part 1, 3.

5. The Espy collection includes eight executions of Hispanics in the Spanish Southwest in the early seventeenth century that are excluded from this study. The area would not become a part of the continental United States until much later, and it seems likely that a much larger number of executions remains undiscovered.

6. The rates for the three ten-year periods, 1606–1615, 1616–1625, and 1626–1635, are excluded from Figure 1.2. They were, respectively, 57.1, 13.1, and 8.7.

7. The estimates for the seventeenth and eighteenth centuries are given in *Historical Statistics*, part 2, 1168. For cautionary notes concerning these estimates, see p. 1152.

8. The number used for the calculation of white executions includes both white and Hispanic executions, since the two groups were not tabulated separately in historical Census reports. The numbers used in preparing Figure 1.2 and later figures and tables, which use population statistics, do not include executions for areas that were not included in the censuses. Thus, for example, executions in Louisiana before 1806 and California before 1846 were excluded.

9. A similar figure is in Ted Robert Gurr, "Historical Trends in Violent Crime: Europe and the United States," in *Violence in America: The History of Crime*, ed. Ted Robert Gurr, 36 (Newbury Park, London, and New Delhi: Sage Publications, 1989).

10. See, in this connection, Friedman, *Crime and Punishment in American History*, 41–42. See also Samuel Walker, *Popular Justice: A History of American Criminal Justice*, 2d ed. (New York: Oxford University Press, 1998), 34–35.

11. *Historical Statistics*, part 2, 1152.

12. The literature on the accuracy of the U.S. Census is extensive. See, for example, the articles in *Social Science History* 15 (Winter 1991), which provide a comprehensive review of the literature on this subject.

13. The rates for the three ten-year periods before 1626 are excluded from Figure 1.3. For whites they were, respectively, 57.1, 13.1, and 8.7. The first African American was executed in the 1636–1645 period; the rate was 16.8.

14. No African Americans were executed during the period 1606–1635 and 1646–1655.

15. The spike in the ratios for the period 1706–1715 is explained by the execution of twenty African Americans for slave revolt in New York in 1712. The second and smaller spike for the period 1796–1805 reflects the execution of at least forty-nine African Americans, also for slave revolt, in Virginia and North Carolina.

16. "Lethal offense," as used here, includes murder, conspiracy to commit murder, accessory to murder, and murder with other crimes, such as burglary and rape. It does not include the attempt to commit murder.

17. As defined here, rape does not include rape combined with murder.

18. The percentage of executions of African Americans for rape in the period 1876–1945 amounted to nearly 90% of all known nonlethal offenses.

CHAPTER 2

1. See, for example, David L. Bodenhamer, *Fair Trial: Rights of the Accused in American History* (New York: Oxford University Press, 1992), 26, 64–65; Eugene D. Genovese, *Roll Jordon Roll: The World the Slaves Made* (New York: Random House, 1976), 25–49; Marvin L. M. Kay and Lorin L. Cary, *Slavery in North Carolina, 1748–1775* (Chapel Hill: University of North Carolina Press, 1995), 70–95; Thomas D. Morris, *Southern Slavery and the Law, 1619–1860* (Chapel Hill: University of North Carolina Press, 1996), esp. 161–261; Kenneth M. Stampp, *The Peculiar Institution: Slavery in the Antebellum South* (New York: Alfred A. Knopf, 1956), 21–23, 206–17, 224–27; George M. Stroud, *A Sketch of the Laws Relating to Slavery in the Several States of the United States of America* (New York: Negro University Press, 1968), 69–95.

2. For discussions of colonial criminal justice, see Lawrence M. Friedman, *A History of American Law* (New York: Simon and Schuster, 1973), 29–90; *Crime and Punishment in American History*, 20–58; Douglas Greenberg, *Crime and Law Enforcement in the Colony of New York* (Ithaca, NY: Cornell University Press, 1974), 70–98; Julius Goebel Jr. and T. Raymond Norton, *Law Enforcement in Colonial New York: A Study in Criminal Procedure, 1664–1776* (Montclair, NJ: Patterson Smith, 1970), especially 384–484, 701–10 reprinted; Samuel Walker, *Popular Justice: A History of American Criminal Justice,* 2d ed. (New York: Oxford University Press, 1998), 11–46, 126–33; Bradley Chapin, *Criminal Justice in Colonial America, 1606–1660* (Athens: University of Georgia Press, 1983), 3–24.

3. The known number executed between 1608 and 1695 is 278. Ten are not included in this table as follows: Two Native Americans were executed in the area defined here as the East North Central region, and eight Hispanics were executed in the area defined here as the Mountain region.

4. In this and the following chapters, the four regions are defined as New England: Connecticut, Maine, Massachusetts, New Hampshire, Rhode Island, and Vermont; Middle Atlantic: New Jersey, New York, and Pennsylvania; South: Alabama, Arkansas, Florida, Georgia, Louisiana, Mississippi, North Carolina, South Carolina, Texas, and Virginia; and Border: Delaware, Kentucky, Maryland, Missouri, Tennessee, West Virginia, and the District of Columbia. Of course, many of these colonies and states did not exist during much of the period considered in this chapter. Regional population totals for the colonial period (1610–1780) were computed from population estimates in the U.S. Bureau of the Census, *Historical Statistics of the United States, Colonial Times to 1970, Bicentennial Edition,* part 2, 1168.

5. James D. Drake, *King Philip's War: Civil War in New England, 1675–1676* (Amherst: University of Massachusetts Press, 1999), esp. 157–62; Jill Lepore, *The Name of War: King Philip's War and the Origins of American Identity* (New York: Alfred A. Knopf, 1998), xi, 23–24, 114, 143, 153, 155, 178.

6. Mary Beth Norton, *In the Devil's Snare: The Salem Witchcraft Crisis of 1692* (New York: Alfred A. Knopf, 2002), 215–17. The same individuals are listed as being executed for witchcraft in the Espy file but with some variation in dates of execution and spelling of names.

7. Wilcomb Washburn, *The Governor and the Rebel: A History of Bacon's Rebellion in Virginia* (Chapel Hill: University of North Carolina Press, 1957), 119, indicates that twenty-three were executed in connection to Bacon's Rebellion of 1676. The Espy file includes twenty-six executions during the period 1676–1685.

8. U.S. Bureau of the Census, *Historical Statistics of the United States*, part 2, 1152, 1168.

9. Ibid., 1168. Daniel Allen Hearn pointed out in *Legal Executions in New England: A Comprehensive Reference, 1623–1960* (Jefferson, NC: McFarland and Company, 1999), 2, that "New England (when compared to some other regions of the country) practiced unusual restraint in the imposition of capital punishment."

10. The known number of executions between 1696 and 1785 is 2,177. Seven executions in the East North Central region and four in the Pacific region are not included in Table 2.3.

11. Friedman, *Crime and Punishment in American History*, 54–55, 165–67.

12. There is a mismatch between those listed as executed for piracy in the Espy file and the number indicated by David Cordingly, *Under the Black Flag: The Romance and the Reality of Life among the Pirates* (New York: Random House, 1995), 245–47. Cordingly indicates that ninety-three were executed for piracy in Boston, Newport, Rhode Island, Williamsburg, Virginia, and Charleston, South Carolina, between 1700 and 1730. Espy lists only sixty-five in the same towns and periods. The major discrepancies are the omission by Espy of thirteen of Blackbeard's crew, indicated by Cordingly as executed in Williamsburg in 1718, and thirty given by Cordingly as executed in Charleston in 1718 rather than twenty-one, according to Espy. However, the version of the Espy data that we have used (described in the Appendix) indicates twenty-six additional executions in Virginia and twenty-three in South Carolina without names or offenses during the period 1716–1725. It is possible that pirates given as executed by Cordingly are among them. Espy also lists seven executed for piracy that do not appear in Cordingly.

13. The Espy file and Kenneth Scott, "The Slave Insurrection in New York in 1712," *New York Historical Society Quarterly* 45 (1961): 43–74, list twenty slaves executed in New York in 1712 with some variations in the spelling of names and dates and methods of execution. The Espy file indicates that four were burned, one was hung in chains, one was broken on the wheel, and then hanged. The Espy file lists the twenty as executed for slave revolt. Scott (ibid., 62–67) indicates that they were indicted and tried for murder, accessory

to murder, or assault. See also Herbert Aptheker, *American Slave Revolts* (New York: Columbia University Press, 1942), 172–73.

14. Thomas J. Davis, *A Rumor of Revolt: The "Great Negro Plot" in Colonial New York* (New York: The Free Press, 1985) ix, 71, 94–95, 120–21, 127, 130, 190, 192, 202, 225, 231, lists thirty-four executed; see also Jill Lepore, *New York Burning: Liberty, Slavery, and Conspiracy in Eighteenth Century Manhattan* (New York: Alfred A. Knopf, 2005), xii, 248–59. The Espy file lists thirty-three as executed between May 11, 1741, and August 29, 1741. Four names are included in Espy that are not in Davis, and two names in Davis do not appear in the Espy file; three names are included in Espy that are not in Lepore, and three names in Lepore are not included in the Espy file. Variations also occur in the spelling of names, as well as minor differences in the methods of execution. See also Aptheker, *American Slave Revolts*, 192–95.

15. Aptheker, *American Slave Revolts*, 172–73, 192–95; Peter H. Wood, *Black Majority: Negroes in Colonial South Carolina from 1670 through the Stono Rebellion* (New York: Knopf, 1974), 313–23.

16. The population estimate is from Ira Berlin, *Slaves without Masters: The Free Negro in the Ante Bellum South* (New York: Pantheon Books, 1974), Appendix I, 396–99.

17. It is likely, as we argue in the appendix and various other places, that the number of executions carried out during the Colonial period was larger than those reported in the Espy collection, and Colonial rates of execution would more nearly equal or exceed English rates during the same period. If that is the case, then the discrepancy between Colonial and more contemporary rates of execution is larger than indicated.

18. Philip Jenkins, "From Gallows to Prison? The Execution Rate in Early Modern England," *Criminal Justice History* 7 (1986): 54, 60, 64, passim.

19. Stuart Banner, *The Death Penalty: An American History* (Cambridge, MA: Harvard University Press, 2002), 5–52, provides a telling account of Colonial executions and attitudes toward the death penalty.

20. The available data give the offense charged for over 70% of known executions prior to 1945, but for only a little over 46% of executions during the Colonial and Revolutionary years.

21. Banner, *The Death Penalty*, 53–70; Friedman, *Crime and Punishment in American History*, 41–44. See also Bradley Chapin, *Criminal Justice in Colonial America, 1606–1660* (Athens: University of Georgia Press, 1983), 55–62; Julius Geobel Jr. and T. Raymond Naughton, *Law Enforcement in Colonial New York: A Study in Criminal Procedure, 1664–1776* (Montclair, NJ: Patterson Smith, 1970), 671–75, 748–59; Greenberg, *Crime and Law Enforcement in the Colony of New York, 1691–1776*, 130–32; Donna J. Spindel, *Crime and Society in North Carolina, 1663–1776* (Baton Rouge, LA: Louisiana State University Press, 1989), 116–25.

22. Banner, *The Death Penalty*, 65–70.

23. Ibid., 70–86.

CHAPTER 3

1. The South, the Border states, New England, and the Middle Atlantic region are defined in chapter 2. The Old Northwest includes Illinois, Indiana,

Michigan, Ohio, and Wisconsin. The West North Central, Mountain, and Pacific regions are examined in chapter 6. Unless otherwise indicated, all regional data used in this and the following chapters were computed from the Inter-university Consortium for Political and Social Research, "Historical, Demographic, Economic, and Social Data: The United States, 1790–1970" (ICPSR 0003) (Ann Arbor, Michigan) by adding the state population totals for each decade.

2. Edward C. Johnson, Gail R. Johnson, and Melissa Johnson Williams, *All Were Not Heroes: A Study of "The List of U.S. Soldiers Executed by U.S. Military Authorities during the Late War"* (Chicago: Authors, 1997), 15–405, lists 235 Union soldiers executed in the Southern and Border states, particularly Virginia, during the war. See also James M. McPherson, *Battle Cry of Freedom: The Civil War Era* (New York: Oxford University Press, 1988). On desertions in the Union Army, see 84, 606, and 720. For desertions in the Confederate Army, see 440, 613–15, and 670.

3. The number of whites legally executed in the Southern and Border regions was greater than during any equivalent ten-year period after 1865. Even so, it is possible that the available data do not record all executions carried out by the Union and Confederate armies. It also is possible that an unknown number of executions were of dubious legality.

4. We know the gender of approximately two thirds of those executed during the period.

5. David J. Bodenhamer, *Fair Trial: Rights of the Accused in American History* (New York: Oxford University Press, 1992), 64–65; Leon F. Litwack, *North of Slavery: The Negro in the Free States, 1790–1860* (Chicago: University of Chicago Press, 1961), esp. 93–97.

6. Johnson et al., *All Were Not Heroes*, 15–405.

7. William J. Bowers, with Glenn L. Pierce and John G. McDevitt, *Legal Homicide: Death as Punishment in America, 1864–1982* (Boston: Northeastern University Press, 1984), 6–11; Raymond T. Bye, "Capital Punishment in the United States," Ph.D. dissertation, University of Pennsylvania (Philadelphia: The Committee on Philanthropic Labor of Philadelphia, 1919), 8–10.

8. See, for example, Alice Felt Tyler, *Freedom's Ferment: Phases of American Social History from the Colonial Period to the Outbreak of the Civil War* (New York: Harper & Row, 1962, reprinted), 1–4, 265–85. See also Louis P. Masur, *Rites of Execution: Capital Punishment and the Transformation of American Culture* (New York: Oxford University Press, 1989), 13–24, 141–59; David J. Rothman, *The Discovery of the Asylum: Social Order and Disorder in the New Republic* (Boston: Little Brown, 1971), esp. 57–78.

9. These issues are discussed in William Francis Kuntz, II, *Criminal Sentencing in Three Nineteenth Century Cities: Social History of Punishment in New York, Boston, and Philadelphia, 1830–1880* (New York: Garland Publishing, 1988), 56–105; Stuart Banner, *The Death Penalty: An American History* (Cambridge, MA: Harvard University Press, 2002), 112–37. See also Michael Stephen Hindus, *Prison and Plantation: Crime, Justice, and Authority in Massachusetts and South Carolina, 1767–1878* (Chapel Hill: University of North Carolina Press, 1989), 183–214. The development of the prison system also provided a more effective alternative to the death penalty.

10. Banner, *The Death Penalty*, 98, 131–37; Bye, "Capital Punishment in the United States," 5–6; Eugene D. Genovese, *Roll Jordon Roll: The World the*

Slaves Made (New York: Vintage Books, 1976), 33; Samuel Walker, *Popular Justice: A History of American Criminal Justice,* 2d ed. (New York: Oxford University Press, 39–46, 80–93).

11. Bye, "Capital Punishment in the United States," 5–6; Friedman, *Crime and Punishment in American History,* 73–74; Hindus, *Prison and Plantation,* 195–200; Masur, *Rites of Execution,* 73–81; Rothman, *The Discovery of the Asylum,* 61–62.

12. For reasons discussed earlier in this chapter, the period 1856–1865 is omitted from the table.

13. Banner, The Death Penalty, 137–43; Berlin, *Slaves without Masters: The Free Negro in the Ante-Bellum South,* 65, 96, 100, 317; Morris, *Southern Slavery and the Law, 1619–1860,* 304–307; George M. Stroud, *A Sketch of the Laws Relating to Slavery in the Several States of the United States of America* (New York: Negro Universities Press, 1968), 69–88.

14. See, for example, Edward L. Ayers, *Vengeance and Justice: Crime and Punishment in the 19th Century American South* (New York: Oxford University Press, 1984), 136–37; Aptheker, *American Negro Slave Revolts,* 165, 231–32, 250, 277, 326, 347–48, 366; Douglas R. Egerton, *He Shall Go Free: The Lives of Denmark Vesey* (Madison, WI: Madison House, 1999), 189, 195, 196, 199; James Lofton, *Insurrection in South Carolina: The Turbulent World of Denmark Vesey* (Yellow Springs, OH: Antioch Press, 1964), 155–81; Winthrop D. Jordan, *Tumult and Silence at Second Creek: An Inquiry into a Civil War Slave Conspiracy* (Baton Rouge: Louisiana State University Press, 1993), 98; Philip J. Schwarz, *Twice Condemned: Slaves and the Criminal Laws of Virginia, 1705–1865* (Baton Rouge, LA: Louisiana State University Press, 1988), 53–54, 195.

15. Eugene Genovese wrote that in the nineteenth century "The burning alive of alleged rapists and murderers . . . declined, although this and other atrocities never disappeared." See *Roll Jordon Roll: The World the Slaves Made,* 69. The Espy collection records only eleven executions by burning, all African Americans, between 1786 and 1825. Since the secondary literature is not specific with respect to the number executed by such methods, we have relied on the Espy collection. However, we know the methods used for only a little over 50% of known Southern executions and for slightly less than 60% of those in the Border region. It is certainly possible, therefore, that use of such methods was more frequent than the Espy collection suggests. In contrast, we know the methods used in almost 90% of executions in New England, almost 80% in the Middle Atlantic region, and approximately 75% of those in the Old Northwest. The Espy collection records the execution of a single Native American by bludgeoning in Ohio in 1810.

16. The following discussion of changing attitudes toward public executions draws upon Banner, *The Death Penalty: An American History,* 144–69, and Masur, *Rites of Execution: Capital Punishment and the Transformation of American Culture, 1776–1865,* 93–116.

17. *Historical Statistics,* 12. For the size of crowds at public executions, see, for example, Banner, *The Death Penalty,* 144–61; Friedman, *Crime and Punishment in American History,* 168–70.

18. Banner, *The Death Penalty,* 154, 343–44. Maine may have been an exception. However, there were no executions in the state from the 1830s

through the 1850s. Public executions were never abolished in Michigan and Wisconsin, but capital punishment was.

19. Banner, *The Death Penalty*, 167–68.

CHAPTER 4

1. Friedman, *Crime and Punishment in American History*, 85.

2. The African American percentage of total population in the South declined from almost 44% in 1870 to nearly 29% in 1940.

3. The reader should recall that unless otherwise indicated, the rates of execution are based on the annual average number of executions during each ten-year period.

4. In calculating rates of execution, we have combined the white and Hispanic categories in the Espy data since, as noted in chapter 1, the Census enumerated and tabulated people of Hispanic derivation as white. In the South and Border states during these years, executions of Hispanics occurred only in Texas. Of the 641 executed in Texas during these years, seventy-three (approximately 11%) are recorded as Hispanics.

5. Bowers, with Pierce and McDevett, *Legal Homicide: Death as Punishment in America, 1864–1982*, 10–11.

6. Bowers et al., *Legal Homicide*, 9; Louis Filler, "Movements to Abolish the Death Penalty in the United States," *The Annals of the American Academy of Political and Social Science* (November 1952): 285: 124–36.

7. Information concerning the offenses charged is known for approximately 50% of known executions during the period 1866 through 1875, for over 70% of those conducted during the next 50 years, and for 98% and 99% of those carried out during the period 1926–1935 and 1936–1945.

8. Banner, *The Death Penalty*, 154–55.

9. Bowers et al., *Legal Homicide*, 45–48.

10. Espy and Smykla, "Executions in the United States, 1608–1991: The Espy File," iii. North Carolina adopted the electric chair in 1910 and changed to the gas chamber in 1936. See Bowers et al., *Legal Homicide*, 13.

11. Ibid., 9.

12. Ibid., 10–13.

13. We know the offenses charged for 77% of the known executions during the period 1866–1875; 83% for the 1896–1905 period; and between 89% and 98% for the remaining ten-year period.

14. *New York Times*, August 8, 9, 1942; Francis MacDonnell, *Insidious Foes: The Axis Fifth Column and the American Home Front* (New York: Oxford University Press, 1995), 131–33.

15. Banner, *The Death Penalty*, 154–55.

16. Walker, *Popular Justice: A History of American Criminal Justice*, 92; Banner, T*he Death Penalty*, 156. According to the St. Louis *Post-Dispatch*, March 20, 2001, the Owensboro hanging was the last hanging conducted without restrictions on the size of the crowd. A year later, in 1937, Roscoe Jackson was hanged in Galena, Missouri, before a crowd of approximately 500. In this case, however, a stockade had been constructed to restrict the number of onlookers. For a brief account of this execution, see also Walker, *Popular Justice*, 92.

17. Bowers et al., *Legal Homicide*, 45–48.

18. Ibid., 12–13.

19. The quotation is from Brown, *Strain of Violence: Historical Studies of American Violence and Vigilantism*, 168. For a discussion of the attitudes and pronouncements of legal figures from all regions of the nation, see pages 145–79. See also Robert P. Ingalls, *Urban Vigilantes in the New South: Tampa, 1882–1936* (Knoxville: University of Tennessee Press, 1988), 1–30; Arthur F. Raper, *The Tragedy of Lynching* (Chapel Hill: University of North Carolina Press, 1933), 1–2. Many of the photographs and postcards reproduced in James Allen, Hilton Als, John Lewis, and Leon F. Litwack, *Without Sanctuary: Lynching Photography in America* (Sante Fe, NM: Twin Palms Publishers, 2000) also suggest that participants and spectators had no fear of legal prosecution as they seemed to pose willingly for photographs with lynching victims.

20. W. Fitzhugh Brundage, *Lynching in the New South: Georgia and Virginia, 1880–1930*, in *Blacks in the New World*, ed. August Meier and John H. Bracey (Urbana: University of Illinois Press, 1993), 1–16; Friedman, *Crime and Punishment in American History*, 189–92; Roger Lane, *Murder in America: A History*, in *The History of Crime and Criminal Justice Series*, ed. David R. Johnson and Jeffrey S. Adler, 152–53 (Columbus: Ohio State University Press, 1997), 152–53; James W. Marquart, Sheldon Ekland-Olson, and Jonathan R. Sorensen, *The Rope, the Chair, and the Needle: Capital Punishment in Texas, 1923–1990* (Austin: University of Texas Press, 1994), 2, 17; Raper, *The Tragedy of Lynching*, 19, 33, 46, 137–38; Wright, *Racial Violence in Kentucky: Lynchings, Mob Rule, and "Legal Lynchings,"* 12–13, 251–305.

21. Jessie Parkhurst Guzman, Lewis W. Jones, and Woodrow Hall, eds., *1952 Negro Year Book: A Review of Events Affecting Negro Life* (New York: Wm. H. Wise & Co., 1952), 277–78.

22. In assessing the older compilations of lynchings, Steward E. Tolnay and E. M. Beck, *Festival of Violence: An Analysis of Southern Lynchings, 1882–1930* (Urbana: University of Illinois Press, 1995), 262, conclude that they probably overstate the number of lynchings. Wright, *Racial Violence in Kentucky,* 4–5, suggests that they may understate the actual number of lynchings.

23. Wright, *Racial Violence in Kentucky,* 40–42.

24. Brown, *Strain of Violence*, 217–218. See also Allen et al., *Without Sanctuary*.

25. Brown, *Strain of Violence*, 211–14, 323–25.

26. Brundage, *Lynching in the New South*, 25–26; Wright, *Racial Violence in Kentucky,* 127–54.

27. Guzman et al., *1952 Negro Year Book*, 277–78.

28. Data for eight of the Southern states included in Table 4.3 and in Figure 4.4 (Alabama, Arkansas, Florida, Georgia, Louisiana, Mississippi, and North and South Carolina) were provided by S. E. Tolnay and E. M. Beck and were used in their book *Festival of Violence*. Data for Virginia are from Brundage, *Lynching in the New South*, 281–83. Data for Texas are from the National Association for the Advancement of Colored People, *Thirty Years of Lynching in the United States, 1889–1918* (New York: Negro University Press, 1969), Appendix II, 43–105; Walter White, *Rope & Faggot: A Biography of Judge Lynch* (New York: Alfred A. Knopf, 1929), table VII, 254–59; Tuskegee Institute, Division of

Behavioral Science Research, Tuskegee, Alabama, "Newspaper Clipping File" (microfilm copy from the University of Illinois Library, Champaign, Illinois); and Chicago *Tribune*, January 1, 1887, January 1, 1888, December 30, 1888.

29. Wright, Racial *Violence in Kentucky*, 19–60. Table 4.4 is compiled from Appendix A, 307–23.

30. Brown, *Strain of Violence*, Appendix 3, 316–18.

31. See, for example, Eric Foner, *Reconstruction: America's Unfinished Revolution, 1863–1877* (New York: Harper & Row, 1988), 119–23; Leon F. Litwack, *Been in the Storm So Long: The Aftermath of Slavery* (New York: Alfred A. Knopf, 1979), 274–82, 289, 303–304.

32. Reasons given for lynching are listed in Brundage, *Lynching in the New South*, 281–83; Wright, *Racial Violence in Kentucky*, 307–23; *Thirty Years of Lynching*, passim; and in data provided by Tolnay and Beck.

CHAPTER 5

1. Bowers et al., *Legal Homicide: Death as Punishment in America, 1864–1982*, 9.

2. *Prisoners Friend*, March 1849, 139.

3. Friedman, *Crime and Punishment in American History*, 168–71; Masur, *Rites of Execution*, 111; Negley K. Teeters and Jack H. Hedblom, *Hang By the Neck: The Legal Use of Scaffold and Noose, Gibbet, Stake, and Firing Squad from Colonial Times to the Present* (Springfield, IL: C. C. Thomas, 1967), 151–53.

4. Bowers et al., *Legal Homicide*, 9, 10–11. Abolition of capital punishment was not absolute in every case. In Michigan, for example, treason continued to be subject to the death penalty.

5. Information is available for approximately 98% of known executions conducted in the Northeastern states from 1866 through 1945. Known offenses range from approximately 96% of executions conducted from 1866 through 1875 to 100% for those conducted from 1926 through 1945.

6. For the dates of adoption of electrocution, see Bowers et al., *Legal Homicide*, 13. For discussions of the movement to adopt electrocution and controversies surrounding its use, see Banner, *The Death Penalty, An American History*, 177–96; Jurgen Martschukat, "The Art of Killing by Electricity: The Sublime and the Electric Chair," *Journal of American History* 89 (December 2002), 909–21. See also Friedman, *A History of American Law*, 517–19; Frank E. Hartung, "Trends in the use of Capital Punishment," *The Annals of the American Academy of Political and Social Science* (November, 1952), 284: 8–19; and Teeters and Hedblom, *Hang By the Neck: The Legal Use of Scaffold and Noose, Gibbet, Stake, and Firing Squad from Colonial Times to the Present*, 446–50.

7. Chicago *Tribune*, January 1, 1887, January 1, 1888, and December 30, 1888; The National Association for the Advancement of Colored People, *Thirty Years of Lynching in the United States, 1889–1918*, Appendix II, 43–105; White, *Rope & Faggot: A Biography of Judge Lynch*, table VII, 254–59; Tuskegee Institute, Division of Behavioral Science Research, Tuskegee, Alabama, "Newspaper Clipping File" (microfilm, reels 221–225, University of Illinois Library, Champaign, Illinois).

8. Guzman et al., *1952 Negro Year Book: A Review of Events Affecting Negro Life*, 277.

9. Ibid.

10. Ibid.

11. Ibid.

12. Ibid.

13. Ibid.

14. Rates of lynching and rates of execution and lynching combined in the East North Central region were based on the population in the capital punishment states, Illinois, Indiana, and Ohio.

15. Richard H. Steckel, "The Quality of Census Data for Historical Inquiry: A Research Agenda," *Social Science History* 15 (Winter 1991): 579–99. The quotation is from p. 581. For sources on the characteristics of data from historical censuses, see chapter 1, note 12.

16. Brown, *Strain of Violence: Historical Studies of American Violence and Vigilantism*, 211–14, 324–25.

17. For differing views concerning the incidence of homicide during the early twentieth century, see Eric H. Monkkonen, *Police in Urban American, 1860–1920* (Cambridge: Cambridge University Press, 1981), 76–77; Roger Lane, "On the Social Meaning of Homicide Trends in America," in *Violence in America: The History of Crime*, ed. Ted Robert Gurr, 55–79 (Newbury Park, CA: Sage Publications, 1989).

18. See, for example, John Higham, *Strangers in the Land: Patterns of American Nativism, 1860–1925*, 2d ed. (New Brunswick: Rutgers University Press, 1992), 39, 90–91, 160, 267–68; Alan M. Kraut, *The Huddled Masses: The Immigrant in American Society, 1880–1921*, 2d ed. (Wheeling, IL: Harlan Davidson, 2001), 173–213.

19. Data for the Italian population in 1910, the center point of the 1906–1915 period, are found in the U. S. Bureau of the Census, *Thirteenth Census of the United States: 1910, Population* (Washington, DC: U.S. Government Printing Office, 1913), 1: 917–24. Italian foreign-born data for 1920, the center point of the period 1916–1925, are in ibid., *Fourteenth Census of the United States: 1920, Population* (Washington, DC: U.S. Government Printing Office, 1922), 2: 698. Italian foreign-stock population data for 1920 are in ibid., 2: 912–23. For Italian foreign-born population in 1930 for the period 1926–1935, see ibid., *Fifteenth Census of the United States: 1930, Population* (Washington, DC: U.S. Government Printing Office, 1932), 3: part 1: 3. Italian foreign-stock population data in 1930 are in ibid., 3: part 1: 54.

20. White native-born population data for 1910, the center point of the period 1906–1915, are found in the U.S. Bureau of the Census, *Thirteenth Census of the United States: 1910, Population*, 1: 146–53. For 1920, white native-born data are in ibid., *Fourteenth Census of the United States: 1920, Population*, 1: 31. White native-born data for 1930 are in ibid., *Fifteenth Census of the United States: 1930, Population*, 2: 36.

CHAPTER 6

1. This perspective draws upon David T. Courtwright, *Violent Land: Single Men and Social Disorder from the Frontier to the Inner City* (Cambridge,

MA: Harvard University Press, 1996), see esp. 1–65; Norbert Elias, *The Civilizing Process: Sociogenetic and Psychogenetic Investigations*, rev. ed., ed. Eric Dunning, Johan Goudsblom, and Stephen Mennel (Oxford: Blackwell, 1994); David Garland, *Punishment and Modern Society: A Study in Social Theory* (Chicago: University of Chicago Press, 1990), esp. chap. 10. See also Richard Maxwell Brown, *No Duty to Retreat: Violence and Values in American History and Society* (New York: Oxford University Press, 1991), chap. 2, 3, esp. 41–48. Brown traces much of Western violence to conflict between the consolidating efforts of emerging capitalist enterprise, on the one hand, and more traditional agrarian values, on the other, a conflict reinforced by, and reinforcing, partisan divisions and Civil War animosities.

2. For a discussion of debates over Western violence, see Roger G. McGrath, *Gunfighters, Highwaymen, & Vigilantes: Violence and the Frontier* (Berkeley: University of California Press, 1984), 261–71; Clare V. McKanna Jr., *Homicide, Race, and Justice in the American West, 1880–1920* (Tucson: University of Arizona Press, 1997), 6–10.

3. McKanna, *Homicide, Race, and Justice*, esp. 39–44, 97–98, 153, 162–63. See also McGrath, *Gunfighters, Highwaymen, & Vigilantes*, 253–54. Disagreement over Western violence compared to violence in other areas turns in part on a basic methodological question. Is it appropriate and useful to employ standardized measures—as percentages or rates per some standard number, such as 100,000—to compare populations of widely differing sizes? For a rejection of the use of this approach in studying the early West or other historical eras, see Robert R. Dykstra, "To Live and Die in Dodge City: Body Counts, Law and Order, and the Case of *Kansas v. Gill*," in *Lethal Imagination: Violence and Brutality in American History*, ed. Michael A. Bellesiles, 213–14 (New York: New York University Press, 1999).

4. The West North Central region includes Iowa, Kansas, Minnesota, Nebraska, North Dakota, South Dakota, and Oklahoma. The Mountain region includes Arizona, Colorado, Idaho, Montana, Nevada, New Mexico, Utah, and Wyoming, and the Pacific Coast is made up of California, Oregon, and Washington.

5. The Espy collection records twenty-nine executions carried out in these regions prior to 1836. These include eight Hispanics executed in the seventeenth century in the Spanish Southwest; fifteen Native Americans and five Hispanics executed in the late eighteenth and early nineteenth centuries in Spanish-controlled California; and one Native American put to death in Iowa Territory in 1834.

6. William W. Folwell, *A History of Minnesota*, 4 vols., rev. ed. (St. Paul: Minnesota Historical Society, 1924), 2: 196–210; Robert M. Utley, *The Indian Frontier of the American West 1846–1890* (Albuquerque: University of New Mexico Press, 1984), 76–81.

7. As an example, in his memoirs Philip H. Sheridan described the arrest of thirteen Indians on March 26, 1856, for attacking whites at the Cascades of the Columbia River. After trial by a military commission, nine were sentenced to death and hanged the following day. See Philip H. Sheridan, *Personal Memoirs of P. H. Sheridan, General, United States Army*, 2 vols. (New York: Charles L. Webster & Company, 1888), 1: 81–84. These "executions" are not included in the Espy collection, nor have we added them to the collection. Hubert Howe

Bancroft, in *Popular Tribunals*, 2 vols., in *The Works of Hubert Howe Bancroft*, vols. 36 and 37 (1887; reprinted, New York: Arno Press, 1967), 1: 158–59, reported that the commander at Fort Sutter in California in the 1850s regularly administered a procedure for the military trial and execution of Native Americans, although Bancroft gave no indication of the numbers executed. See also Edmond S. Meany, *History of the State of Washington* (New York: Macmillan Company, 1909), 178, 195, 215–16, for additional examples of the execution of Native Americans with and without trial.

8. U.S. Bureau of the Census, *Historical Statistics of the United States, Colonial Times to 1970, Bicentennial Edition*, 1: 25.

9. The necessity of combining the two groups in calculating rates of execution introduces a greater possibility of distortion for the West, particularly the Southwest, than for the rest of the nation. The Hispanic population of this subregion was significantly larger than in the rest of the nation, and the combination of the two groups may give the impression that non-Hispanic whites were executed at higher rates than was actually the case.

10. The timing and extent of Census enumerations are succinctly given in ibid., 1: 3–4. Asian population data are found in the U.S. Bureau of the Census, *Thirteenth Census of the United States: 1910, Population*, 1: 141; ibid., *Fifteenth Census of the United States: 1930, Population*, 2: 3; ibid., *Sixteenth Census of the United States: 1940, Population*, part 1, vol. 2: 52.

For population data on the Native American population, see *Thirteenth Census of the United States: Population*, 1: 141; "The Indian Population of the United States and Alaska," *Fifteenth Census of the United States*, 2–3; *Sixteenth Census of the United States: 1940*, part 1, vol. 2: 52.

11. U.S. Bureau of the Census, *Historical Statistics*, 1: 3. The 1930 Mexican population totals are in the U.S. Bureau of the Census, Fifteenth *Census of the United States: 1930, Population*, 2: 3.

12. To repeat a point made earlier, we do not treat the Espy collection as a sample in either the dictionary or technical sense of that word. The collection was not intended as a sample but is an effort to collect information on the total universe of legal executions carried out in American history. Thus we often treat small numbers as real values—as approximations of historical reality—not as the possibly erroneous products of inadequate sampling.

13. It would probably be possible to exaggerate the degree of organization that vigilante "trials" sometimes involved. Thomas J. Dimsdale, the historian of the Montana vigilante movement in the 1860s, tells of the leader of a vigilante band who asked his men to line up on one side of the road if they favored hanging two captives and on the other side to free them. Every man "voted" to hang them and, wrote Dimsdale, "the doom of the robbers was sealed." See *The Vigilantes of Montana or Popular Justice in the Rocky Mountains* (Norman: University of Oklahoma Press, 1953), 131. Hubert Howe Bancroft described numerous "executions" when vigilante organizations conducted such "trials" and other instances when there was no pretense of legal procedure. In volume 1, Bancroft focused on the lynchings carried out by the "mobocracy"; volume 2 concentrated on the actions of the San Francisco Committee of Vigilance. See Bancroft, *Popular Tribunals*, 1, 2, passim. See also Brown, *Strain of Violence*, 95–133.

14. Michael J. Pfeifer, *Rough Justice: Lynching and American Society, 1874–1947* (Urbana and Chicago: University of Illinois Press, 2004), 3, emphasis.

15. Brown, *Strain of Violence*, esp. chapter 6. See also Friedman, *Crime and Punishment in American History*, 179–87; *A History of American Law* , 320–21, 505–506; Lane, *Murder in America: A History*, 177; Walker, *Popular Justice: A History of American Criminal Justice*, 76–77.

16. Brown, in *Strain of Violence*, Appendix 3, 305–19, sometimes gives the approximate number killed by vigilantes and in some instances lists the numbers killed during more or less extended time periods. As a consequence, a detailed comparison with population is often not possible.

17. Ibid., 130–33, Appendix 3, 305–19.

18. Bancroft, *Popular Tribunals*, 1: 515.

19. Brown, Strain *of Violence*, note 41, p. 352, Appendix 3, 306–307.

20. Guzman, 1952 *Negro Year Book*, 277.

21. The discussion of lynching in the Western regions is based on the sources cited in note 6, chapter 5.

22. Bancroft, *Popular Tribunals*, 1, passim.

23. Bowers et al., *Legal Homicide: Death as Punishment in America, 1864–1982*, 11.

24. Ibid., 8–10.

25. Ibid., 13.

26. One Asian American was executed in the South in 1877 and one in the East North Central region in 1939. They are not included in Table 6.6.

27. U.S. Bureau of the Census, *Thirteenth Census of the United States: 1910, Population*, 1: 141.

28. See, for example, Stephen J. Leonard, *Lynching in Colorado, 1859–1919* (Boulder: University Press of Colorado, 2002) 123–27, 146; Pfeifer, *Rough Justice: Lynching and American Society, 1874–1947*, 47, 49.

29. Brown, *Strains of Violence*, 162–63. Roosevelt's views were ambiguous in that he sympathized with Western vigilantism but was very critical of lynching in the South. See H. W. Brands, *T. R.: The Last Romantic* (New York: Basic Books, 1997), 496–500.

30. The argument here draws upon Courtwright, *Violent Land*, 21–25.

CHAPTER 7

1. Guzman et al., *1952 Negro Year Book: A Review of Events Affecting Negro Life*, 277–78.

2. It should be kept in mind that the Bureau of the Census tabulated Hispanics with other whites. During the period 189–1905, thirty-six Hispanic Americans and 472 other whites were executed.

3. The occupations of a number of the second group of executions supplied to us by Espy consisting of 4,139 cases may be known but were not included in the data we received. Judging from what is known about occupations of the executed from Espy's data obtained from the Inter-university Consortium for Political and Social Research, however, probably the occupation of most of these additional cases is unknown. In the data obtained from the ICPSR

a higher proportion of missing data on occupation (and age as well) is found for those executed before the twentieth century and in the South and Border regions. In the second group of 4,148 cases, nearly 83% of the executions occurred in the South and Border regions, and nearly 85% of the 4,148 executions took place before 1896. See the Appendix in this book.

4. Kathleen McGuire, Ann L. Pastore, and Timothy J. Flanigan, *Bureau of Justice Statistics Sourcebook of Criminal Statistics—1992* (Washington, DC: U.S. Government Printing Office, 1993), 597.

5. Courtwright, *Violent Land*, esp. 1–46; Roger Lane, *Murder in America: A History*, 122–23, 127–28, 183; Michael Tonry, *Malign Neglect: Race, Crime, and Punishment in America* (New York: Oxford University Press, 1995), 29–31.

6. Patterns in state records of the age of those executed are suggested by "Executions under State Authority: An Inventory," compiled by Negley K. Teeters and Charles I. Zibulka and first published in its entirety in William J. Bowers, *Executions in America* (Lexington, MA: D. C. Heath, 1974), 200–401. The inventory is based on state records with age as one of the variables. The inventory is republished in Bowers et al., *Legal Homicide: Death as Punishment in America, 1864–1982*, 396–523, with corrections by M. Watt Espy. Both versions of the inventory show the same general pattern of missing data on age.

7. The age of nine of those executed is given as under fifteen. The age range fifteen through thirty-four is used to allow comparison with data from the U.S. Censuses.

8. On the basis of data for New York City, Eric H. Monkkonen, *Murder in New York City* (Berkeley: University of California Press, 2001), 101–102 suggests that this age distribution may be largely a phenomenon of the late twentieth century.

9. Washington State Department of Corrections, Division of Prisons, "Persons Executed at the Washington State Penitentiary since 1904." Four pages, no date of publication.

10. U.S. Bureau of the Census, *Historical Statistics of the United States, Colonial Times to 1970, Bicentennial Edition*, 1: 380.

11. Washington State Department of Corrections, Division of Prisons, "Persons Executed at the Washington State Penitentiary since 1904."

12. For a brief but cogent discussion of this view, see Monkkonen, *Murder in New York City*, 11–16.

13. In defining urban population, we have used the Census definition as residence in places of 2,500 population or greater.

14. The median rates of executions for all states and territories and including all executions without regard for race or ethnicity were for 1876–1885, .23; 1916–1925, .11; and 1936–1945, .075.

15. Because some of the counties included rural areas, the comparisons tend to inflate the rates of execution for the cities.

16. Hugo Adam Bedau and Michael L. Radelet, "Miscarriages of Justice in Potentially Capital Cases," *Stanford Law Review* 40 (November 1987): 72–73, puts the number executed in error from the period 1905–1945 at twenty-one. Bedau and Radelet also provide evidence (p. 35 and passim) that from 1900 to 1949, an additional eighty-four were wrongfully convicted of homicide or rape and sentenced to death but not executed. However, see also Stephen J.

Markham and Paul G. Cassell, "Protecting the Innocent: A Response to the Bedau-Radelet Study," and Bedau and Radelet, "The Myth of Infallibility: A Reply to Markham and Cassell," both in *Stanford Law Review* 41 (November 1988): 121–70; Michael L. Radelet, Hugo Adam Bedau, and Constance E. Putnam, *In Spite of Innocence: Erroneous Convictions in Capital Cases* (Boston: Northeastern University Press, 1992). For a brief but penetrating discussion of the problems of error presented by capital punishment, see Scott Turow, *Ultimate Punishment: A Lawyer's Reflection on Dealing with the Death Penalty* (New York: Farrar, Straus and Giroux, 2003), passim.

17. Lane, *Violent Death in the City: Suicide, Accident, and Murder in Nineteenth-Century Philadelphia* (Cambridge, MA: Harvard University Press, 1979), 114–41. See also Lane, *Murder in America*, 181–88; Courtwright, *Violent Land*, 270–80.

18. Courtwright, *Violent Land*, 30, 237–40; Lane, *Murder in America*, 348–52; *Violent Death in the City*, 102–103; Humbert S. Nelli, *The Business of Crime: Italians and Syndicate Crime in the United States* (New York: Oxford University Press, 1976), 3–23.

19. Clare V. McKanna Jr., "Seeds of Destruction: Homicide, Race, and Justice in Omaha, 1880–1920," *Journal of American Ethnic History* 14 (Fall 1994): 7–10. For a recent discussion of the relevant literature on the "subculture of violence," see Steven F. Messner, Robert D. Baller, and Matthew P. Zevenbergen, "The Legacy of Lynching and Southern Homicide," *American Sociological Review* 70 (August 2005): 633–36.

20. *Historical Statistics* gives numbers and rates of homicides for the period 1900–1970 (p. 414), but not by race or ethnic group. Moreover, the data are misleading. They are for the "Death Registration Area," which did not include all states until 1933. For 1900 through 1905, for example, only ten states and the District of Columbia were included. See ibid., 44–45, 408.

21. Jeffrey S. Adler, "'The Negro Would Be More Than an Angel to Withstand Such Treatment:' African-American Homicide in Chicago, 1875–1910," in *Lethal Imagination: Violence and Brutality in American History*, ed. Michael A. Bellesiles, 301–304. (New York: New York University Press, 1999); Monkkonen, *Murder in New York City*, 138–44; Lane, *Violent Death in the City*, 103–105; McKanna Jr., "Seeds of Destruction: Homicide, Race, and Justice in Omaha, 1880–1920," 7. Because of the characteristics of available source material, homicides are not consistently counted in the same way in these publications.

22. For a discussion of the legal position of African Americans in the North, see Leon F. Litwack, *North of Slavery: The Negro in the Free States, 1790–1860* (Chicago: University of Chicago Press, 1961), esp. 93–103.

23. This evidence is summarized most recently in David Cole, *No Equal Justice: Race and Class in the American Criminal Justice System* (New York: The New Press, 1999), esp. 1–15, 132–57. See also David J. Bodenhamer, *Fair Trial: Rights of the Accused in American History* (New York: Oxford University Press, 1992), 48–91; Jerome G. Miller, *Search and Destroy: African American Males in the Criminal Justice System* (New York: Cambridge University Press, 1996), 48–88; Tonry, *Malign Neglect*, 3–80.

24. Negley K. Teeters and Charles J. Zibulka, "Executions under State Authority: An Inventory," in *Legal Homicide: Death as Punishment in America*,

1864–1982, William J. Bowers, with Glenn L. Pierce and John G. Mcdevitt, 395–523 (Boston: Northeastern University Press, 1984), indicate whether or not those executed had appealed and the level of appeal. We know of no systematic and comprehensive data on the appellate history of those executed under local authority.

25. Bowers et al., *Legal Homicide*, 62–63, 73–87, provide an extended discussion of the patterns of appeal for executions under state authority, including racial and regional differences.

26. Bodenhamer, *Fair Trial*, 48–91; Friedman, *Crime and Punishment in American History*, 296–300; Walker, *Popular Justice*, 74–79.

27. Hindus, *Prison and Plantation*, 183–214, Masur, *Rites of Execution*, esp. 13–24, 255–70; Rothman, *The Discovery of the Asylum: Social Order and Disorder in the New Republic*, 57–78; Schwarz, *Twice Condemned*, 23–28; Alice Felt Tyler, *Freedom's Ferment: Phases of American Social History from the Colonial Period to the Outbreak of Civil War* (New York: Harper Torchbooks, 1962; originally published in 1944), 265–85.

28. Walker, *Popular Justice*, 142–44; Dorothy O. Johansen and Charles M. Gates, *Empire of the Columbia: A History of the Northwest* (New York: Harper and Row, 1967), 458.

29. James A. Davis, Tom W. Smith, and Peter V. Marsden, General Social Surveys, 1972–2002: (Cumulative file) (Computer file). 2nd ICPSR version. Chicago, IL: National Opinion Research Center (producer), 2003. Storrs, CT: Roper Center for Public Opinion Research, University of Connecticut/Ann Arbor, MI: Inter-university Consortium for Political and Social Research (distributors), 2003.

30. William G. Mayer, *The Changing American Mind: How and Why American Public Opinion Changed: 1960–1988* (Ann Arbor: University of Michigan Press, 1992), 263–70, 358; Benjamin I. Page and Robert Y. Shapiro, *The Rational Public: Fifty Years of Trends in American's Policy Preferences* (Chicago: University of Chicago Press, 1992), 92–94, 402–403.

CHAPTER 8

1. See, for example, Ted Robert Gurr, "Historical Trends in Violent Crime: Europe and the United States," in *Violence in America: The History of Crime*, ed. Ted Robert Gurr, 21–54 (Newbury Park, London, and New Delhi: Sage Publications, 1989); Roger Lane, "On the Social Meaning of Homicide Trends in America," ibid., 55–79; Eric H. Monkkonen, "Diverging Homicide Rates: England and the United States," ibid., 80–101.

2. Unless otherwise indicated, all data bearing upon executions since 1977 used in this chapter are from Debora Fins, "Death Row U.S.A: A Quarterly Report, Fall, 2003. A Quarterly Report by the Criminal Justice Project of the NAACP Legal Defense and Educational Fund, Inc." The Death Penalty Information Center Web site, http://www.deathpenaltyinfo.org.

3. Bureau of Justice Statistics, *Sourcebook of Criminal Justice Statistics Online*, Table 6.80, 2005. http://www.albany.edu/sourcebook/pdf/t6802005.pdf. Table 6.80 was adapted from NAACP Legal Defense and Educational Fund, Inc., "Death Row U.S.A.: Summer, 2005," New York: NAACP Legal Defense and Educational Fund, Inc., 2005. (Mimeographed), 1, 30, 31.

4. Ibid.

5. Ibid.

6. U.S. Bureau of the Census, Table DP-1, "Profile of General Demographic Characteristics: 2000." Census 2000 Summary File. http://www.census.gov. The number of Native Americans put to death was very small, as Table 8.1 indicates. However, the Native American population also was small, a little less than 1% of the total population in 2000. The high ratio for Native Americans in the Pacific region, shown in Table 8.3, reflects one Native American put to death out of a total of twelve executions.

7. Thomas P. Bonczar and Tracy L. Snell, "Capital Punishment 2000," *Bureau of Justice Statistics Bulletin* (Washington, DC: U.S. Department of Justice, Office of Justice Programs, 2002), 5–8.

8. U.S. Bureau of the Census, *Statistical Abstract of the United States: 2000*, Table 12, "Resident Population by Age and Sex," http://www.census.gov.

9. Ibid., Table 210, "Educational Attainment by Selected Characteristics," http://www.census.gov.

10. The execution rates in Table 8.4 for the two later time periods are not fully comparable to those for the earlier periods. The ethnic categories employed by the Death Penalty Information Center and other groups include Hispanics, Non-Hispanic African Americans, and Non-Hispanic Whites. In calculating rates for the latter two periods, we have used comparable ethnic categories employed by the U.S. Bureau of the Census. However, the Hispanic category was not used in the U.S. Censuses of 1940 and earlier. Rather, those of Hispanic origin (usually, it appears, people of Mexican descent) were classified as white (U.S. Bureau of the Census, *Historical* Statistics, 3, 4). As noted at several points in preceding chapters, in order to calculate execution rates for the years prior to 1945, we combined the White and Hispanic categories employed in the Espy file. Since in U.S. Censuses prior to 1950 racial classifications usually were based on the observations of Census enumerators, it is probable that some Hispanics also were classified with racial groups other than whites. Comparison is further complicated by some inconsistency in the ethnic classification procedures employed by the various states in reporting executions. See U.S. Bureau of Justice Statistics, *Sourcebook of Criminal Justice Statistics Online*, Appendix 15, 4. http://www.albany.edu/sourcebook.

11. In this respect, see also Banner, *The Death Penalty*, 189, and Laurie E. Ekstrand et al., *Death Penalty Sentencing: Research Indicates Pattern of Racial Disparities, Report to Senate and House Committees on the Judiciary* (Washington, DC: General Accounting Office [GAO/GGD-90-57], February 1990).

12. Research has tended to concentrate on comparisons of African Americans to whites. Relatively less attention has been directed to Hispanics and Native Americans, although both groups are overrepresented in some jurisdictions, perhaps because of ambiguities in the way Hispanics are enumerated and the very small number of Native Americans.

13. Alfred Blumstein, "On the Racial Disproportionality of United States' Prison Populations," *The Journal of Criminal Law and Criminology* 73:3 (Autumn 1982): 1259–81. The quotation is from p. 1261.

14. Alfred Blumstein, "Racial Disproportionality of U.S. Prison Populations Revisited," *University of Colorado Law Review* 64:3 (1993): 743–60.

15. For example, see Patrick A. Langan, "Racism on Trial: New Evidence to Explain the Composition of Prisons in the United States," *The Journal of Criminal Law and Criminology* 76:3 (Autumn 1985): 666–83; William Wilbanks, *The Myth of a Racist Criminal Justice System* (Monterey, CA: Brooks/Cole Publishing, 1987), 149–59. For discussions of this literature, see Wilbanks, op. cit., passim; Janet L. Laurite and Robert J. Sampson, "Minorities, Crime, and Criminal Justice," in *The Handbook of Crime and Punishment*, ed. Michael Tonry, 58–84 (New York: Oxford University Press, 1998); and for a more critical discussion, see Michael K. Brown, Martin Carney, Elliott Currie, Troy Duster, David B. Oppenheimer, Marjorie M. Shultz, and David Wellman, *White-Washing Race: The Myth of a Color-Blind Society* (Berkeley: University of California Press, 2005).

16. Robert D. Crutchfield, George S. Bridges, Susan R. Pitchford, "Analytical and Aggregation Biases in Analyses of Imprisonment: Reconciling Discrepancies in Studies of Racial Disparity," *Journal of Research in Crime and Delinquency* 31:2 (May 1994): 166–82. See also Brown et al., *White-Washing Race: The Myth of a Color-Blind Society*, 138–39.

17. Roy L. Austin and Mark D. Allen, "Racial Disparity in Arrest Rates as an Explanation of Racial Disparity in Commitment to Pennsylvania's Prisons," *Journal of Research in Crime and Delinquency* 37 (May 2000): 200–20; Brown et al., *White-Washing Race: The Myth of a Color-Blind Society*, 139–47.

18. David C. Baldus, George Woodworth, and Charles A. Pulaski Jr., *Equal Justice and the Death Penalty: A Legal and Empirical Analysis* (Boston: Northeastern University Press, 1990), esp. chap. 12, 394–425.

19. U.S. General Accounting Office, *Death Penalty Research Indicates Pattern of Racial Disparities* (Washington, DC: General Accounting Office, 1990), 1–6.

20. David C. Baldus, George Woodworth, David Zuckerman, Neil Alan Weiner, Barbara Broffitt, "Racial Discrimination and the Death Penalty in the Post-Furman Era: An Empirical and Legal Overview, with Recent Findings from Philadelphia, *Cornell Law Review* 83 (September 1998) 1713–16.

21. Ibid., 1662–16.

22. Ibid., 1660–61, 1742–45.

23. *Sourcebook of Criminal Justice Statistics, 2003*, Table 3.127, p. 309, Table 3.128, p. 310. http://www.albany.edu/sourcebook/pdf/section3.pdf.

24. As we read it, this seems the general thrust of this point of view. See, for example, John J. DiLulio Jr., "My Black Crime Problem, and Ours," in *Race, Crime and Justice: A Reader*, ed. Shaun L. Gabbidon and Helen Taylor Green, 73–85 (New York and London: Routledge, 2005); Dinesh D'Souza, *The End of Racism: Principles for a Multiracial Society* (New York: The Free Press, 1995), 477–556; John H. McWhorter, *Losing the Race: Self-Sabotage in Black America* (New York: The Free Press, 2000), 212–62; Stephan Thernstrom and Abigail Thernstrom, *America in Black and White: One Nation, Indivisible* (New York: Touchstone, 1997), 258–85, 531–45.

25. Examples of this point of view are Brown et al., *White-Washing Race*, 131–60; Sheri Lynn Johnson, "Race and Capital Punishment," in *America's Death Penalty: Beyond Repair?*, ed. Stephen P. Garvey, 121–43 (Durham, NC: Duke University Press, 2003); Tonry, *Malign Neglect*, 9–47, 79–80, 181–82, 207–209.

CHAPTER 9

1. Norbert Elias, *The Civilizing Process: Sociogenetic and Psychogenetic Investigations,* rev. ed., ed. Eric Dunning, Johan Goudsblom, and Stephen Mennel (Oxford: Blackwell Publishers, 1994); Garland, *Punishment and Modern Society: A Study in Social Theory,* esp. chapter 10.

2. Elias, *The Civilizing Process,* 367.

3. Ibid., 365–67.

4. Ibid., 369.

5. Ibid., 370.

6. Although concerned with a somewhat different issue, Roger Lane provides an insightful discussion of the role of the school system and industrial labor in suppressing some types of violence. See Lane, *Violent Death in the City,* 118–41.

7. Garland, *Punishment and Modern Society,* 213–47, esp. 243–46. See also Elias, *The Civilizing Process,* 414–21.

8. See Banner, *The Death Penalty in American History,* 53–75.

9. Garland, *Punishment and Modern Society,* 220–27.

10. It is easy to recognize that historically established white authorities did not protect African Americans and other racial and ethnic minority groups from lynching and other forms of persecution. It also is clear that the historical tendency in many jurisdictions to treat crimes by African Americans against African American victims as less serious and less worthy of attention than crimes against white victims meant that African Americans were not treated equally before the law and legal authorities. The evidence is less clear, but it is probably that crimes against Native Americans, Hispanics, and Asians also were treated as less important than crimes against whites, which had the similar effect of denying equal protection by the law.

11. Garland, *Punishment and American Society,* 222–25.

APPENDIX

1. M. Watt Espy and John Ortiz Smykla, *Executions in the United States, 1608–1991: The Espy File* (computer file). Second ICPSR ed. Compiled by John Ortiz Smykla, University of Alabama. Ann Arbor, MI: Inter-university Consortium for Political and Social Research (producer and distributor), 1992, i–v.

2. This total excludes eight executions recorded in the 1640s in the Spanish Southwest.

3. Bowers, *Executions in America,* 200–401.

4. Bowers et al., *Legal Homicide,* 395–523. The corrections are summarized on p. 395. For descriptions of Espy's work, see pp. 43–45, 396–97; see also Espy and Smykla, *Executions in the United States,* i–iv.

5. Negley K. Teeters, *Scaffold and Chair: A Compilation of Their Use in Pennsylvania, 1682–1962* (Philadelphia: Pennsylvania Prison Society, 1963), 62–65, 168–84, 192–229. Teeters also published the names of persons executed before 1835 in "Public Executions in Pennsylvania, 1682–1834," *Journal of the Lancaster County Historical Society* (1960).

6. G. S. Rowe, *Embattled Bench: The Pennsylvania Supreme Court and the Forging of a Democratic Society, 1664–1809* (Newark: University of Delaware Press, 1994), 67, 68, 162, gives the numbers executed during various periods of Pennsylvania history. These are generally in agreement with the numbers of executions included in the Espy collection for the same periods. However, it is also indicated that eighty-seven executions took place during the ninety-five years prior to 1777. The Espy collection indicates 114 during these years. Rowe refers to Negley K. Teeters, "Public Executions in Pennsylvania, 1682–1834," *Journal of the Lancaster Historical Society* 64 (1960) and to the 1987 version of the Espy file but also indicates on p. 349 that "most figures regarding executions used in this study are taken from my own study (in collaboration with Jack D. Marietta) of crime in Pennsylvania between 1681 and 1800."

7. Daniel Allen Hearn, *Legal Executions in New York: A Comprehensive Reference, 1639–1963* (Jefferson, NC: McFarland and Company, 1997); *Legal Executions in New England: A Comprehensive Reference, 1623–1960* (Jefferson, NC: McFarland and Company, 1999).

8. Hearn, *Legal Executions in New York*, 1, 328–29; *Legal Executions in New England*, 2–3.

9. Wright, *Racial Violence in Kentucky, 1865–1940: Lynchings, Mob Rule, and Legal Lynchings*, 225–31.

10. John D. Bessler, *Legacy of Violence: Lynch Mobs and Executions in Minnesota* (Minneapolis: University of Minnesota Press, 2003), 293, passim.

11. Leonard, *Lynching in Colorado, 1859–1919*, 62, 173–74. Table A.2 (p. 173) gives only nineteen executions. However, 1889 is dropped from the table, and a legal execution in that year is referred to on p. 62.

12. Ibid., 4, 17–20.

13. Monkkonen, *Murder in New York City*, 113.

14. Randolph Roth, " 'Blood Calls for Vengeance!' The History of Capital Punishment in Vermont," *Vermont History* 65 (1997): 10–25.

15. Hindus, *Prison and Plantation*, 103–104.

16. Ibid., 157.

17. Philip J. Schwarz, *Twice Condemned: Slaves and the Criminal Laws of Virginia, 1705–1865* (Baton Rouge: Louisiana State University Press, 1988), ix, 15.

18. Ibid., 236.

19. Donna J. Spindell, Crime *and Society in North Carolina, 1663–1776* (Baton Rouge: Louisiana State University Press, 1989), 25–28, 135.

20. Marvin L. Michael Kay and Lorin Lee Cary, *Slavery in North Carolina, 1748–1775* (Chapel Hill: University of North Carolina Press, 1995), 76–77.

21. For North Carolina the first execution in the Espy file took place in 1726, and the first in South Carolina in 1718. However, the *Historical Statistics*, 1168, indicates that both of the Carolinas had at least a limited white and African American population as early as the 1660s and 1670s. It is difficult to believe that no executions took place prior to those listed in the Espy file.

22. For a discussion of plantation justice in North Carolina, see Kay and Cary, *Slavery in North Carolina*, 73–75. For South Carolina, see Hindus, *Prison and Plantation*, 137–39.

23. Spindell, *Crime and Society in North Carolina,* 133–34. Kay and Cary, in *Slavery in North Carolina,* point out that "North Carolina passed no law before 1774 making it a crime to attack, wound, disable, maim, or kill a slave," 75.

24. Hindus, *Prison and Plantation,* 132–33.

25. For discussions of slave courts in North and South Carolina, see Kay and Cary, *Slavery in North Carolina,* 70–95; Hindus, *Prison and Plantation,* 131–37; Spindell, *Crime and Society in North Carolina,* 23–24.

26. Hindus, Prison and Plantation, 151, 154.

27. This is not to suggest that the legal system as it concerned slaves— or, for that matter, free African Americans—was fair or just. It was neither. It is only to say that in some unknown number of instances it is impossible to know whether legal requirements, such as they were, were actually followed.

28. With all due deference to the much-vaunted honor claimed by the Southern plantation aristocracy, such petitions do not necessarily prove that slaves were executed for alleged wrongdoing as opposed to being killed in accidents or in some other fashion.

29. For a discussion of some of these issues as they bear upon the early West, see Leonard, *Lynching in Colorado,* 3–7. See also his comments on the treatment, or lack thereof, of lynching by earlier historians of the West.

30. Ibid., 3.

Index

Adultery, 41

African Americans: bias against, 162–163; Border region executions, 75–91, 149; Civil War executions of, 58; colonial executions, 30*tab*, 33, 34, 37*tab*, 43; in colonial/revolutionary period, 28, 29; criminal justice system and, 27; death for nonlethal crimes by, 73*fig*; death penalty for rape by, 25; on death row, 174*tab*; disenfranchisement of, 68, 77; disparities in prison population, 177–181; disproportionate execution of, 2, 9, 12–15, 13*tab*, 19, 20*fig*, 43, 44, 53, 54, 69, 106, 108, 125, 138, 139*tab*, 149, 160, 173; East North Central region executions, 103*fig*, 104, 105*tab*; executions for nonlethal offenses, 23, 24*fig*, 25, 64, 80*fig*; gender and executions of, 15; ghettoization of, 111; inability to testify against whites, 44, 55, 63; lack of access to legal counsel, 44, 111; large Southern population, 52; legacy of exclusion from civilizing process, 187, 188; legal system bias against, 55, 81; lynching of, 81–91, 106, 108, 109*fig*, 110, 132, 133*tab*, 134*tab*, 141*tab*; mistrust of white institutions by, 161; Mountain region executions, 120–129; New England region executions, 96, 97*tab*, 99*fig*; Northeast region executions, 149; Pacific region executions, 120–129; population increases among, 54; prohibition on jury duty, 55, 63; rates of execution of, 17*fig*, 22*fig*; ratio of executions to whites, 139*tab*, 143*tab*; ratio of lynchings to whites, 140, 141*tab*; segregation of, 68, 77; Southern region executions, 67–75, 81–91, 149, 171, 172*tab*; Western region executions, 149; West North Central region executions, 120–129

Alabama: end of public executions, 74; Hispanic executions, 52; lynching in, 88; Native American executions, 52; shift to private executions, 65

Alabama Law Center, University of, 6

Appeals, 74

Arizona: Asian executions, 127*tab*; centralization of executions, 135; discretionary sentencing in, 136; elimination of capital punishment in, 137; Hispanic executions, 122, 127*tab*; Native American executions, 127*tab*; white executions, 127*tab*

Arkansas: African American executions, 72; lynching in, 88; Native American executions, 52, 69

Arson, 44

Asians: on death row, 174*tab*;
  disproportionate execution of,
  126, 127–128*tab*, 138; East North
  Central region executions, 104,
  105*tab*; lynching and, 133*tab*,
  134*tab*; Mountain region executions, 120–129, 150; New
  England region executions, 96,
  97*tab*, 98; Pacific region executions, 120–129, 150; populations
  in Western region, 126; ratio of
  executions to whites, 139*tab*

Bacon's Rebellion, 29
Baldus, James, 179
Bancroft, Hubert Howe, 130, 136
Beck, E.M., 7
Bessler, John D., 199
Bestiality, 41
Blasphemy, 41
Blumstein, Alfred, 178
Border region, 34, 75–91; African
  American executions, 30*tab*,
  32*tab*, 34, 37*tab*, 53, 53*tab*, 55,
  55*tab*, 75–91, 149, 172*tab*,
  177*tab*; Asian executions, 53*tab*;
  changes in defining capital
  offenses in, 63; colonial executions, 29, 30*tab*, 32*tab*, 33, 37*tab*;
  death row population in, 174*tab*;
  disproportionate execution of
  African Americans in, 43, 44*tab*;
  dominance of agricultural sector
  in, 48; early republic executions,
  49, 51, 53*tab*, 55*tab*, 56*tab*;
  executions for nonlethal offenses
  in, 62*tab*; Hispanic executions,
  53*tab*; impact of Civil War on,
  67; increase/decline in use of
  death penalty in, 51; lynching in,
  82, 85, 88, 110, 132, 149;
  methods of executions, 42; Native
  American executions, 30*tab*, 34,
  53*tab*, 76*tab*, 172*tab*; persistence
  of public executions, 187; ratio of
  African American/Asian executions
  to white in, 139*tab*; ratio of
  African American to white

lynchings in, 141*tab*; reluctance to
  give up local control of execu-
  tions, 79; slavery in, 33, 75; total
  known executions, 193*tab*;
  violence in, 48; white executions,
  32*tab*, 34, 37*tab*, 51, 53*tab*, 55,
  55*tab*, 76*tab*, 172*tab*, 177*tab*
Bowers, William J., 196
Branding, 28, 41
Breaking on the wheel, 40, 42, 44
Brown, Richard Maxwell, 8, 82, 88,
  111, 130, 131
Brundage, W. Fitzhugh, 8
Bureau of Justice Statistics, 173
Burglary, 23
Burning, 40, 42, 64

California: Asian executions, 122,
  128*tab*; death row population in,
  171; discretionary sentencing in,
  136; Hispanic executions, 122,
  128*tab*; lynching in, 130, 132,
  144; Native American executions,
  128*tab*; population growth, 123;
  white executions, 128*tab*
Capital punishment. *See also* Death
  penalty; Executions: abolishment
  of, 72; alternatives to, 28, 59–60;
  centralization of control over, 4;
  changes in incidence of, 48–60;
  changes in technology of, 75, 95;
  during Civil War, 67; in colonial/
  revolutionary period, 27–45; as
  deterrent, 28, 59, 60; discretionary
  use of, 72, 79, 95, 136; disparity
  in use of, 3; in early republic, 47–
  56; efforts to abolish, 165; English
  use of, 38–39; as form of violence, 3; gender and, 9, 10, 15,
  16, 43, 54, 69, 77, 123; history
  of, 2, 3, 4, 5–8; increase/decline in
  use of, 4, 9, 72; increase in use
  after Reconstruction period, 67;
  lack of uniformity in, 2; legitimacy of, 47; as means of coping
  with crime and violence, 16;
  mitigation of punishment in, 41;
  popular support for, 164, 165,

166, 169; practical bases for reform of, 59–60; racial disparity in, 25; rates of execution and, 16–21; regional patterns, 42–45; restoration of, 136, 165, 167, 169; restrictions on, 21, 23; social perspectives, 147–166; Southern use of, 67–75, 81–91; variation in, 2; violent offenses and, 3

Cary, Lorin L., 201

Cattle theft, 136

Citizenship, 163

Civil War: cause of increase in executions, 51; desertion in, 51; disruption of, 67; effect on incidence of executions, 10; executions by Union Army during, 57; lynching during, 82

Colonial/revolutionary period, 27–45; change and development in, 28; death penalty during, 38–42; eighteenth century, 31–38; executions, 27–45; population growth during, 28; race and region during, 42–45; seventeenth century, 28–31

Colorado: centralization of executions, 135; discretionary sentencing in, 136; elimination of capital punishment in, 137; Hispanic executions, 122, 127*tab*; white executions, 127*tab*

Committees of vigilance, 129

Commutations, 74

Connecticut: African American executions, 31, 96; Asian executions, 98; capital punishment use in, 58; centralization of executions, 94; colonial executions, 29; early republic executions, 58; Italian-Americans in, 113*tab*; use of electrocution in, 95

Counterfeiting, 23, 39, 41

Courts: federal, 4

Crime: European immigrants blamed for, 111, 112; leading to execution, 40; military, 51; mitigation of punishment for, 41; reduction in charges for, 41

Crime, capital, 21–26; changes in definitions of, 3, 23, 28, 59, 60–64; consequences beneficial to whites, 23, 24; redefining, 3, 59, 60–64, 77, 78; redefinitions as "white only," 63, 74; reduction in, 25

Crime, nonlethal, 23, 24, 40; death penalty for, 63, 73*fig*; ethnic bias in execution for, 23, 24, 73*fig*

Crime, organized, 111

Crime, sexual, 39, 41. *See also* Rape

Criminal justice system: African Americans and, 27; bias against lower status persons, 164; colonial, 27–45; development of, 2; discrimination against African Americans in, 3, 78, 111; early reform efforts, 47, 48; greater uniformity in, 169; harshness of early system, 27, 28; national, 169; racial bias in, 162–163; in relation to executed persons, 162–163

Death: colonial attitudes on, 39, 40

Death penalty. *See also* individual regions: changes in administration of, 186; during Civil War, 75; contemporary use of, 167–189; decline in with institutional development, 144; discrimination and, 177–181; doubts about deterrence value of, 47, 59, 60; efforts to curb use of, 47; frequency of use, 1; increase and/or decline in use of, 18, 25, 28, 33, 68, 167, 184, 186; jury decisions on, 72; legal use of, 1; limited to crimes involving death of victim, 72, 74, 79, 90, 91, 95, 135, 136; mandatory, 72; national perspective, 9–26; outside the law, 81–91; patterns in use of, 167, 168, 169; post-1945, 167–189; racial discrimination and, 179, 180; racial/ethnic disparities in current use of, 171; for rape, 74, 79;

Death penalty *(continued)*
reduction of offenses subject to,
60–64; religious opposition to, 47,
59; reprieves from, 41, 59–60;
seen as appropriate by majority,
164; seen as excessive, 59; social
perspectives, 147–166; use by
colonists, 16, 18, 39, 40
Death Penalty Information Center, 6
Delaware: colonial executions, 29;
elimination of public executions,
65, 79; lynching in, 88; relinquishes local control of executions, 79
Desertion, 51
Discrimination: arrest rates and,
178; in criminal justice system,
111, 178, 179, 180; death penalty
and, 177–181
Dismemberment, 40, 42

Early republic period, 47–56;
economic development in, 48;
frequency of executions, 48–54;
population growth during, 49, 50;
reform efforts in, 47, 48
East North Central region: African
American executions, 50*tab*, 55,
55*tab*, 103*fig*, 104, 105*tab*,
172*tab*, 177*tab*; Asian executions,
104, 105*tab*; capital punishment
in, 102–110; death row population in, 174*tab*; disproportionate
execution of African Americans in,
106, 108; early republic executions, 49, 50*tab*, 55*tab*, 56*tab*;
Hispanic executions, 50*tab*, 104,
105*tab*; lynching in, 106; migration of African Americans to, 104;
Native American executions,
50*tab*, 104, 105*tab*; population
growth in, 104; ratio of African
American/Asian executions to
white in, 139*tab*; total known
executions, 193*tab*; white executions, 50*tab*, 55, 55*tab*, 103*fig*,
105*tab*, 172*tab*, 177*tab*

Electrocution, 75, 79, 95
Elias, Norbert, 4, 184, 185, 186, 187
Enlightenment values, 47
Espy, M. Watt, 5, 6, 7, 36, 125,
126, 150, 191, 192, 195, 196,
197, 198, 199, 200, 201
Espy Summary Data, 193*tab*
Ethnicity: diversity of in Northeast
region, 93; of executed persons,
148–150; executions and, 9,
12–15, 13*tab*, 29, 33
Executed persons, 147–158; age
groups, 152–156, 160, 161;
attitudes of legal/law enforcement
community toward, 164; criminal
justice system and, 162–163;
educational levels, 156, 160–161;
effect of stereotypes on, 164;
employment of, 161; ethnicity,
148–150; gender imbalances, 160,
161; guilt/innocence of, 160;
immigrant groups, 161; local
values and attitudes and, 163–166;
minority group, 152; occupations
of, 150–152; popular attitudes
toward, 163–166; professionals,
151; race, 148–150; reasons for
execution of, 158–166; regional
origin, 148–150; socioeconomic
status of, 173; status of, 150–152;
values/behavioral norms of, 161;
"white-collar," 151
Executions. *See also* individual
regions: of African Americans, 9,
12–15, 13*tab*, 17*fig*; alternatives
to, 28; of Asians, 13*tab*; average
annual, 11*fig*; carried out locally,
74; centralization of conduct of,
74, 75; changes in methods of,
64–66; changes in offenses leading
to, 60–64; characteristics of
persons in, 5, 6; in colonial/
revolutionary period, 27–45;
deterrent effect of, 66; in early
republic, 9, 47–56; in East North
Central region, 102–110; effect of
Revolutionary and Civil Wars on,

10; ethnicity and, 9, 12–15, 13*tab*, 29, 33; extreme methods of, 39, 40, 42, 65; frequency of, 10–16, 95–110; gender and, 9, 10, 15–16, 43; of Hispanics, 13*tab*; identification of early deaths by, 10; increase/decline in use of, 16, 31; of Italian-Americans, 112, 113*tab*; local, 6; mass, 35; in Middle Atlantic region, 29; of Native Americans, 9, 13*tab*; in New England region, 29, 95–100; for nonlethal offenses, 40, 41, 79; in Northeast region, 93–117; private, 74, 94, 183, 186; public, 64, 65, 74, 75, 95, 183; rate of urbanization and, 157–158; rates of, 16–21, 36*tab*, 37; record keeping and, 75; for religious beliefs, 39; semiprivate, 79; shifted to prisons, 65; in Southern region, 29; state level, 74, 94, 96; stays of, 74; surges caused by events, 18; symbolic, 41; underreporting of, 18, 19; vigilante, 129–135; for war-related offenses, 35; of whites, 12–15, 17*fig*; "witnesses" to, 94

Florida: death row population in, 173; lynching in, 88
Foreign born-foreign stock, executions of, 111–114, 113*tab*
Forgery, 23, 39, 41
France, 36
Friedman, Lawrence, 2, 68

Garland, David, 4, 184, 186, 187
Gender: capital punishment and, 9, 10, 15–16, 43, 54, 69, 77, 123; death row population and, 173, 174; violence and, 144
General Social Survey, 165
Georgia: end of public executions, 74; execution by burning in, 64; lynching in, 88; Native American executions, 52; shift to private executions, 65

Hanging, 35, 40, 42, 64, 65, 75; public, 79
Hearn, Daniel Allen, 197
Hindus, Michael, 200, 202
Hispanics: death penalty for rape by, 25; on death row, 174*tab*; disproportionate execution of in Western region, 126, 127–128*tab*; early republic executions, 52; East North Central region executions, 104, 105*tab*; execution of, 13*tab*, 69; lynching and, 83, 84*tab*, 133*tab*; Mountain region executions, 150; New England region executions, 97*tab*; Pacific region executions, 120–129, 150; populations in Western region, 126; Southern region executions, 69, 70*tab*, 171, 172*tab*
Historical Statistics of the United States, 8
Horse stealing, 135, 136

Idaho: Asian executions, 127*tab*; centralization of executions, 135; discretionary sentencing in, 136; lynching in, 130, 131; white executions, 127*tab*
Illinois: executions at local level in, 94; Italian-Americans in, 113*tab*; lynching in, 106, 108; use of electrocution in, 95
Inter-university Consortium for Political and Social Research (ICPSR), 6, 8, 191
Incest, 41
Indiana: centralization of executions, 94; lynching in, 106, 108; population growth in, 49
Industrialization, 48
Iowa: elimination of death penalty in, 137, 170; lynching in, 130
Italian-Americans, 112, 113*tab*, 114

Jamestown (Virginia), 29
"Jim Crow" practices, 68, 74, 77, 110, 111

Kansas: centralization of executions, 135; discretionary sentencing in, 136; elimination of capital punishment in, 137; lynching in, 130, 133; reinstitution of capital punishment, 136

Kay, Marvin L. Michael, 201

Kentucky: hanging in, 81; lynching in, 82, 83, 88; relinquishes local control of executions, 79; use of electrocution in, 79

Kidnapping, 136

King Philip's War, 29

Lane, Roger, 161

Legal system. *See also* Criminal justice system: bias against African Americans in, 81; discretionary use of death penalty by, 72, 95, 136; intimidating conditions at trials, 81; lynching and, 68; racially discriminatory, 25; socioeconomic status and, 25

Leonard, Stephen J., 199, 203

Lincoln, Abraham, 122

Louisiana: colonial executions, 36; executions for nonlethal offenses in, 64; Hispanic executions, 52; local executions, 75; lynching in, 88; Native American executions, 52

Lynching, 65, 69, 81–91; of African Americans, 68, 132, 133*tab*; African American/white rates, 140, 141*tab*; approval for, 1; of Asians, 133*tab*; in Border region, 85, 87*fig*; cancels decline in legal use of death penalty, 90, 91; as covert action, 82; as criminal act, 1; disproportionate execution of African Americans by, 81–91; in East North Central region, 106; geographical distribution of, 83; of Hispanics, 83, 84*tab*, 133*tab*; lack of records of deaths by, 81; legal system and, 1, 68; meaning of, 82; in Middle Atlantic region, 100; of Native Americans, 133*tab*;

in New England region, 96; prevention of, 1, 74; relation to capital punishment, 2; as ritualized spectacles, 82, 90; as societal protection, 81; terror aspect of, 82, 90; in Western region, 129–135; white mob rioting and, 82; of whites, 83, 84*tab*, 86*fig*, 87*fig*, 89*tab*, 132, 133*tab*

Maine: African American executions, 96; centralization of executions, 94; elimination of death penalty, 95, 170

Maryland: colonial executions, 29; lynching in, 88; relinquishes local control of executions, 79

Massachusetts: African American executions, 31, 96; Asian executions, 98, 138; capital punishment use in, 58; centralization of executions, 94; colonial executions, 29; early republic executions, 58; elimination of death penalty in, 170; Italian-Americans in, 113*tab*; piracy in, 35

McDevitt, John, 196

McKanna, Clare, 161

Michigan: early republic executions, 51; elimination of death penalty, 58, 94, 95, 165, 170; lynching in, 106; Native American executions, 51

Middle Atlantic region: African American executions, 30*tab*, 32*tab*, 34, 37*tab*, 50*tab*, 55*tab*, 177*tab*; centralization of executions, 94; changes in defining capital offenses in, 60; colonial executions, 29, 30*tab*, 32*tab*, 34, 35, 37*tab*; death row population in, 174*tab*; disproportionate execution of African Americans in, 43, 44*tab*; diversity in, 100; early republic executions, 49, 50*tab*, 55*tab*, 56*tab*; executions for nonlethal offenses in, 40, 41, 61*tab*; Hispanic executions, 50*tab*;

lynching in, 100; methods of executions, 42; migration of African Americans to, 102; Native American executions, 30*tab*, 34, 50*tab*; ratio of African American/ Asian executions to white in, 139*tab*; ratio of African American to white executions, 143*tab*; reform efforts in, 49; slavery in, 33; total known executions, 193*tab*; use of capital punishment in, 100–102; white executions, 32*tab*, 34, 37*tab*, 50*tab*, 55*tab*, 172*tab*, 177*tab*

Minnesota: elimination of capital punishment in, 135, 137, 170; Native American executions, 122

Minorities. *See also* individual groups: disproportionate execution of, 2

Mississippi: end of public executions, 74; local executions, 75; lynching in, 88; shift to private executions, 65

Missouri: elimination of capital punishment in, 79; lynching in, 83, 88; relinquishes local control of executions, 79; use of lethal gas in, 79

Monkkonen, Eric H., 199

Montana: discretionary sentencing in, 136; lynching in, 130; white executions, 127*tab*

Mountain region: African American executions, 120–129, 172*tab*, 177*tab*; Asian executions, 120– 129, 150, 172*tab*; death penalty in, 120; death row population in, 174*tab*; disproportionate execution of African Americans in, 125; gender ratio in, 144; heavy use of capital punishment in early years, 120, 121; high degree of violence in, 129; Hispanic executions, 120– 129, 150, 172*tab*; lynching in, 130, 132, 133*tab*, 134*tab*; Native American executions, 120–129, 172*tab*; ratio of African American

to white executions, 139*tab*, 143*tab*; ratio of African American to white lynchings in, 141*tab*; total known executions, 194*tab*; white executions, 120–129, 171, 172*tab*, 177*tab*

Murder: accessory to, 136; attempted, 136

Mutilation, 28, 82, 90, 142

National Association for the Advancement of Colored People (NAACP), 8

National Science Foundation, 6

Native Americans: Abenaki, 200; Border region executions of, 76*tab*; colonial executions, 29, 30*tab*, 33, 34, 35; in colonial/ revolutionary period, 28, 29; death penalty for rape by, 25; on death row, 174*tab*; early republic executions, 52; East North Central region executions, 104, 105*tab*; execution of, 9, 13*tab*, 44, 69, 126, 127–128*tab*, 173; legacy of exclusion from civilizing process, 187, 188; lynching and, 133*tab*; Mountain region executions, 120– 129; New England region executions, 97*tab*; Pacific region executions, 120–129; population on reservations, 125–126; Santee Sioux, 122; Southern executions, 69, 70*tab*; West North Central region executions, 120–129; wrongful deaths of, 142

Nebraska: lynching in, 130

Nevada: Asian executions, 127*tab*; centralization of executions, 135; discretionary sentencing in, 136; Hispanic executions, 127*tab*; Native American executions, 127*tab*; white executions, 127*tab*

New England region: African American executions, 30*tab*, 32*tab*, 34, 37*tab*, 50*tab*, 55*tab*, 99*fig*, 177*tab*; capital punishment in, 95–100; centralization of

New England region *(continued)*
executions, 96; changes in defining
capital offenses in, 60; colonial
executions, 29, 30*tab*, 31, 32*tab*,
34, 35, 37*tab*, 43; death row
population in, 174*tab*; disproportionate execution of African
Americans in, 43, 44*tab*, 98; early
republic executions, 49, 50*tab*,
55*tab*, 56*tab*; executions for
nonlethal offenses in, 40, 41,
61*tab*; female executions, 43;
Hispanic executions, 50*tab*;
increase and/or decline in use of,
33, 37; methods of executions, 42;
Native American executions, 29,
30*tab*, 34, 50*tab*; population
growth in, 29, 31, 33; rare use of
death penalty in, 98; ratio of
African American/Asian executions
to white in, 139*tab*; reform efforts
in, 49; sexual offenses in, 41; shift
to private executions, 65; total
known executions, 193*tab*; white
executions, 29, 32*tab*, 34, 37*tab*,
50*tab*, 55*tab*, 99*fig*, 172*tab*,
177*tab*
New Hampshire: centralization of
executions, 94; hangings in, 95
New Jersey: centralization of
executions, 94; colonial executions, 29; Italian-Americans in,
113*tab*; lynching in, 100
New Mexico: centralization of
executions, 135; discretionary
sentencing in, 136; Hispanic
executions, 122, 128*tab*; white
executions, 128*tab*
New York: centralization of executions, 94; colonial executions, 29;
early republic executions, 51;
Italian-Americans in, 113*tab*;
lynching in, 100; Native American
executions, 51; slave revolts in,
35; use of electrocution in, 95
North Carolina: execution by
burning in, 64; lynching in, 88
North Dakota: elimination of death
penalty in, 137, 170

Northeast region: African American
executions, 95–110, 149; changes
in capital punishment in, 94–95;
comparison of rates of executions
and lynchings with other regions,
115*tab*, 116, 117*tab*; diverse
ethnicity in, 93; lynching in, 95;
migration of African Americans
to, 93; racial/ethnic tension in,
110–117; urbanization in, 93,
157; use of death penalty in,
93–117

Ohio: centralization of executions,
94; death row population in, 173;
early republic executions, 51;
Italian-Americans in, 113*tab*;
lynching in, 106, 108; Native
American executions, 51; population growth in, 49
Oklahoma: African American
population in, 125; lynching in,
132, 133; Native American
executions, 122, 127*tab*; white
executions, 127*tab*
Old Northwest region: population
growth in, 49
Oregon: Asian executions, 128*tab*;
discretionary sentencing in, 136;
elimination of capital punishment
in, 137, 165; population growth,
123; white executions, 128*tab*

Pacific region: African American
executions, 120–129, 172*tab*,
177*tab*; Asian executions, 150,
172*tab*; death penalty in, 120;
death row population in, 174*tab*;
disproportionate execution of
African Americans in, 125; gender
ratio in, 144; heavy use of capital
punishment in early years, 120,
121; high degree of violence in,
129; Hispanic executions, 150;
lynching in, 130, 132, 133*tab*,
134*tab*; Native American executions, 120–129, 172*tab*; ratio of
African American to white
executions, 139*tab*, 143*tab*; ratio

of African American to white lynchings in, 141*tab*; shifts to state jurisdiction, 135; total known executions, 194*tab*; white executions, 120–129, 171, 172*tab*, 177*tab*

Pennsylvania: centralization of executions, 94; colonial executions, 29; death row population in, 171; Italian-Americans in, 113*tab*; lynching in, 100

Pfeifer, Michael, 129

Pierce, Glenn, 196

Piracy, 35

Prisoners' Friend, 94, 200

Poisoning, 44

Pressing, 42

Pulaski, Charles, 179

Race: bias, 162–163; effect on likelihood of death sentence, 179; of executed persons, 9, 12–15, 148–150; prejudice, 25, 136; riots, 111

Rape, 23, 25, 63, 79, 81, 136; death penalty for, 74, 91, 95

Reconstruction period: increase/decline in use of capital punishment during, 67, 68; lynching during, 82

Redding, David, 200

Revolutionary War: effect on incidence of executions, 10

Rhode Island: abolishment of death penalty, 58; colonial executions, 29; elimination of death penalty, 95, 170; piracy in, 35

Robbery, 23, 41, 135

Roosevelt, Theodore, 142

Roth, Randolph, 200

Rowe, G. S., 200

Salem (Massachusetts), witchcraft in, 29, 40

Schwarz, Philip J., 201

Segregation, 68; imposition by whites, 85; institutionalization of, 77

Severance of appendages, 41

Shooting, 64

Slavery, 202; abolishment of, 48, 55; in Border region, 33, 75; as dominant labor system, 33; elimination of, 67; lynching in states where legal, 149; meaning of, 68; in Middle Atlantic region, 33; occupations of, 151; rebellions, 26, 35, 36, 44, 63, 64; resistance to, 26; in Southern region, 33; white power and, 68

Smykla, John Ortiz, 6

Social: bias, 2; bureaucratization, 148; conflict, 3; development, 4; differentiation, 184; diversity, 48; integration, 184; order, 3; organization, 184; perspectives on death penalty, 147–166; relations, 4

Socioeconomic status: of death row population, 173, 174, 175, 176; differences in, 4; of executed persons, 3, 150–152, 158–166, 173; legal system and, 25

South Carolina: execution by burning in, 64; lynching in, 88; piracy in, 35

South Dakota: centralization of executions, 135; elimination of capital punishment in, 135, 137

Southern region: African American executions, 67–75, 81–91, 149, 171, 172*tab*, 177*tab*; Asian executions, 53*tab*, 172*tab*; changes in defining capital offenses in, 63; colonial executions, 29, 30*tab*, 32*tab*, 33, 34, 37*tab*, 43; death row population in, 173, 174*tab*; disproportionate execution of African Americans in, 43, 44*tab*; dominance of agricultural sector in, 48; early republic executions, 49, 51, 52, 53*tab*, 55*tab*, 56*tab*; executions for nonlethal offenses in, 40, 41, 61*tab*; female executions, 43; Hispanic executions, 53*tab*, 69, 70*tab*, 171, 172*tab*; impact of Civil War on, 67; increase/decline in use of death penalty in, 33, 51; lynching in,

Southern region *(continued)*
82, 83, 86*fig,* 88, 110, 132, 149;
methods of executions, 42;
migration of African Americans
from, 93; Native American
executions, 30*tab,* 34, 52, 53*tab,*
69, 70*tab,* 172*tab*; no abolishment
of capital punishment in, 72;
persistence of public executions,
187; ratio of African American to
white executions, 139*tab,* 143*tab*;
ratio of African American to
white lynchings in, 141*tab*;
restoration of death penalty in,
170; slavery in, 33; total known
executions, 193*tab*; violence in,
48; white executions, 32*tab,* 34,
37*tab,* 51, 53*tab,* 55, 55*tab,* 68,
70*tab,* 71*fig,* 172*tab,* 177*tab*
Spain, 36
Spindell, Donna J., 201
Steckel, Richard, 108
Stono Rebellion (1739), 35
Stroud, George, 63
New Jersey, Supreme Court of, 179

Teeters, Negley, 196, 197
Tennessee: elimination of capital
punishment in, 79; execution by
burning in, 64; lynching in, 83,
88; relinquishes local control of
executions, 79; use of electrocution in, 79
Terrorism, 68, 110, 142
Texas: death row population in,
173; Hispanic executions, 52, 69,
171, 172*tab*; lynching in, 83, 88
Theft, 23, 39, 41; death penalty for,
24, 74
Tolnay, Stewart, 7
Torture, 64, 90, 142

United States Census, 8, 112
United States General Accounting
Office (Government Accountabilty
Office), 179
Urban/rural distribution of execu-
tions, 148, 157–158, 159*tab*

Utah: centralization of executions, 135;
discretionary sentencing in, 136

Vermont: centralization of executions, 94; elimination of death
penalty in, 170
Vigilantism, 129–135; "instant,"
131; as "mobocracy," 131, 132,
136, 142; support from prominent
figures, 187; treated as necessary,
142
Violence: age groups involved, 152–
156; in Border region, 48; capital
punishment as form of, 3;
contemporary rejection of, 185;
decline in, 186; frontier conditions
and, 144; gender imbalance and,
144; incidence of, 3; lack of
civilizing experiences for those
practicing, 187; legal suppression
of proclivities for, 187; legitimate
exercise of, 187; regulation of, 4;
role of, 3; as routine element in
life, 185, 186; self-restraint and,
184, 185; in Southern region, 48;
subcultures of, 161; Western
states, 119
Virginia: African American executions, 72; capital offenses in, 63;
colonial executions, 29; Hispanic
executions, 52; increase in
frequency of executions, 29;
Jamestown execution, 9; lynching
in, 88; piracy in, 35

Washington: Asian executions,
128*tab*; discretionary sentencing
in, 136; elimination of capital
punishment in, 137; Hispanic
executions, 126, 128*tab*; Native
American executions, 128*tab*;
population growth, 123; white
executions, 128*tab*
Washington, D.C.: elimination of
death penalty in, 170; lynching in,
88; use of electrocution in, 79
Western region: African American
executions, 149; African Ameri-

cans migration to, 125; capital punishment in, 119–145; disproportionate execution of African Americans in, 138, 139*tab*; disproportionate number of males in, 119; ethnic differences in, 117, 119; homicide rates in, 119; institutional change/development in, 135–137; lack of incarceration facilities in, 129; lynching in, 129–135; modification of capital punishment in, 135–137; persistence of public executions, 187; racial/ethnic patterns in, 122–129; vigilantes in, 129–135

West North Central region: African American executions, 120–129, 172*tab*, 177*tab*; Asian executions, 172*tab*; centralization of executions, 135; death penalty in, 120; death row population in, 174*tab*; gender ratio in, 144; heavy use of capital punishment in early years, 120, 121; lynching in, 130, 132, 133*tab*, 134*tab*; Native American executions, 120–129, 172*tab*; ratio of African American to white executions, 139*tab*, 143*tab*; ratio of African American to white lynchings in, 141*tab*; total known executions, 194*tab*; white executions, 120–129, 172*tab*, 177*tab*

West Virginia: elimination of death penalty in, 170; elimination of public executions, 79; relinquishes local control of executions, 79

Whipping, 28, 41

Whites: Border region executions of, 76*tab*; Civil War executions of, 58; colonial executions, 29, 30*tab*, 33, 34, 37*tab*, 43; in colonial/revolutionary period, 28, 29; convictions for offenses against African Americans, 63; death penalty for nonlethal offenses, 23, 73*fig*; on death row, 174*tab*; desire to maintain control after elimination of slavery, 68; East North Central region executions, 103*fig*, 105*tab*; efforts to establish racial supremacy, 85; executions and, 12–15; executions for nonlethal offenses, 80*fig*; intergroup tensions among, 111; lynching and, 83, 84*tab*, 86*fig*, 87*fig*, 89*tab*, 106, 132, 133*tab*, 134*tab*, 141*tab*; Mountain region executions, 120–129, 171, 172*tab*; "native stock," 112, 113*tab*; New England region executions, 96, 97*tab*, 99*fig*; Pacific region executions, 120–129; rates of execution of, 17*fig*, 20*fig*, 22*fig*; ratio of executions to African Americans, 139*tab*, 143*tab*; ratio of lynchings to African Americans, 140, 141*tab*; redefinition of capital crimes for, 74; Southern executions of, 68, 70*tab*, 71*fig*; testimony against, 44; West North Central region executions, 120–129

Wife beating, 136

Wisconsin: elimination of death penalty, 59, 94, 95, 170; lynching in, 106

Witchcraft, 29, 39, 40

Women. *See* Gender

Woodworth, George, 179

Wright, George C., 8, 82, 88, 198, 199

Wyoming: Asian executions, 128*tab*; centralization of executions, 135; discretionary sentencing in, 136; lynching in, 130; Native American executions, 128*tab*; white executions, 128*tab*

Zibulka, Charles, 196